DAILY LIFE OF

AFRICAN AMERICAN SLAVES IN THE ANTEBELLUM SOUTH

Recent Titles in
The Greenwood Press Daily Life Through History Series

The Colonial South
John Schlotterbeck

A Medieval Monastery
Sherri Olson

Arthurian Britain
Deborah J. Shepherd

Victorian Women
Lydia Murdoch

The California Gold Rush
Thomas Maxwell-Long

18th-Century England, Second Edition
Kirstin Olsen

Colonial New England, Second Edition
Claudia Durst Johnson

Life in 1950s America
Nancy Hendricks

Jazz Age America
Steven L. Piott

Women in the Progressive Era
Kirstin Olsen

The Industrial United States, 1870–1900, Second Edition
Julie Husband and Jim O'Loughlin

The 1960s Counterculture
Jim Willis

Renaissance Italy, Second Edition
Elizabeth S. Cohen and Thomas V. Cohen

Nazi-Occupied Europe
Harold J. Goldberg

DAILY LIFE OF
AFRICAN AMERICAN SLAVES IN THE ANTEBELLUM SOUTH

PAUL E. TEED AND
MELISSA LADD TEED

The Greenwood Press Daily Life Through History Series

BLOOMSBURY ACADEMIC
NEW YORK • LONDON • OXFORD • NEW DELHI • SYDNEY

BLOOMSBURY ACADEMIC

Bloomsbury Publishing Inc, 1359 Broadway, New York, NY 10018, USA
Bloomsbury Publishing Plc, 50 Bedford Square, London, WC1B 3DP, UK
Bloomsbury Publishing Ireland, 29 Earlsfort Terrace, Dublin 2, D02 AY28, Ireland

BLOOMSBURY, BLOOMSBURY ACADEMIC and the Diana logo
are trademarks of Bloomsbury Publishing Plc

First published in the United States of America by ABC-CLIO 2020
Paperback edition published by Bloomsbury Academic 2026

Copyright © Bloomsbury Publishing Inc, 2025

Cover Photo: Slaves sit waiting to be sold (Pictures Now/Alamy Stock Photo)

All rights reserved. No part of this publication may be: i) reproduced or transmitted in
any form, electronic or mechanical, including photocopying, recording or by means of
any information storage or retrieval system without prior permission in writing from
the publishers; or ii) used or reproduced in any way for the training, development or
operation of artificial intelligence (AI) technologies, including generative AI technologies.
The rights holders expressly reserve this publication from the text and data mining
exception as per Article 4(3) of the Digital Single Market Directive (EU) 2019/790.

Bloomsbury Publishing Inc does not have any control over, or responsibility for,
any third-party websites referred to or in this book. All internet addresses given
in this book were correct at the time of going to press. The author and publisher
regret any inconvenience caused if addresses have changed or sites have
ceased to exist, but can accept no responsibility for any such changes.

Library of Congress Cataloging-in-Publication Data

A catalog record for this book is available from the Library of Congress.

ISBN: HB: 978-1-4408-6324-0
PB: 979-8-2164-3936-3
ePDF: 978-1-4408-6325-7
eBook: 979-8-2160-7132-7

Series: The Greenwood Press Daily Life Through History Series

For product safety related questions contact productsafety@bloomsbury.com.

To find out more about our authors and books visit www.bloomsbury.com
and sign up for our newsletters.

CONTENTS

Preface		ix
Introduction		xiii
Timeline of Events		xix
Glossary		xxiii
1.	ECONOMIC LIFE	1
	The Planters' Economy	3
	The Agricultural Cycle	5
	The Chesapeake and Tobacco	8
	Cotton	11
	Sugar	15
	Rice	18
	Slave Hiring	20
	Reproduction and the "Fancy Trade"	24
	Domestic Work	27
	Independent Production	29
	Document: Solomon Northup, *Twelve Years a Slave* (1853)	33

2.	**DOMESTIC LIFE**	39
	The Slave Trade	40
	Bonds of Affection	46
	Courtship and Marriage	51
	Pregnancy and Childbirth	57
	Parenting Enslaved Children	59
	Document: Henry Brown, *Narrative of the Life of Henry Box Brown* (1851)	62
3.	**MATERIAL LIFE**	67
	Food	69
	Slave Quarters	81
	Clothing	87
	Documents: Interview with Tempie Cummins (1937) and Charles Ball, *Slavery in the United States* (1837)	91
4.	**RELIGIOUS LIFE**	97
	The African Spiritual Legacy	99
	Christianity and Conversion	105
	Origins of the Black Church	109
	Religion and Daily Life	113
	Religion and Rebellion	117
	Document: Peter Randolph, *Sketches of Slave Life: Or, Illustrations of the "Peculiar Institution"* (1855)	120
5.	**POLITICAL LIFE**	125
	Paternalism: The Ideology of Plantation Government	126
	The Politics of Fieldwork	131
	The Politics of the Big House	136
	Disrupting the Plantation Hierarchy	139
	Enslaved People and American Politics	144
	Document: Louis Hughes, *Thirty Years a Slave: From Bondage to Freedom* (1896)	148

6.	INTELLECTUAL LIFE	153
	Slavery and Literacy in the Antebellum South	155
	The Meanings of Literacy	162
	Slave Narratives: Ex-Slaves as Organic Intellectuals	166
	Folk Medicine: Healing Knowledge in the Slave Community	172
	Document: Thomas Jones, *The Experience of Thomas H. Jones, Who Was a Slave for Forty-Three Years* (1862)	175
7.	RECREATIONAL LIFE	179
	Music	180
	Dancing	188
	Holidays and Festivities	191
	Children's Games	196
	Storytelling	197
	Document: William Wells Brown, *My Southern Home* (1880)	202
Bibliography		207
Index		215

PREFACE

This book examines the daily life of slaves in the antebellum era, which began in 1815 and ended in 1860 on the eve of the Civil War. This was a period of dynamic growth in the United States, with the population, the physical size of the nation, and its economy all expanding dramatically. Influenced by the economic trends in the nation as a whole, slavery was not a static institution in the decades before the Civil War. The growth of the cotton economy in the South revolutionized the slave system during these years and fundamentally reordered the lives of the enslaved workers who produced this highly valuable crop. As the cotton revolution spread from coastal states into the Mississippi Valley and beyond, slaves were forcibly relocated from their homes and families to these new regions of the South where a whole new set of factors affected how they lived. In this same period, the international slave trade was banned, and a thriving domestic trade in black men, women, and children emerged as a profitable element of the Southern economy. The rise of the antislavery movement during the 1830s also dramatically affected enslaved people as it offered slaves an ideology of resistance and made slaveholders increasingly anxious. This book, therefore, is careful to note both continuities and discontinuities in the experiences of enslaved people who were caught in an institution undergoing dramatic expansion and facing growing challenges.

This book has benefited from the pioneering work of countless scholars who have painstakingly reconstructed the lives of enslaved people in the antebellum South. A key theme emerging from this rich literature is that the experiences of slaves were not all the same, and thus there is not one way to describe their lives but many. In this book, readers will find that several important factors shaped the lives of slaves, including the region of the South where they lived, the crop they cultivated, the size of the plantation or farm where they resided, the wealth and disposition of their owners, and the composition of the surrounding slave population. At the same time however, the one unifying theme that shaped the lives of all enslaved people regardless of their occupation or location was their status as property under the law and their vulnerability to the power of the white men and women who owned them.

This examination of daily life is arranged topically, and each chapter concludes with a document that illustrates an issue central to that aspect of daily life. The volume begins by examining the economic life of slaves because the organization of labor on Southern plantations and in the urban South is the starting point for understanding their daily experiences under the institution of chattel slavery. Since most enslaved people lived and worked on cotton plantations, much of the chapter will focus on patterns of work in that context. But because a significant minority of slaves cultivated rice, sugar, and tobacco, consideration is given to the substantially different conditions that shaped life in those systems. Urban slaves, who often possessed valuable artisanal skills, make up a final but important category of enslaved workers. The incessant use of violence to spur and maintain high levels of productivity also receives attention here as does the relative profitability of plantations and their "peculiar" system of forced labor.

Our attention then shifts to the consequences of defining human beings as property on all other aspects of daily life. The chapter on domestic life draws on a wealth of recent historical scholarship about African American families under slavery, including their response to slave sales; their childrearing and naming practices; and their efforts to maintain bonds of affection, including marriage, within a system that attempted to deprive them of essential control over these intimate details of their lives. The nature and quality of domestic life for the enslaved was shaped powerfully by their material circumstances, which is explored in detail in the next chapter. The examination of the material life of slaves makes use of both documentary and archaeological evidence to explore the dwellings, clothing, food, and other material aspects of enslaved people's lives. While slaveholders allotted (to varying degrees) basic necessities to their slaves, evidence shows that African Americans supplemented their diets when possible, altered their clothing to fit their own tastes and customs, and turned cabins into homes.

The following four chapters focus on the rich culture of enslaved people, specifically their religious, political, intellectual, and recreational lives. Examining the religious lives of enslaved people provides a unique opportunity to explore the role of cultural syncretism in their daily experiences. Slave religion, as historians have shown, was a mix of West African traditions and Anglo-American revival Christianity. This chapter considers the role of covert "hush harbor" churches or "praise houses" located on the margins of plantation life and their distinctively liberationist version of the Christian gospel. At the same time, the use of ritual techniques such as call and response singing and the "ring shout" sacred dance opens a window on the African roots of the black church. The chapter on political life explores the ways in which slaves, covertly and overtly, contested the power of the white plantation hierarchy and critiqued the larger system of slavery. The chapter also shows that all forms of slave resistance, even the most subtle, were inherently political acts undertaken in opposition to the formidable system of legal oppression that was constructed in the antebellum South.

The chapters on intellectual and recreational life extend the examination of slave culture. The former explores the insatiable desire for literacy and knowledge on the part of enslaved people. Though most Southern states criminalized the teaching of literacy skills to slaves, many sources attest to the existence of strong intellectual traditions among them. The chapter also points out the enormous contribution to American literary culture made by ex-slaves like Frederick Douglass, who wrote autobiographical accounts of their lives under slavery and leveled a searing critique of the institution. The final chapter examines the role of recreational activities, especially music and dance, in the lives of enslaved African Americans and uses the details of these activities as additional evidence for the survival of West African traditions. While the chapter examines the ways in which slaveholders attempted to limit or co-opt slaves' recreational activities, it ultimately argues that that enslaved people effectively used recreation as an additional antidote to the dehumanizing effects of the system under which they lived.

ACKNOWLEDGMENTS

We would like to thank several people for their assistance in the completion of this book. The staff of the Zahnow Library at Saginaw Valley State University were helpful in obtaining source materials, and the university supported the project by granting a sabbatical leave. Kaitlin Ciarmiello at ABC-CLIO/Greenwood has been a pleasure to work with, and we are grateful for her timely answers to our many questions. As always, we thank our daughters, Emilia and Lucy, whose constant love and support has inspired and sustained us through the long process of writing this book.

INTRODUCTION

Nearly all historians of the United States have identified slavery as a central factor in the making of the modern nation and argue that its brutal legacy of racism remains deeply embedded in American society down to the present day. Although there is no way to understand the nation's past without reckoning with the multifaceted impact of slavery, many Americans clearly find the subject disturbing and out of step with images of the nation emphasizing freedom and equality. Indeed, recent controversies over middle school and high school social studies curricula and over textbook adoptions around the country have centered on their presentation of slavery and its role in American life. Despite a scholarly consensus on the central role of slavery in causing the Civil War, for example, state education officials in Texas only recently adopted curricular standards acknowledging that fact. One widely used high school textbook produced by a mass-market publisher, moreover, was challenged by parents in 2015 for using the generic and sanitized word "workers" to describe Africans kidnapped from their homeland and forced to labor under terrible conditions in the Americas. Most recently, conflict over the presence of monuments to leaders of the overtly proslavery Confederate States of America has generated an intense debate in the country over the realities of life for African Americans on the plantations of the Old South.

Many Americans seem unwilling or unable to confront this aspect of their nation's past, with nearly 41 percent of respondents to a 2015 Marist poll denying that slavery was the main cause of the Civil War (Ehlinger 2015).

Yet even as these issues roil the public debate, teachers face enormous difficulty in presenting their students with an accurate understanding of slavery and its role in American history. In a survey compiled by the Southern Poverty Law Center, for example, teachers reported that school districts and state boards of education provide only lukewarm support for teaching about slavery and that assigned textbooks inadequately address the subject. When asked if the textbook they use does "a good job of covering slavery," only 8 percent strongly agreed, while 18 percent either disagreed or strongly disagreed (SPLC 2018, 29). In addition, teachers acknowledge that slavery is a topic that sometimes creates an uncomfortable classroom environment as it raises questions about the character of the nation and about the source of racial inequality in contemporary America. The logical result of these limiting factors is a striking lack of knowledge among high school seniors about the history, character, and meaning of American slavery. In a 2016 poll consisting of eighteen historical questions conducted by Survey USA, only 32 percent of seniors knew that slavery was abolished by the Thirteenth Amendment and less than half knew that the Middle Passage referred to the horrific process by which kidnapped Africans were brought to the Americas as slaves. Thus, while slavery has become a more important topic than ever, Americans lack essential knowledge about its history.

What is perhaps even more surprising is that the general public's declining knowledge about the history of slavery is occurring at a time when historians of the institution are making huge strides in understanding it. In recent decades, the study of American slavery has attracted some of the most talented and innovative historians of our time. Using a wide range of sources and techniques, scholars have explored nearly every aspect of the system of chattel slavery from its inception in colonial Virginia through emancipation. We know more than ever before about the economic impact of slavery on the nation's development, the role of the slave trade in the emergence of cotton production, the brutal methods by which slaveholders dramatically increased staple crops, the experience of enslaved women in the plantation houses of the antebellum South, the diet of slaves, their religious lives, and the material circumstances they confronted on a daily basis. Accurate information about all these topics is also more accessible than ever as the digitization of archival sources has made plantation records, interviews with ex-slaves, slave narratives, and other critical documents available to anyone with access to the Internet. In the past, serious inquiry about slavery required extensive travel to special collections departments and archives around the country, but digitization has placed the raw materials of historical work at the fingertips of students.

Like any scholarly field, the history of slavery has generated interpretive disagreement among its practitioners. For some time, debate has centered around the degree to which enslaved people were able to resist the dehumanization and violence inherent in slavery and to carve out a world that was culturally autonomous from that of their masters. Scholars who emphasize the "agency" of enslaved people have pointed to evidence that West African cultural patterns, including religious practices, naming traditions, family and community structures, agricultural techniques, and material customs, demonstrate that many enslaved people were able to protect themselves from the worst emotional and psychological effects of slavery. Other historians, represented most recently in works by Walter Johnson and Edward Baptist, have argued that slavery was, at its core, a system of forced labor governed by the ruthless logic of capitalist production that demanded higher and higher levels of material output for the world market in cotton. The extent to which enslaved people were able to exert "agency" or "autonomy" over their own lives, these scholars insist, was conditioned and sometimes totally compromised by the terrible labor demands made on their bodies. The differences between these two approaches should not be overstated, but they form the basic plane on which current historiographical debates are taking place.

The approach taken in this book seeks to blend the best elements of the most recent literature on the history of slavery. In its most basic form, antebellum slavery was a system that defined enslaved people as chattel property, a form of ownership that imposed almost no restrictions upon the ability of slaveholders to buy, sell, and use their slaves at will. The daily lives of slaves, then, were shaped profoundly by the recognition that their most basic relationships to family, friends, and community could be severed by masters who chose to sell them to slave traders or other planters. Fear of physical punishment or abuse weighed heavily on the minds of enslaved people, but their dread of sale and separation from loved ones was perhaps their most overriding fear. In many of the chapters that follow, the existence of a market in slaves will cast a defining shadow over aspects of daily life. Their religious faith, for example, often provided consolation to those who had lost their nearest and dearest to sale, while the intellectual and political values of enslaved people often revolved around scathing critiques of their masters' crass decisions to place profits over human relationships. In their musical and recreational activities, enslaved people worked to create social bonds and shared memories they hoped would survive the possibility of loss and separation.

But the "chattel principle," as one former slave called it, shaped many other aspects of slaves' lives as well, including the rhythms of their work, their material circumstances, and their relationships with slaveholders. As property with a dollar value nearly as great as the land itself, slaves were a central element of their owners' assets, and their productive labor was indispensable to the profitability of the plantations, farms, and shops where they worked. This meant that slaveholders interacted with their slaves primarily out of economic self-interest and sought to extract maximum value from their labor at as low a cost as possible. On plantations, where the vast majority of enslaved people lived and worked, an unrelenting routine of year-round labor and a carefully measured allotment of food, clothing, and shelter sharply circumscribed the time and ability of slaves to realize their individual, familial, and communal aspirations. Despite the rhetoric of racial paternalism that they constantly used to defend and justify the system of slavery, Southern planters were enmeshed in a capitalist system of cash-crop production that required them to use their human property to the fullest in their headlong pursuit of profit. Plantations were not, as slaveholders contended, extended families but rather labor camps in which enslaved workers' lives were forced to conform to the demands of cotton, sugar, tobacco, or other staple crop production. Physical abuse, poor diet, shoddy clothing, and medical neglect were, unfortunately, outgrowths of a system that defined slaves as chattel and that valued them only insofar as they contributed to the economic interest or social aspirations of their owners.

Yet the dire consequences of defining slaves as property are only one half of the story of the slaves' daily lives that is told here. Enslaved men, women, and children refused to accept the terms of this brutal, dehumanizing system and used all their cultural, intellectual, and physical resources to resist it. Like other oppressed people in history, African American slaves were acutely conscious of the weaknesses in the system and exploited gaps in the slaveholders' power wherever it was possible. Although slaves lacked political rights, for example, they understood that plantations operated according to a hierarchy in which white masters, mistresses, and overseers had specific responsibilities and exerted distinctive forms of power. Playing whites off against each other, especially owners and overseers, was a means by which slaves protected themselves against overwork or various forms of abuse. Recognizing that slaveholding families liked to see themselves as benevolent, evangelical Christians, slaves appealed to such values and received permission to build churches of their own where they developed a covert critique of slavery and where a distinctive brand of liberation theology was born. While they rejected the paternalistic defense of the oppressive system, enslaved people used its terms to their advantage wherever possible, and the richness of their religious, recreational, political, and intellectual lives testified to the success of their endeavors.

Another main theme that emerges in this work on the daily lives of enslaved people is the persistence of African cultural practices into the world of antebellum slaves. Though there is a wide-ranging debate among historians over the extent of cultural transmission from West Africa to the United States, the evidence for significant continuity is overwhelming. Despite the power of slaveholders to impose their cultural norms on the people they owned as property, the West African elements of slave culture in the United States gave enslaved people an alternative set of values through which to construct a world of their own. Many slaves converted to Christianity during the great revivals of the early nineteenth century, for example, but the circumstances of their conversions allowed them to express and enact their new faith in ways that were consistent with their African spiritual heritage. Alongside their Christianity, moreover, slaves practiced conjure, fortune telling, divination, and other African practices that allowed them to navigate the treacherous waters of American slavery. In their recreational lives, slaves preserved critical aspects of African dance and musical culture in ways that helped to create a strong sense of community in a world in which slave communities existed under the ever-present possibility of disruption through sale. All these elements suggest that while the daily life of slaves was powerfully shaped by both the power of the master and the demanding realities of the plantation regime, slaves embraced their own human vitality and sought to create lives of their own.

The daily lives of slaves in the antebellum South as presented here are, therefore, a dynamic story of oppression and resistance.

The evidence of this, as we shall see, can be found most compellingly in the words of the slaves themselves as found in the various narratives they wrote before and after emancipation and in the hundreds of interviews they recorded during the 1930s. Indeed, those narratives and interviews focused directly on daily life rather than on abstract discussions of the institution of slavery. In the end, it seems that what former slaves remembered most about their experience under the cruel burden of human bondage was the ways in which they had somehow made it through each day despite the violence and brutality they experienced. It was in their daily struggles for human dignity that the slaves found hope for the future and the strength to continue the fight against a system designed to crush out their dreams for freedom.

REFERENCES

Ehlinger, Samantha. 2015. "Did Slavery Cause Civil War? Many Americans Don't Think So." McClatchy, August 6.

SPLC. 2018. Teaching Hard History: American Slavery. Southern Poverty Law Center. https://www.splcenter.org/sites/default/files/tt_hard_history_american_slavery.pdf

TIMELINE OF EVENTS

The following is a list of some of the key political and economic events that affected the development of slavery in the United States.

1619 The first slaves arrive in Virginia.

1662 Virginia decides that the freedom or enslavement of black children would follow the condition of their mother.

1777 In its state constitution, Vermont prohibits slavery.

1787 The Northwest Ordinance bans slavery in the Northwest Territory (Illinois, Indiana, Michigan, Ohio, and Wisconsin).

1790 In the first U.S. census, slaves outnumber whites in South Carolina.

1794 Eli Whitney invents the cotton gin, a device that separates the cotton seed from the lint. This allows for the widespread production of cotton and the spread of slavery into the Lower South.

1800 Gabriel Prosser, an enslaved blacksmith, leads an unsuccessful slave revolt in Richmond, Virginia. He and twenty-five others are hanged. In response, state legislatures pass laws prohibiting the education of slaves and their public assembly.

There are 900,000 slaves in the United States.

1801	The United States produces 40 million pounds of cotton.
1803	The United States purchases the Louisiana territory from France.
1804	A slave revolution occurs in Haiti.
1808	The United States outlaws the international slave trade. The law banning the importation of slaves goes into effect, but it is poorly enforced.
1816	The African Methodist Episcopal (AME) Church, the first all-black religious denomination, is founded.
1820	As part of the Missouri Compromise, Missouri joins the United States as a slave state and Maine as a free state. Slavery is prohibited in the Louisiana territory north of Missouri's southern border.
1822	Denmark Vesey is accused of and then executed for planning a slave revolt in Charleston, South Carolina.
1829	Mexico abolishes slavery.
1830	There are two million slaves in the United States.
1831	The United States produces 322 million pounds of cotton.
	Nat Turner, an enslaved preacher in Virginia, leads a slave uprising of between sixty and eighty rebels. This rebellion results in the death of fifty-seven whites. Approximately twenty-four rebels are killed in combat or executed by the state. Enraged white patrollers kill many more slaves in response to Nat Turner's rebellion.
	In Boston, William Lloyd Garrison founds an antislavery newspaper, *The Liberator*.
1833	Abolitionists meet in Philadelphia to found the American Anti-Slavery Society, an organization dedicated to the immediate, uncompensated emancipation of slaves.
1836	The U.S. Congress passes the "Gag Rule," banning the discussion of any abolitionist petitions. Thousands of petitions are sent to Congress, but they are not acknowledged in the official record. This ban is in effect until 1844. Former president John Quincy Adams, now serving in the House of Representatives, opposes the Gag Rule and attempts to read antislavery petitions.
1839	The slave ship *La Amistad*, which had been seized by the illegally enslaved Africans on board, is captured by an American naval vessel off the coast of Long Island, New York. The

	case galvanizes abolitionists and generates sectional conflict over the fate of the Africans.
1840	There are 2.5 million slaves in the United States.
1841	The United States produces 559 million pounds of cotton.
1845	Frederick Douglass publishes his autobiography of his experiences as a slave in Maryland. It is the most famous example of the narratives written by former slaves.
1848	The United States and Mexico sign the Treaty of Guadeloupe-Hidalgo, which cedes millions of acres of land to the United States and reignites the political debate over the expansion of slavery into western territories.
1849	Henry "Box" Brown escapes slavery by mailing himself in a wooden crate from Richmond, Virginia, to Philadelphia, Pennsylvania.
1850	As part of the Compromise of 1850, Congress passes a stronger Fugitive Slave Law that limits the rights of the accused to defend themselves and punishes anyone who aids fugitives.
	There are 3.2 million slaves in the United States.
1851	The United States produces 1.1 billion pounds of cotton.
1852	Harriet Beecher Stowe publishes her best-selling novel, *Uncle Tom's Cabin*.
1853	Margaret Douglass is arrested, convicted, and imprisoned for teaching Richmond slaves to read.
1854	The Kansas-Nebraska Act repeals the Missouri Compromise, which states that all territory acquired in the Louisiana Purchase north of the southern border of Missouri would be free. Instead, popular sovereignty—a vote by residents in the territory—will be used to determine if Kansas and Nebraska will be free or slave states.
1856	A bloody civil war begins in Kansas between proslavery and free-state forces.
1857	In *Dred Scott v. Sandford*, the Supreme Court declares that African Americans are not citizens and that Congress cannot bar slavery in the territories.
1859	In October, John Brown carries out a raid on the federal arsenal in Harpers Ferry, Virginia. His plan is to seize the arsenal and use the weapons stored there to arm slaves. He is convicted and executed for treason against the state of Virginia.

1860	The *Clotilda* arrives in Mobile Bay in Alabama, carrying a cargo of 110 enslaved Africans. After the slaves are unloaded, Captain William Foster burns the ship to destroy the evidence of his criminal activity. This is the last slave ship to unload in the United States.

Abraham Lincoln is elected president. Lincoln, the first Republican president, receives 40 percent of the popular vote and virtually no support from Southern states. In response, South Carolina passes the "Ordinance of Secession" in December and dissolves its connection to the United States.

There are 3.9 million slaves in the United States. The United States produces 1.5 billion pounds of cotton.

1861	By February, Mississippi, Florida, Alabama, Georgia, Louisiana, and Texas secede from the Union and join with South Carolina to create the Confederate States of America. In June, Virginia, North Carolina, Arkansas, and Tennessee secede and join the Confederacy.

1863	President Abraham Lincoln issues the Emancipation Proclamation freeing slaves in all areas of the rebellious South and authorizes the recruitment of African American soldiers. It goes into effect on January 1.

1865	The Thirteenth Amendment to the U.S. Constitution abolishes slavery.

GLOSSARY

The following is a list of key terms and definitions used in the various chapters of this book.

Agency: An interpretive concept meaning that despite the enormous power of slaveholders, enslaved people creatively forged an identity and culture independent of those who owned them.

Anti-literacy laws: A series of laws passed in slave states that prohibited the teaching of literacy skills to slaves and free black people.

Ashcake: A bread commonly eaten by enslaved people, made from cornmeal, water, and sometimes salt that was cooked in the fire covered in ashes. Once cooked the ashes were removed. *See hoecake.*

Big House: The name given to the slave owner's home.

Brer Rabbit: An animal trickster figure appearing in many slave folktales who repeatedly outwits and triumphs over more powerful rivals.

Brer Wolf: An animal figure appearing in many slave folktales whose attempts to capture and eat Brer Rabbit are frustrated by the rabbit's superior guile.

Chattel principle: The idea that enslaved people were owned as property by slaveholders and could be bought and sold at will.

Chesapeake: The geographic and cultural region that encompasses Maryland and Virginia.

Coffle: A group of slaves chained together, usually to travel to a slave market.

Concubine: A woman sold to a buyer as a slave mistress.

Conjure: A West African–derived practice based on a belief in the spiritual or magical power or roots, amulets, charms, or other objects to influence human behavior.

Conversion: A process of commitment to the Christian religion, often accompanied by emotional intensity and a deep feeling of personal transformation.

Corn shucking or cornhusking: Annual events when slaves gathered in large groups to shuck corn and then participate in music, dancing, and other recreational activities.

Cotton gin: A mechanical device that separated cotton lint from seeds and allowed for the production of a vastly larger volume of cotton each year in the South.

Domestic slave trade: The sale of slaves within the United States. In the antebellum era, three-quarters of a million slaves from the Upper South were sold to the Lower South.

"Fancy trade": The buying and selling of enslaved women for prostitution or concubinage.

Frolic: A term that slaves often used to describe dances or other celebratory events that included music and storytelling.

Great Dismal Swamp: A large swamp in southeastern Virginia and northeastern North Carolina between Elizabeth City, North Carolina, and Norfolk, Virginia.

Hoecake: A bread commonly eaten by enslaved people, made from cornmeal, water, and sometimes salt that was cooked on the back of a gardening hoe in a fire. See ashcake.

Independent production: The production of food, clothing, or other items by slaves for their own use or sale.

Jumping the broom: A ritual to celebrate a marriage that involved two people holding the ends of a broom while the couple jumped over it.

Junkanoo: An Afro-Caribbean masquerade procession involving large groups of slaves dressed in a variety of ornate, brightly colored costumes.

Lowcountry: A geographic and cultural region along the coast of South Carolina and Georgia where rice is grown.

Lower South: The part of the southern United States where cotton was grown. It includes South Carolina, Georgia, Florida, Alabama, Mississippi, Louisiana, and Texas.

Organic intellectual: A member of an oppressed class who obtains the intellectual tools to challenge the dominant system of power and who speaks out on behalf of other members.

Glossary

Overseer: A white employee of the plantation owner who was charged with direct supervision of slaves and their work.

Paternalism: The main proslavery ideology of the slaveholders which insisted that the system of slavery was a morally legitimate social arrangement based on the innate superiority of whites.

Patting: A coordinated series of rhythmic claps on the knees, hands, and shoulders in time with singing and dancing.

Petit Gulf cotton: The most common form of cotton produced in the American South during the antebellum era.

Pit schools: Secret places on the plantation, sometimes holes in the ground covered by branches, where illegal learning took place.

Plantation mistress: The wife of the planter.

Planter: The owner of a plantation complex that included land, slaves, and other means of production.

"Playing possum": A term used by slaveholders to describe slaves who feigned illness.

Praise house: Wooden houses constructed by slaves where Christian worship, including ring shouts, took place.

Quills: Simple flutes made by slaves in which small tubes of varying lengths and thicknesses were tied together to allow different pitches.

Rations: The weekly food allotment that slave owners provided enslaved people.

Ring shout: A religious ritual in which worshippers formed a moving circle and sang, shouted, clapped, and stomped their feet in rhythmic patterns.

Sea Islands: A series of small barrier islands off the coast of South Carolina, Georgia, and Florida where a large slave population produced cotton and rice.

Sickhouse: Structures built on some plantations to house slaves who were ill or unable to work.

Slave hiring: A system in which slave owners hired out surplus slaves for a set period of time. The hirer pays the owner a fee and provides food, clothing, and lodging for the slave.

Slave narratives: Autobiographical writings by ex-slaves describing the nature of life under the system of human bondage.

Slave quarters: The small cabins, usually made of logs, that enslaved people lived in.

Slave spirituals: Religious songs composed and sung by enslaved people as they worshipped and worked.

Slave trader: An individual whose primary economic activity was the buying and selling of slaves.

System of gang labor: The most common system of labor on Southern plantations in which slaves worked sunup to sundown six days per week.

Task system of labor: A system of labor organization common in the lowcountry of South Carolina and Georgia in which slaves were assigned a particular task each day rather than a set number of hours to work in the field.

Upper South: The northern portion of the southern part of the United States, including Virginia, Maryland, North Carolina, Tennessee, and Arkansas.

1

ECONOMIC LIFE

When Sarah Gudger looked back at her time as a slave in North Carolina, she emphasized the centrality of work to her experiences: "Jes wok, an' wok, an' wok. I nebbah know nothin' but wok" (Rawick 1974, 14: 352). From sunup to sundown, six, sometimes seven, days a week, masters dictated what work needed to be done and at what pace. Enslaved people did whatever work they were ordered to perform, from hoeing and plowing to chopping wood. At the end of the workday, they returned to their quarters to prepare a meal, grind corn for the next day, and then get a few hours of sleep before the process began again. The intense labor demands made upon the daily lives of enslaved people reflect the fundamentally economic basis of the slave system and the determination of planters to extract the maximum productive capacity from the human beings they owned. Although slaves worked in many distinct capacities and contexts across the landscape of the South, they were all subjected to a labor regimen that valued them not as human beings but as commodities that could be turned to profit.

Although proslavery propaganda defended Southern plantations as extended families, in reality, they were economic units of production that specialized in a cash crop, namely, rice, cotton, sugar, or tobacco. The acquisition of western lands and the removal of Native Americans opened up huge expanses for agricultural production that tempted people to move west and take advantage of the wealth to be made in the expanding cotton and sugar markets. To cultivate and harvest their staple crops, planters extracted unpaid labor from individuals whom the law deemed to be property. As property, enslaved people could be bought and sold, used up and replaced as needed, without regard for their needs or feelings. Instead, enslaved people were judged for what they could produce for their owners. Prospective buyers were interested in slaves' strength, skills, and suitability for particular forms of work. Former bondperson Louis Hughes remembered buyers asking "What can you do?" Men were asked: "Can you plow? Are you a blacksmith? Have you ever cared for horses? Can you pick cotton rapidly?" (Hughes 1897, 7–8). Buyers also inquired if women had particular skills, especially as cooks and seamstresses. The labor performed by enslaved people was crucial to the success of Southern plantations.

Because plantations were businesses, planters routinely made economic calculations about how much profit they could expect based on the number of acres they owned, the price of the staple crop, and the number of "hands" they could exploit. As a result, the vast majority of slaves engaged in some form of fieldwork. Their days were long, and their labor was exhausting. The human body, often with the aid of only the simplest implement like a hoe, planted, cultivated, and harvested staple crops that fueled economic growth in antebellum America. The economic life of enslaved people was dictated first by the work requirements of their owners, who determined what labor needed to be performed, as well as the pace of work and the hours. If slaves failed to meet the requisite standards, they would be punished. Whipping was the favored form, and it could occur for any reason. Even if slaveholders possessed enormous power, they could not impose their will in all circumstances, and enslaved people resisted their owners' demands by feigning illness, working slowly, or running away. To avoid disruptions, especially at harvest time, or to keep slaves working at a specific pace, slaveholders negotiated with slaves, making small concessions, like offering extra food, days off, or Christmas bonuses. While the master controlled most of the day, enslaved people carved out time to produce items that could be consumed or traded for other necessities. When considering the economic life of slaves, therefore, the perspective of both slaveholders and the enslaved needs to be considered. By examining both perspectives, we can then recognize that the value slaveholders placed on their slaves was not the value that enslaved people placed on their own bodies and souls. As in other aspects of their lives, enslaved people created their own limited, but important, sphere of economic activity.

THE PLANTERS' ECONOMY

In order to fully understand the economic lives of enslaved people, it is crucial to recognize the basic functions of the plantation economy in which their lives and labor were situated. To grow a staple crop, landowners faced numerous challenges in the hope of reaping a substantial profit, often placing themselves in debt to purchase land, labor, and machinery. Such debt could take many years to pay off, and at any point planters' profits might sink because of falling commodity prices or low yields due to disease, an early frost, or too little rain. Deeply aware of such risks, landholders hoped to improve their chances by carefully studying their agricultural practices and identifying areas that could be made more efficient. They looked for more drought- or frost-resistant strains of cotton and sugar, hoping to improve their returns. Regardless of what staple crop was being grown, planters sought to maximize the productivity and efficiency of their labor supply. That meant that enslaved people worked in all weather, especially in the unremitting heat and humidity that allowed staple crops like cotton and sugar to flourish, and they were exposed to numerous diseases, including malaria and cholera. Frederick Douglass emphasized that "it was never too hot or too cold, it could never rain, blow, hail, or snow, too hard for us to work in the field" (Douglass 1845, 63). Planters explored new means of managing their workforce so that the productivity of each field hand increased. While some utilized positive incentives to induce slaves to work faster, most planters relied on punishment as the mechanism to make enslaved people work at an ever-increasing pace.

As property, slaves had a value that slave owners calculated not only at the point of sale but yearly. Slave owners kept an inventory in which they listed the estimated market value of each slave they owned. Those enslaved people rated as "prime hands" had the highest productivity and therefore the highest value. A number of factors affected this rating, including skill, size, strength, age, and health. Planters used a fractional system to classify everyone on the plantation based on how productive they were as laborers. Children, for instance, were usually classified as "quarter hands," and as they aged, they moved to half, three-quarters, or full hands. A person too old or ill to work would have been classed as having no value. In their records, planters listed how many slaves they owned and then calculated how many "full hands" they added up to. Historian Caitlin Rosenthal has argued that "by rating their workers as partial hands, planters rendered the enslaved as abstract units of labor, many of which could be summed to make a whole" (Rosenthal 2018, 147). Slave owners understood that the value of their "human capital" appreciated or depreciated annually. Scars on the back of an enslaved person, for instance, would have been seen as evidence of disobedience and would have caused the person's value to decline. Running away also caused depreciation. In his narrative, Henry Bibb demonstrated his understanding of these calculations and explained that he was sold to a Kentucky slave trader "at a depreciated price because I was a runaway" (Bibb 1849, 203).

The number of slaves on a farm or plantation and the requirements of specific staple crops affected the form of labor management. On small landholdings with fewer than ten slaves, masters usually worked in the fields alongside their slaves and could personally confirm that work continued at the required pace. On larger plantations, planters hired overseers or estate managers to decide what tasks needed to be performed on a day-to-day basis. Most regions in the South relied on a system of gang labor, where slaves worked from sunup to sundown under the supervision of an overseer whose job it was to enforce the required pace. If anyone failed to keep up, that person was punished. Talking during the workday could lead to a whipping, as could arriving late, breaking a hoe, or missing weeds. Despite being threatened with whipping, some slaves did slow their pace as soon as the overseer moved out of sight. Tobacco's need for constant attention and the regimented nature of sugar cultivation made the gang system an efficient form of labor management. The workday began at dawn after a bell or horn sounded to wake all the tired bodies from their sleep. After working for a couple of hours, enslaved people stopped for breakfast and then returned to the fields. A second break was taken at midday, and then work continued until nightfall. Planters established work rules—when enslaved people needed to start work, when they ate their meals or nursed their children, and how quickly they needed to work. While the master controlled most of their day, enslaved people controlled their time at night and on Sundays, the traditional day off.

A different form of slave management emerged in rice cultivation, one that measured a day's work not in the number of hours worked but in the completion of a specific task, like a quarter acre of hoeing or splitting one hundred rails. The task system emerged in the rice fields of South Carolina and Georgia in the eighteenth century. By the antebellum era, specific definitions of what constituted "a day's work," negotiated between owners and enslaved people, had become customary practice, but conflict did occur between overseers and field hands if work was left undone or was deemed of poor quality. The task system required that slaves work hard, but it allowed them more autonomy to determine the pace of their labor. If they worked intensively to finish their allotted task, then they would have time to do their own work, hunting, fishing, or cultivating their provision garden. Under the task system, enslaved people had a customary right to their time, a commodity in much smaller supply under the gang system.

THE AGRICULTURAL CYCLE

While significant differences existed based on the form of slave management, the agricultural cycle meant that there were some basic similarities in the experiences of all slaves. At the beginning of each year, the land needed to be cleared of any debris from the previous season. Machinery and farm implements, ditches, and irrigation systems would also need to be repaired. Once these tasks had been completed, a cycle of plowing, planting, weeding, and harvesting would begin. Whether it was tobacco, rice, cotton, or sugar, harvest was the most exhausting time of the year. Facing hot weather, long days, and sometimes a feverish pace, enslaved people worked by hand to harvest crops. Mechanization emerged slowly in the processing of rice and sugar, but the picking of cotton and the cutting of rice stalks and sugarcane relied exclusively on human power. Once harvested, the crop then needed to be ginned, threshed, cured, or ground before being packed for sale. Fieldwork, therefore, varied seasonally—different work was required at different points of the agricultural cycle, with harvesting being the most arduous.

During the agricultural cycle, there was slack time when the staple crop did not require any attention. In those instances, masters shifted their slaves to other productive work, especially the cultivation of the corn that would be consumed on the plantation. At harvest time, the corn was pulled off the stalks and carted home to be shucked. A landowner might put enslaved people to work shucking corn when it was too wet or too dark to tend the staple crop, or he might have it shucked in one night by requesting neighboring

The expansion of slavery in antebellum America was driven by the demand for cotton, which slaves in this illustration were harvesting. Enslaved people from South Carolina to Texas worked long hours in the fields as masters increased the pace at which slaves were required to pick cotton. (Library of Congress)

planters to send their slaves to help. Francis Fedric described one corn shucking party when slaves split into teams to see which one could finish their pile first. As they shucked, the captains of the teams led the companies in song, and once they had finished in the early morning, the slaveholder provided supper for all the workers. Fedric remembered this occasion as a fun and joyous respite from a rigorous agricultural cycle. In addition to cultivating corn, enslaved people butchered hogs and then smoked the meat so that it would not become infested with worms. It was substantially cheaper for landholders if their farms produced most of the food that would be consumed during the year.

In addition to the seasonal nature of work responsibilities, the age and gender of individual slaves affected the nature of the labor they performed. Antebellum America generally constructed clear distinctions between the roles of white men and women, and common belief held that white women were physically delicate and therefore ill suited to hard physical labor. Yet while prescriptive literature suggested that white women should not perform fieldwork, no such prohibition existed for African American women. In most instances, enslaved men and women performed whatever jobs were needed. Historian Deborah Gray White has noted that women might even fill the role usually performed by an ox, attaching leather straps to their shoulders so they could haul logs. Yet slaveholders did observe certain gender distinctions in the work roles they assigned, and tasks that required the most strength—felling trees with axes or splitting boards—were usually performed by men. Women, in contrast, monopolized tasks associated with cooking and clothing: grinding corn into meal, spinning, sewing, weaving, and washing. Titled positions on plantations—carpenter, driver, or blacksmith—were also reserved for men. Historian Susan O'Donovan has found that men performed a wider assortment of jobs on plantations than women did and men's work usually involved a greater degree of mobility. If cotton needed to be transported to a local merchant for sale or timber needed to be taken to a local mill, O'Donovan aptly noted that "slave men monopolized the seats on planters' wagons and oxcarts" (O'Donovan 2007, 38).

Identifying a gendered division of labor, Deborah Gray White has argued that, in general, men plowed and women hoed. In rice cultivation, a clear line existed, and only men plowed, but in cotton, the division was more permeable. While men did most of the plowing, enslaved women used one type of plow that removed the weeds from between rows of cotton. Northern visitors to the South commented on the unexpected sight of women using a plow. Frederick Law Olmsted observed that enslaved women in Mississippi "twitched their plows around on the head-land, jerking their reins, and yelling to their mules, with apparent ease, energy, and rapidity." He even denied that their gender "unfitted them for the occupation" (Olmsted 1860, 81). Many former slaves agreed with Olmsted's observations, and George Fleming commented that when women plowed they often could not be distinguished from men because they wore breeches. Mary Minus Biddle, who operated a plow in Florida, was said to "handle it with the agility of a man" (Rawick 1974, 17: 33). Mandy Rollins recalled that she "usta wuk like a mule" cutting down trees, hoeing, plowing, stripping cane, and pulling corn. She stressed that she did "mos' erething dat a man eber did" (Tanner 2014, 81). Many former slaves expressed pride that they could perform the hardest work that men could do. When Mary Frances Webb recounted the experiences of her grandmother in slavery, she emphasized her strength: "She plowed and hoed the crops in the summer and spring, and in the winter she sawed and cut cord wood just like a man" (Rawick 1973, 7: 314).

Age was also a factor in work assignments as young children performed light tasks like weeding; feeding the sheep, hogs, or cows; and bringing wood to the kitchen. They toted water, washed dishes, and answered the doorbell. Ebenezer Brown remembered gathering eggs and picking up fruit that fell off the trees and feeding it to the hogs. Brown also churned butter, and when he saw "lil'l lumps uf butter stickin on de handle I wud take my finger an' wipe it off an' den suck my finger" (Berlin, Favreau, and Miller 1988, 94). Katie Darling took care of her master's children, and as soon as she was "big enough to tote a cow pail" she milked the cows (Berlin, Favreau, and Miller 1988, 89). Yet even as small children were assigned work that befitted their physical size, it is important to recall that they were valued in economic rather than human terms just as their parents were. The fact that children could be put to work on lighter tasks meant that their mothers and fathers could be put into the fields at harvest time.

THE CHESAPEAKE AND TOBACCO

While there were many common features in the agricultural work that enslaved people performed on plantations throughout the South, important differences existed as well, depending upon the crop that slaves were required to produce. The tobacco economy of the Chesapeake region, the cotton-producing region of the Deep South, the sugar plantations of Louisiana, and the rice fields of South Carolina and Georgia all had distinctive rhythms of production that shaped the daily lives of slaves. Slaves were required to master the skills necessary for the cultivation of these different staple crops, and the physical demands that each crop placed upon enslaved workers waxed and waned over the course of the year. Some production cycles required nearly year-round work, which left little time for slaves to engage in their own economic activities, while others were punctuated by off times. Thus, in order to understand the economic lives of enslaved people in the plantation South, it is important to examine the four most important crops that shaped their working days.

In the Chesapeake region of Virginia and Maryland, slaves were mainly engaged in the production of tobacco, which had become the primary export commodity from Virginia soon after the colony's founding. African slaves did not replace indentured servants as the principal source of labor in the cultivation of the staple crop until the last third of the seventeenth century, but they soon became inseparable from the tobacco economy. Unlike wheat, which required little attention between planting and harvesting, tobacco needed attention throughout the growing cycle. In early

January, tobacco seeds were planted in special seedbeds and covered with branches to protect the small plants from damaging frost. In late April or May, the seedlings were transplanted into the main fields where they were planted in long rows. Before the seedlings could be transplanted, however, the fields needed to be prepared. First, they were plowed or hoed to raise a four-inch mound called a tobacco hill so that water would flow away from the plants. Enslaved people used a stick to make a hole in the ground, and then they placed a seedling inside it and then pressed down the soil around the plant. At this stage, planters hoped for rain, because without it, the seedlings would die.

As tobacco plants grew, they required constant attention. At least three times during the growing season, the plants needed to be weeded. Small children were often used to crawl between the plants and pick any weeds growing close to the tobacco. In addition, the top of the tobacco plant was cut off so that it did not flower, and all suckers, or secondary shoots, were removed. Planters wanted the tobacco plant's energy focused on the growth of the leaves. In addition, planters waged a daily war against the various worms that could destroy the leaves. Enslaved children were tasked with examining the tobacco leaves and picking off and killing every worm they found. At age eight, Robert Ellet worked in the fields "a-worming tobacco," and he learned to do it so effectively that his master received a purchase offer. Simon Stokes disliked the job, remembering a cruel overseer with a sharp eye who made the young boy eat any worms he failed to remove from the leaves. When Nancy Williams did not pick worms as carefully as her master wanted, he stuffed a handful of worms into her mouth. Williams did not know how many worms she swallowed, but she acknowledged that she "picked em off careful arter dat" (Perdue, Barden, and Phillips 1976, 85, 322). In addition to worms and insects that could harm the plant, too much or too little water could spell disaster. If tobacco plants were too wet or too dry for an extended period of time, the leaves began to decay quickly and an entire field could be lost in as few as four days. If the leaves were near maturity, they needed to be immediately cut and cured; otherwise the crop would be lost.

Finally, planters needed to decide when the leaves were ready to be cut. If they waited too long, a frost could destroy the plant, and experienced growers usually relied on the appearance of the leaves as their guide, looking for changes in color and thickness. Tobacco leaves were usually picked when they were starting to brown.

Former bondman Gabe Hunt emphasized the importance of determining when the tobacco was ready: "Pick 'em too soon dey don't cure, an you pick 'em too late dey bitters" (Perdue, Barden, and Phillips 1976, 148). In most cases, cutting tobacco began in September, and enslaved people needed to break the leaves off carefully to avoid bruising them. As they cut the tobacco, their fingers became covered in a sticky gum that would not wash off. Once cut, tobacco leaves then needed to be hung to dry in barns. The process of curing took many days, and planters again needed to rely on their experience to determine when the process was complete. If left to dry too long, the leaves would crumble and disintegrate; if the leaves were not dry enough, they would rot. In wet weather, fires could be lit in the barns to promote drying. Once perfectly cured, the leaves were taken down, and the stems were removed. The final stage involved the leaves being pressed together and packed into hogsheads for transportation to market.

In addition to cultivating tobacco, numerous other jobs needed to be performed by enslaved people in the Chesapeake region. Men with artisanal skills worked as carpenters repairing buildings, as blacksmiths fixing wagon wheels, and as coopers making barrels. These skilled workers were often hired out to work for a neighboring planter. Most slaves, however, would perform fieldwork, and the learning process began when they were young. Josiah Henson remembered that as a young boy in Maryland he was required "to carry buckets of water to the men at work, to hold a horse-plough, used for weeding between the rows of corn, and as I grew older and taller, to take care of master's saddle-horse." His tasks changed as he grew in strength, with the trajectory toward fieldwork. When a hoe was put into his hands, Henson "was soon required to do the day's work of a man" (Henson 1849, 6). With the ambition to be more than a field hand, however, Josiah Henson exposed that the overseer was cheating the master and was promoted to the position of superintendent of farmwork. One of his new responsibilities was to transport the crops to market and sell the corn, wheat, and tobacco for the best price he could find. When Henson returned after a long day, hungry and tired, his only reward was his master's criticism that he had not commanded higher prices for the produce.

Even if Chesapeake masters like Henson's promoted slaves to positions of responsibility, they were careful to keep power and control clearly demarcated. Masters used punishment to assert their authority whenever they believed that slaves were not sufficiently subservient. Masters watched their slaves carefully to see that they were where they were supposed to be and doing the work that had been assigned to them. If slaves failed to work as ordered, they were punished, sometimes brutally. When he was only in his teens, Jermain Loguen had a piece of wood shoved through the roof of his mouth by his drunken master simply because the handle of a hoe fell off. Masters often made no allowance for age or inexperience. When ordered to take a team of oxen to get a load of wood, Frederick Douglass, who had never performed this task before, proved unable to control the oxen, and they ran until becoming entangled in trees and the cart turned over. After extricating the oxen and righting the cart, Douglass proceeded on his way, chopping wood and loading the cart for the return journey. Unfortunately, he again lost control of the team, and they rushed through a gate, catching it on the cart and breaking it. When Douglass told his master about the mishaps, he was whipped for wasting time and destroying property.

COTTON

While the demands of tobacco production gave birth to American slavery and remained the dominant system in the Chesapeake region into the antebellum period, cotton production became the South's most lucrative crop, increasing from 1.4 million pounds produced in 1800 to 2 billion pounds in 1860. Having developed new, steam-powered looms, British textile manufacturers eagerly imported the short-staple cotton that was grown in the southern part of the United States. As the profitability of cotton soared after the cotton gin made it possible to separate the seed from the lint mechanically, the demand for labor increased sharply in the southwestern portion of the United States. To meet the demand of planters in places like Georgia, Mississippi, and Louisiana, enslaved people in the Chesapeake were sold to traders who transported them to slave markets in distant cities, especially New Orleans. Used to the established work routines in tobacco, corn, or wheat cultivation in Virginia and Maryland, enslaved people underwent a disorienting transition to cotton agriculture on the frontier. Land needed to be cleared; trees needed to be felled; and cotton needed to be planted, tended, and harvested. Slave owners increased the pace of production, and each year enslaved people were forced to tend more acres and pick more cotton. When the price of cotton went up in Great Britain, enslaved people quickly felt the effect at a faster pace and a whip that was used more frequently.

Cultivating cotton in long parallel rows of evenly spaced plants required skill and hard work. Planters in the Mississippi Valley developed a new strain in 1820, called Petit Gulf cotton, that bloomed earlier, produced a high-quality cotton, and was easier to pick. Experience taught enslaved people how closely to sow the seeds so that the plants had enough room to grow without becoming entangled with other plants. As the plants grew, field hands thinned and weeded with hoes and plows, and grasses and weeds were removed so that they did not draw necessary nutrients away from the growing plants. Overseers and masters checked to see that the work had been done properly, whipping slaves who let a stray weed escape their notice. When Charles Ball was sold from Maryland to a South Carolina cotton planter, for example, he experienced a highly regimented work pattern for weeding cotton plants. The slaves were divided into groups of eleven, with one person in each group designated as the captain. Simon, the captain of Ball's group, was assigned the first row, and he set the pace for all the others. The overseer kept his whip out in case anyone fell behind, but Ball stated with some satisfaction that he "had no difficulty in learning how the work was to be performed" (Ball 1837, 148). When former bondman John Brown was operating a plow to remove the grass and weeds crowding cotton plants, it malfunctioned, and he had to stop frequently to avoid harming the cotton plants. Because Brown was not plowing evenly and quickly, his master viciously kicked him between the eyes, shattering his nose and damaging his right eye. Despite the blood pouring from his nose and eye, Brown was expected to continue on with his work.

While some agricultural labor, like cutting down trees or repairing fences, required strength, Charles Ball believed that "the art of picking cotton" was less about strength and more about "the power of giving quick and accelerated motion to the fingers, arms, and legs." A day's work was measured in pounds of cotton picked, and each picker was assigned a daily quota. Failure to meet that quota would result in whipping. Picking cotton could consume up to six months on a large plantation—beginning in September and continuing until January or February. Planters and overseers looked for ways to speed up picking cotton. Cotton pickers were each given a sack that hung around their neck. Walking between the rows of cotton, the picker removed all cotton from open bolls on their right and left. Charles Ball remembered: "In this way he picks half the cotton from each of the rows, and the pickers who come on his right and left, take the remainder from the opposite sides of the rows" (Ball 1837, 210–211). Former bondman John Brown recalled the back pain caused by "constant stooping" while picking cotton and the soreness when the sharp boll cut "the flesh round the nails" no matter how much care was taken by the picker (Brown 1855, 176).

The cotton plant continued to grow and send out new blossoms until the first frost. Because cotton matured at different rates, the same plant was picked three to six times during the harvest season. In the first picking, the bolls at the bottom were ready, and with each successive picking, the cotton picker moved higher up the plant. Frost did not harm the ripened cotton, and so picking could continue during winter. Mary Reynolds emphasized how unpleasant this was: "The times I hated the most was pickin' cotton when the frost was on the bolls. My hands git sore and crack and bleed" (Tanner 2014, 6). They lit a small fire in the fields, and when their fingers were too painful to continue, they would run to warm their hands.

Picking cotton rapidly, however, was more difficult than it at first appeared. Children on cotton plantations were given smaller quotas than adults, and from a young age they developed the manual dexterity to pick cotton efficiently. When adults without any experience in cotton first picked it, they realized how difficult it was to meet the required pace. When purchased by a South Carolina cotton planter, Charles Ball easily learned how to tend the cotton plants, but picking was a different matter. Though Ball was strong and adept at many agricultural tasks, he found that at picking he "was not equal to a boy of twelve or fifteen years of age." On his first day, he picked 38 pounds of cotton, while others picked 20 pounds more than him. Determined to learn the skill, Ball was soon able to pick more than 50 pounds of cotton. Though Ball improved, he was convinced that anyone who did not start picking cotton before the person was twenty-five would not become "a crack picker" (Ball 1837, 215, 217). Solomon Northup, who had been kidnapped and sold into slavery as an adult, observed cotton pickers who had "a natural knack, or quickness," which allowed them to pick rapidly with both hands. They executed their work "with a precision and dexterity that was incomprehensible to me" (Northup 1853, 166, 178). Northup's movements, on the other hand, were slow and awkward, as the inexperienced picker seized the boll in one hand and deliberately removed the cotton in the other. He lacked the coordination to easily deposit the cotton into his basket, often dropping it onto the ground. When he stooped to pick it up, his sack would swing from side to side, damaging the branches with unripe cotton. When Northup did not improve, his master made the calculation that hiring him out to a sugar planter for a few months would be a better use of his labor.

Planters invested in land and slaves to make a profit, and the more cotton produced on their land, the more money they made. When drawing up estimates of how much cotton to plant given the amount of available labor, planters calculated that each slave would be responsible for five acres of cotton. Charles Ball believed that it was possible for a single person to plant and tend five acres, but come harvest, the picker "will find the labour more than he can perform, if the cotton is to be picked clean from the plants" (Ball 1837, 214–215). If five acres yielded 10,000 pounds of seed cotton, Ball estimated that it would take one person more than six months to pick it, assuming 60 pounds per day. Harvesting cotton required the most labor and took up the largest amount of time in the agricultural cycle, and business-minded planters kept daily records of how much cotton each slave picked.

Antebellum planters did not have the benefit of any new mechanical device that would decrease the amount of time it took to harvest the crop. In order to increase productivity, planters required that their "hands" work more quickly. Over the course of the nineteenth century, planters forced enslaved people to pick faster so that more cotton could be harvested. At the beginning of the nineteenth century, for example, South Carolina plantations averaged less than 30 pounds per day per picker. Twenty years later, Mississippi cotton plantations had increased that average to between 50 and 80 pounds per day. That number continued to climb in the 1840s, and many Mississippi slaves averaged more than 200 pounds. In *The Half Has Never Been Told*, historian Edward Baptist has calculated that "the total gain in productivity per picker from 1800 to 1860 was almost 400 percent" (Baptist 2014, 128). The records of one Natchez, Mississippi, planter demonstrate the massive increase in the pace of work by the eve of the Civil War. In 1859, Robert Stewart recorded that his weaker pickers routinely picked between 100 and 200 pounds, while his skilled pickers could pick between 400 and 500 pounds per day. But the daily record was held by Oskar who picked 615 pounds (Rosenthal 2018, 101).

To increase production, some planters offered incentives, like paying slaves to pick on Sundays or paying them for each pound they picked beyond their quota. Mary Reynolds recalled that at Christmas time the "highes' cotton picker gits a suit of clothes"

(Tanner 2014, 11). Former bondman Henry Bibb, however, demonstrated that overseers often used incentives as tricks. In one case, an overseer offered a prize to the individual who picked the most cotton. The lure of a $2 prize induced enslaved people to work quickly, but the amount of cotton they picked on that day became their quota for succeeding days. Alongside incentives, planters used the threat of punishment to encourage enslaved people to pick faster. If the basket did not weigh enough, then enslaved people understood they would be whipped. Describing the bull whip as a "dreadful instrument of torture," Georgia slave John Brown explained that the six-foot-long plaited strips of leather could be used to "draw blood, or cut clean through to the bone" (Brown 1855, 130). Whips and other torture devices caused enslaved people to experience significant fear when the cotton they picked was weighed at the end of the day. Brown found that when he exceeded the 100-pound quota, he was expected to continue to pick more. His master used the whip to encourage Brown to continue to increase his pace, and, by this means, he reached 160 pounds per day. When Israel Campbell picked only 90 pounds of the required 100 pounds, he was whipped for each pound he was under. To avoid future punishment for failing to pick enough cotton, Campbell placed a melon at the bottom of his basket before it was weighed. He emptied the cotton out of sight of the overseer and then returned to the cotton house after everyone had left to remove the incriminating evidence. Because the deception worked, he continued to employ it whenever he feared his basket was short. He also decided to share his strategy with others who were having similar trouble meeting their quota. Campbell reported that "before the season was over every one of the delinquents knew how to save their backs, and they found it much easier to pick melons and pumpkins than to have their backs cut to pieces" (Campbell 1861, 38).

SUGAR

Growing sugarcane in the United States was a race against the weather. It required a minimum of nine months of frost-free days, and only portions of Louisiana could offer that. In contrast, cane grew for as much as twenty months in the Caribbean before being harvested, and the extra time made the cane juice high in sucrose. Louisiana planters wanted to let the cane grow as long as possible, but they needed to harvest it prior to a frost. The introduction of a more frost-resistant sugarcane in the early nineteenth century helped increase the area in Louisiana where it could be grown. The Louisiana sugar industry also expanded during the antebellum era because of a protective tariff, technological innovations like steam-powered mills, cheap land, and a steady supply of slave labor. More than other staple crops, sugar was industrialized and regimented. Planters sought new methods of getting more productivity from their workers and improvements in cultivation. A growing demand for sugar existed in the antebellum era, with consumption quadrupling in less than twenty years. The start-up costs for sugar production, however, were much higher than those for cotton or tobacco because of the expensive equipment needed to process cane. Initially these mills relied on oxen to operate the machines that crushed the cane, but by the end of the antebellum era, about 80 percent of the sugar plantations used steam engines in their mills. These new mills could crush and grind cane at a faster rate, which required changes in the speed with which cane arrived at the mill. Sugar required more investment in machinery than other staple crops, with $20 per acre invested in machinery compared to $10 in rice and $1.60 in cotton. As a result of these costs, large plantations became the norm in sugar cultivation, and historian Richard Follett has demonstrated that sugar mills had enormous fuel requirements—three to four cords of wood were needed for each hogshead of sugar produced. As the cypress swamps were deforested and wood was becoming scarce, planters switched to bagasse burners that utilized a cheaper alternative, dried cane husks.

The requirements of cultivation and processing created grueling working conditions for enslaved people in Louisiana's cane fields. The number of slaves working in sugar quadrupled between 1827 and 1850. When purchasing slaves for their sugar plantations, masters had both an age and gender preference. Richard Follett has found that 85 percent of the slaves sold to Louisiana sugar planters were men. Because of the strength required in sugar cultivation, planters also preferred that the men they purchased were young. As the size of plantations grew larger, so too did the yield per field hand. Productivity increased from two acres per hand at the beginning of the nineteenth century to more than five acres per hand in the 1850s. These punishing working conditions took their toll on enslaved people's bodies, as overwork and poor nutrition left them susceptible to various diseases and early death.

Numerous tasks needed to be performed on sugar plantations, and landholders divided them up so that everyone, regardless of age or gender, had productive work. Ceceil George remembered,

"Everybody worked,—young an' ole, if yo' could only carry two or three sugar cane, yo' worked" (Tanner 2014, 168). One work group focused on plowing rows in the soil, while another group repaired drainage canals, and only after these tasks had been completed could the cane fields be planted. Describing the coordinated efforts of three gangs to plant cane, Solomon Northup explained that the first gang cut off the tops of the stalks, leaving only the healthy portion. The second gang took the prepared stalks and placed them on the ground. Finally, the third gang covered the stalks with soil. As the cane grew, slaves would hoe the fields, removing weeds until the cane had reached the stage where it no longer needed constant attention. At this point they were assigned additional work like growing corn, cutting the wood that would be required to keep the sugar mills operating twenty-four hours a day at the processing stage, and maintaining the levees that held back the Mississippi River.

Cutting cane began in September. Wielding a thin, sharp, 15" blade, enslaved people first cut off the leaves from the stalk and then the unripe part at the top of the cane. All of the unripe part needed to be removed, or else it would sour the molasses. Next the stalk was cut at the root and then laid in a pile. Enslaved children would follow those cutting the cane and pick up the stalks and place them in a cart to be transported to the sugar mill. All of these actions needed to be performed rapidly and repeatedly. When sugar mills used animal power, they worked at a considerably slower pace than those that were steam powered. The result of the shift to steam-powered mills in the 1830s and 1840s was that enslaved people needed to cut the cane more quickly to keep pace with the mechanized sugar mills. The work was arduous and monotonous, and everyone needed to keep the pace or risk punishment from overseers and black drivers. Solomon Northup was given the whip and directed "to use it upon anyone who was caught standing idle." If he failed to discipline inefficient workers, Northup understood "there was another one for my own back" (Northup 1853, 194). Once the cane arrived at the mill, enslaved children quickly unloaded the carts and placed the cane on a conveyor belt that carried it into the mill where it was ground and the juice extracted. The technical, skilled positions were reserved for men, and they often came to know more about the sugar-making process than the estate manager or overseer. The juice was boiled in open kettles until the liquid had evaporated and granulation had occurred. The sugar was then packed into hogshead with holes for the molasses to drain out.

As they tried to beat the frost, planters could not afford delays during the grinding season. They kept the mills running twenty-four hours a day, and enslaved people worked sixteen- to eighteen-hour shifts. Remembering the grueling schedule, Albert Patterson stated, "We'd work in the fields in the day an' make sugar at night" (Tanner 2014, 110). Hunton Love recalled being so tired after harvesting sugarcane all day that he "wuz too tired to do ennythin' but go to sleep." But planters needed enslaved people like Patterson and Love to cooperate during harvesting, reasoning that if slaves worked slowly or broke the machines, productivity would fall. Fearing resistance to the grueling pace of work, planters offered incentives. Those enslaved people who worked in the sugar mills, for instance, were given calorie-rich cane juice to drink. This made such an impression on Hunton Love that he referred to the sugar house as the "cane juice place" (Tanner 2014, 126). They were also given extra food and other bonuses to promote efficiency. Yet ultimately the threat of violence was deemed to be the most effective means of forcing enslaved people to maintain the ferocious pace. Thomas Hamilton remarked that during harvest time, "the fatigue is so great that nothing but the severest application of the lash can stimulate the human frame to endure it" (Follett 2005, 290).

RICE

Like tobacco, cotton, and sugar, the specific demands associated with rice cultivation profoundly affected the daily lives of enslaved people, and the conditions for fieldwork on a rice plantation were especially challenging. In addition to months of toil in the hot sun, they worked in swampy conditions that bred malarial mosquitoes and were home to numerous snakes. Each day, field-workers were assigned a particular task to complete. Over the years, it was determined, for example, that a slave should sow a half acre per day. Overseers and black drivers supervised the daily work in the fields, ensuring that all tasks were completed. Though slaves were whipped if they failed to finish their assigned tasks, planters also offered incentives for slaves to work hard. If slaves did not miss a single day's work because of ill health, for instance, they received an extra bushel of rice. Annual prizes were awarded to slaves who demonstrated special skill in plowing and hoeing. Carelessness, by contrast, was punished. Historian Charles Joyner explained that one South Carolina overseer "administered twelve lashes each to eight women for 'hoeing corn bad'" (Joyner 1984, 53).

An enormous amount of labor needed to be performed on rice plantations before the first seeds were planted. Beginning in December, the fields needed to be prepared. Groups of women would burn the tall stubble from the previous season, and then the soil needed to be loosened, turned, and leveled. Before 1830, enslaved people completed this task with a hoe, which was extremely arduous, while after 1830, the use of animals and a plow made the task somewhat easier. Planters made the shift to a plow once the price of slaves increased, hoping to reduce the risk of overwork or injury to field hands whose labor was the key to their profit. Historian Leslie Schwalm has found that this work was divided along gender lines. Only men used the plow even though the work was similar to what women did with a hoe. In addition to preparing the fields for planting, the irrigation system on rice plantations needed to be checked and repaired. Referred to as "mudwork," enslaved people repaired any breaks in the banks or the floodgates and scooped mud from the ditches, while standing up to their hips in muddy water. Before planting could begin, historian Charles Joyner has explained that seed rice was soaked in mud and then dried so that it did not float to the surface when the fields were flooded.

Sowing rice, which began in mid-March, required more skill than other staple crops. Women on rice plantations were assigned this task, and mothers taught their daughters how to expertly throw seeds into the furrows. After the seeds had been planted, the fields were then alternately flooded and drained during the growing season. Once the rice began to sprout, the fields needed to be weeded and hoed. Charles Ball stated that "watering and weeding the rice is considered one of the most unhealthy occupations on a southern plantation" because enslaved people stayed in the mud and water for weeks at a time (Ball 1837, 204). Beginning at age twelve, children began working in the rice fields, with their parents teaching them how to hoe, plow, and sow. But for nearly two months at the end of the growing season, rice required little attention, and enslaved people were assigned to other work until harvest. Whenever the rice did not need attention, most field hands switched their attention to growing crops like corn, potatoes, or sweet potatoes for the plantation. During the slack time, enslaved people were assigned various tasks, but stripping the fodder from the corn stalks was considered the most exhausting and unappealing.

The rice harvest began in the middle of August. To cut rice, enslaved people grasped the stalks with one hand and wielded a sickle in the other, and the stalks of rice were left to dry before being bundled together. Enslaved women placed the bundles on their heads and carried them to flat-bottomed boats so that they could be transported for processing. Initially by hand and later by machines, grains were loosened from the stalk and then separated from the chaff, and finally, a mortar and pestle were used to remove the grain from the hull. Broken rice would be consumed on the plantation, while the whole grains were sold. Though not used for commercial sale, other parts of the plants had uses on the plantation, with the husks used as fertilizer and the stubble as livestock bedding. Once the harvest of rice and other food crops had finished, attention turned to preparing for the next growing season.

The cultivation of rice included numerous skilled jobs, from plowing even rows to separating rice grain from the hull without breaking it. In addition, carpenters were needed to perform a variety of tasks. With only hand tools, they built plantation houses, slave cabins, and barns. Carpenters also constructed the irrigation system that flooded the rice fields and the row boats and canoes used to transport the rice after the harvest. Skill was required to make the special baskets that were used during the winnowing process when the chaff was separated from the grain. Many former slaves expressed pride in the work they performed to transform the swampy lowcountry into productive rice plantations.

SLAVE HIRING

Hiring slaves out was one option for slave owners who had more slaves than they could profitably use, and January 1 was the traditional hiring day around the South. Harriet Jacobs remembered that on New Year's Eve, enslaved people gathered to "wait anxiously" to find out who would be hired and where they would be sent (Jacobs 1861, 25). Some deals were handled privately between neighbors, while others employed an auctioneer to organize the bidding. In these transactions, a contract was signed between the owner and the hirer stipulating the length of time the slave would be hired for (usually one year) and the rate. This system offered poorer white Southerners the opportunity to employ slave labor without the cost of slave purchase and gave slave owners a mechanism to respond flexibly to changing economic conditions. In the Chesapeake, slave owners often had surplus labor because of the natural increase in the slave population, the decline in tobacco cultivation, and the corresponding increase in grain production. As many planters switched to wheat, they did not need as much labor as when they grew tobacco. While some owners responded to these changes by selling slaves to the lower South, others rented them instead. When caterpillars destroyed his cotton crop in 1845, for example, Edwin Epps hired out his slaves in one of the sugar parishes in Louisiana. He had no interest in selling, but he needed to reduce his expenses and bring in cash to get through the financial crisis. Hiring out was the best option for Epps because it offered him a source of income and it saved the expense of paying for the slaves' upkeep. James Pennington argued that masters also saw slave hiring as a means to "get among their slaves useful trades" (Pennington 1849, 4). Hiring out enslaved boys to tradesmen taught them skills as a blacksmith or stone mason that they could then profitably utilize on their master's plantation.

Enslaved men and women were hired out to perform a variety of jobs—working in agriculture; in domestic service; and in industrial sectors like tobacco factories, coal mines, and building canals and railroads. While domestic and agricultural work was comparable whether enslaved people worked for an owner or an employer, urban areas offered distinct experiences. Cities like Richmond, Virginia, depended heavily on slave labor, and enslaved people worked as porters at train stations and as waiters, cooks, and chambermaids in hotels and were employed in forging iron, milling flour, making soap, and, most important, processing tobacco. By 1860, Richmond had fifty-nine tobacco factories, and slaves performed necessary work flavoring chewing tobacco and producing chewing plugs. Henry Brown, who worked in a tobacco manufactory, explained that slaves worked between fourteen and sixteen hours a day removing stems from the tobacco leaves and adding a licorice and sugar flavoring that gave "the tobacco that sweetish taste which renders it not perfectly abhorrent to those who chew it" (Brown 1851, 41). Once flavored, the tobacco was then pressed, packaged, and shipped to market. Enslaved people hired to stem the tobacco leaves or twist tobacco plugs found the work repetitive, the hours long, and the punishment severe. Henry Brown, for instance, witnessed the beating of one slave simply because he was ten minutes late for work.

Given the influx of hundreds of slaves to work in mills, factories, and foundries, employers rarely offered housing, and hired slaves used board money to live apart from their owners. Living out meant that after the workday ended enslaved people controlled their time and could move around the city, shopping or visiting friends, a freedom of movement not possible on the plantation. In cities like

Richmond, some enslaved people spent their leisure time drinking, gambling, gossiping, dancing, and playing billiards. Parties were opportunities for men and women to socialize without being surveilled, and some white Southerners worried that unsupervised leisure activities promoted insolence and resistance. Court records indicate that some hired slaves did become defiant, sometimes refusing to perform certain tasks, arriving late, and leaving early.

Because of the need for large numbers of workers, companies building roads, canals, or railroads offered the best rates for slave hiring. This work paid the highest but also had the greatest risks because of dangerous working conditions. David Cecelski has argued, however, that "canal digging was the cruelest, most dangerous, unhealthy, and exhausting labor in the American South" (Cecelski 2001, 109). Not only was the work itself exhausting, but the conditions were awful. One task that slaves performed was to remove vines, trees, and roots along the path of the canal. Moses Grandy, who was hired to work as a canal digger near the Great Dismal Swamp, described being "up to the middle or much deeper in mud and water, cutting away roots and baling out mud" (Grandy 1843, 35). As canal diggers literally struggled to keep their heads above water, they also had to avoid the snakes that inhabited the swamps. Along with digging the canals, enslaved people maintained them, removing debris from the canal, repairing wooden locks, and shoring up the banks against erosion. Discipline was harsh, and any slave who could not complete his assigned task would be whipped. Grandy observed a slave who was flogged, pickled, a process where pork brine was put on the person's bleeding back to increase the pain, and then tied up all day as flies and mosquitoes settled on his injured back.

The opening of canals and the advent of steamboats increased commercial activity by making transportation quicker and cheaper, but they also created opportunities for independence and even escape. Moses Grandy piloted a boat hauling goods from Elizabeth City, North Carolina, to Norfolk, Virginia, along the 22 miles of Dismal Swamp Canal. He became skilled at navigating rivers and at making connections with people who needed their goods hauled. Frederick Douglass was hired out to a shipbuilder in Baltimore to learn how to caulk a ship so that the hull was watertight. In one year, Douglass became an experienced caulker who could "command the highest wages," sometimes as much as $9 a week. As a result, Douglass was permitted to find his own employment and return to his master each Saturday night to deliver his wages.

Slaves hired to work on boats traveling up and down the Mississippi River could escape when they docked in Northern cities to unload passengers and trade goods. When William Wells Brown, for instance, was hired as a steward to wait on steamboat passengers as they traveled the Mississippi River, he "thought of leaving the boat at some landing-place, and trying to make my escape to Canada" (Brown 1849, 30). The mobility of bondmen like Douglass, Brown, and Grandy provided opportunities to resist the control of their master and to consider the best way to achieve freedom.

When slave owners and hirers made their contracts, they often separated families, just as a sale did. Some employers would hire women and their young children, but as soon as the children reached the age of ten, they would be hired out alone. The experience of Henry Bruce demonstrates this process. In 1845, he and his siblings were hired out with their mother, but the next year, when Bruce was ten, he was separated from his family and hired to work in a tobacco factory. Enslaved people did not simply submit to the hiring agreements between white Southerners. Some slaves attempted to influence these transactions by asking that the contract protect their ability to visit family, by requesting that a particular white Southerner hire them, or by threatening to run away if they were hired to someone for whom they did not want to work (Martin 2004, 56, 61, 66).

Although slave owners hired out surplus slaves so that they could make money, they also risked their property in these transactions. If mistreated, abused, or neglected, hired slaves might become sick or injured. Frances Kemble argued that the "chief aim" of those who hired slaves was "to get as much out of them, and expend as little on them, as possible" (Kemble 1863, 71). To protect their long-term property interest, some owners took seriously slaves' complaints that employers were abusive and interceded on their behalf. As Jonathan Martin has demonstrated, this "dual mastery" between slave owner and hirer allowed enslaved people the opportunity to exploit the division of power. When employers contracted to hire slaves, they were responsible for feeding, clothing, and housing them. Some employers, however, promised more than they delivered, and this became a point of negotiation between hirers, owners, and slaves. When Henry Bruce was hired to a farmer, for example, who served food in dirty dishes, Bruce refused to eat it. Ultimately his master accommodated his wishes, and Bruce walked to his master's farm 1 mile away each day for his meals. While not all slave owners negotiated with slaves to get them to accept a hiring arrangement, some found the criticisms of the hirer persuasive enough to intervene.

REPRODUCTION AND THE "FANCY TRADE"

Slave owners calculated the value of an enslaved woman based on a number of factors. Some like age, health, and physical strength were common to their assessment of both men and women, but female slaves had a value for slave owners beyond their ability to pick cotton or sew a dress. A woman's ability to reproduce also had economic value for slave owners. After traveling through the South, Frederick Law Olmsted observed that "a slave woman is commonly esteemed least for her working qualities, most for those qualities which give value to a brood-mare" (Olmsted 1862, 57). The reality was a simple one: when an enslaved woman bore a child, the slave owner profited. In 1819, Thomas Jefferson responded to the death of five young enslaved children by instructing his overseers to allow "breeding women" more time to raise their children and to worry less about how much they worked in the fields. Jefferson concluded that "a child raised every 2. years is of more profit than the crop of the best laboring man" (Jefferson 1819). As a result of this logic, some slave owners believed they could interfere with the private lives of enslaved people by selecting partners and even breeding their slaves. When an enslaved woman named Critty, for example, did not bear any children with her first husband, "she was compelled to take a second husband" (Brown 1855, 17). But when Critty still did not produce any offspring, she was sold. Her owner calculated that Critty's worth depended upon her ability to reproduce, and when she failed, he had no further use for her.

Because the system of slavery defined enslaved women as property, owners claimed the right to control their bodies, to expect that they produce children, and to assault them sexually. These circumstances led Harriet Jacobs to conclude that "slavery is terrible for men, but it is far more terrible for women." She emphasized that women experienced unique "wrongs, and sufferings, and mortifications" (Jacobs 1861, 119). The work of enslaved men and women differed, therefore, because women could face sexual assault and exploitation from their master, his sons, overseers, and any guests on the plantation. Under slavery, sexual coercion took many forms as white men claimed mastery over an enslaved woman's body. James Norcum uttered vile sexual suggestions to the teenaged Harriet Jacobs, threatening her with punishment if she told anyone.

John Brown stated that as he and the rest of the slave coffle were being transported to market, a slave trader and his white associates "brutally ill-used" a female slave over a period of several days until he sold her (Brown 1855, 19). In law, the rape of an enslaved woman by her owner was not a crime. With the circumspection common to nineteenth-century narratives, Elizabeth Keckley described a painful time in her life when a white man "with base designs . . . persecuted" her for four years, and she became a mother (Keckley 1868, 39). Slave owners like William Walker also purchased enslaved women as their slave mistresses. Walker informed Cynthia that she had a choice to live with him or to be sold "as a field hand on the worst plantation on the river" (Brown 1849, 46). She became Walker's mistress and housekeeper, but he did not uphold his end of the bargain. Ruthlessly asserting his rights as a property owner, Walker sold Cynthia and her four children as soon as he married. He first exploited Cynthia and then profited financially from her reproductive labor.

A market in women considered sexually attractive to white men emerged, and the "fancy trade" drew planters and businessmen who wanted to purchase a concubine. Brenda Stevenson has argued that buyers usually selected concubines who were described as "pretty white." In particular, white men highly prized women who had light skin, straight hair, and blue eyes (Stevenson 2013, 107). Women were dressed in silk clothes and jewelry and presented for sale in the New Orleans market, and evidence suggests that these sales could bring high prices. Walter Johnson has stated that the sale of women at times "reached three hundred percent of the median prices paid in a given year" (Johnson 1999, 113). Solomon Northup described a slave trader's refusal to sell a light-skinned child because "there were heaps and piles of money to be made of her" when she was older. Because Emily was "an extra handsome, fancy piece," the trader estimated that a buyer would spend as much as $5,000 for her (Northup 1853, 86–87). Former slave Mary Reynolds remembered that her master bought a well-dressed, light-skinned enslaved woman and set her up in a cabin separated from the slave quarter. The stated reason for her presence was that, as a skilled seamstress, she would make clothes for the white family. Over time, however, there was gossip that she was the master's slave mistress, and he was the father of her children. Not only did these women experience sexual coercion at the hands of white men, but they also faced the rage of the plantation mistress who blamed enslaved women for the actions of her husband. To pacify a jealous wife, slave owners would often sell the enslaved women and the children to whom they had given birth.

The experiences of Corinna Hinton demonstrate how domestic and sexual labor could be interwoven. Richmond slave trader Silas Omohundro purchased Hinton, and she became his concubine, bearing him several children. In addition, Hinton assisted Omohundro in his business, providing food to slaves kept in his jail before their sale and acquiring the clothes they would wear at the auction. In particular, Hinton dressed "fancy girls" in expensive clothes to raise their value and operated Omohundro's boardinghouse. As she assisted a slave trader, she in turn earned money and fine clothes for herself. Historian Alexandra Finley has argued that Hinton "took the domestic and reproductive labor for which she was valued and attempted to use it for her own economic advantage" (Finley 2017, 430).

While white men appropriated enslaved women's bodies for their own purposes, white women also wanted to utilize their reproductive labor. White families entered the marketplace seeking enslaved women who could serve as wet nurses for their children. Stephanie Jones-Rogers has argued that the use of enslaved women to suckle white infants created "a demand for the intimate labor that such nurses performed in southern homes" (Jones-Rogers, 2019, 101–102). When Gertrude Thomas needed a wet nurse for her baby, her father offered her the services of an enslaved woman on his plantation who had recently lost her child. If arrangements could not be made privately, numerous white families placed advertisements in the newspaper to hire or purchase a wet nurse. Some women who were available for hire had young children, and so the breast milk would be divided between two infants. But not all white families wanted the milk to be shared, and so some advertisements stipulated that the hirer preferred a wet nurse "without incumbrance" (*Daily Dispatch* 1852, 2). Enslaved mothers deemed healthy and possessing an adequate supply of milk moved from one household to another as their labor was needed. In some cases, formal sales or hiring transactions occurred, but in others, white women made short-term arrangements with their neighbors and exchanged the labor of a wet nurse for a field hand.

White families also called on the service of enslaved black women as midwives, when both slaves and white women were in labor. Mildred Graves, a former slave from Hanover County, Virginia, was a skilled midwife who was regularly hired out to white families in the area. Graves remembered with pride her most difficult case when a white women named Mrs. Leake requested that Graves assist her instead of two Richmond doctors. Working all through the night, Graves explained, "I did ev'ything I knowed an' somethings I didn' know. I don' know how I done it, but anyway a son was born dat mornin' an' dat boy lived." Even the Richmond doctors who had scoffed at her as a witch doctor conceded that she had done well (Perdue, Barden, and Phillips 1976, 120–121). Unlike medical doctors who learned their trade at school and in books, enslaved midwives derived their skills as healers from their mothers or grandmothers who passed on their knowledge from one generation to the next. Midwives used their knowledge of herbal remedies to assist in births and dispensed cloves and whiskey, for instance, to reduce labor pains. Midwives also treated common illnesses like cough, toothache, and backache. Ransom Sidney Taylor stated that his mother was a healer who "used roots, herbs, and grease" to make them well (Rawick 1974, 15: 339). Other healers favored herbal teas to ward away fevers. Midwives performed a variety of tasks connected to healing—administering medicine, preparing food for those who were ill, and cleaning soiled clothes and bed linen. Sharla Fett has noted that "midwifery and sickcare, along with cooking and sewing, were among the few specialized labor roles reserved for enslaved women" (Fett 2002, 112).

DOMESTIC WORK

While most enslaved people spent their lives as field-workers, many large plantations used the labor of a small percentage of enslaved people in a variety of domestic contexts. There were cooks, maids, gardeners, nurses, coachmen, and manservants who kept the household running. On smaller landholdings, enslaved people performed both agricultural and domestic work. Annie Hawkins's mother, for instance, worked in the fields during the day but returned to cook dinner for the planter's family. Women's domestic work involved cleaning—windows, carpets, clothes, floors, and dishes. They polished wood and prepared meals for the family and larger ones when the family entertained. Enslaved women took care of their master's children, and they spun, wove, and sewed. Slaves who worked in the Big House often received better food and clothes than field hands but were at the beck and call of their mistress twenty-four hours a day. Enslaved women were often forced to sleep on the floor in the doorway of their mistress's room in case she had need of them during the night. In general, house slaves were subject to the daily whims and moods of the mistress in a way that field hands were not.

Young children, women, and people over fifty years often performed domestic work as cooks, grooms, gardeners, or maids. They made soap and hauled water to wash the clothes. Young girls would set and clear the table, mind young children, empty chamber pots, or fetch items the mistress wanted. Male children often did basic jobs like sweeping, running errands, bringing water or wood to the household, and cleaning boots. Being young, however, did not protect children from cruel punishment. At the age of four, Lizzie Hobbs began taking care of her owner's daughter, and she was assured that if she performed well she could become a maid when she was older. Lizzie's basic job was to stop the baby from crying by rocking the cradle and shooing away flies. On one occasion, she rocked too hard, the baby fell out of the cradle, and Lizzie was whipped for being careless. When Tom Hawkins started as a houseboy, his job was to keep his mistress's fire going all night. If she needed him and he slept through her cries, however, she would hit him with a stick. Whenever Tom did something she did not like during the day, his mistress usually pulled his hair or ears to show her displeasure. If Louis Hughes did not understand his mistress's orders when he was helping her prepare the loom for weaving, he "did not fail to receive the customary blow, or blows, from her hand" (Hughes 1897, 41).

In most popular understandings of slavery, violence was meted out by men. Field hands who worked too slowly were whipped by an overseer or the master. But within the plantation household, mistresses supervised the work performed there and exerted independent authority over enslaved people. Historian Thavolia Glymph has demonstrated that plantation mistresses used violence—sometimes brutal and sadistic violence—to achieve mastery over their slaves, without risking their status as "ladies." This violence ranged from pulling hair and slapping faces to severe whippings and burnings. Louis Hughes observed his mistress "pinch and choke" a weaver who displeased her (Hughes 1897, 40). Southern women used devices that "ran the gamut from brooms, tongs, irons, shovels, and their hands to whatever was most readily available" (Glymph 2008, 35). The offense committed did not have to be large; any displeasure could engender cruelty. Austin Steward emphasized that his mistress "was continually finding fault with some of the servants." When angered, Mrs. Helm would strike "them over the head with a heavy iron key, until the blood ran" or whip them "with a cowhide, which she always kept by her side when sitting in her room" (Steward 1857, 24). Slaves were whipped if they were not deferential, if the mistress believed they stole food, or if they failed to remove a stain from a piece of clothing. Frederick Douglass described a mistress who whipped the maids every time they passed by her chair to make them work faster. When the baby Delia Garlic was minding hurt its hand, the child's mother "picked up a hot iron" and burned Delia's arm and hand. In another instance, Delia's mistress called her a "black devil" and hit her in the head with a stick (Berlin, Favreau, and Miller 1998, 10). Enslaved women might be beaten without cause simply because the mistress feared that her husband was having a sexual relationship with them.

Masters and mistresses possessed enormous power to compel the labor of enslaved people and mete out punishment if the work was not completed to their satisfaction. Violence and fear were key elements of white domination of black lives. Yet their power was not total. Around the edges of the economic life controlled by slave owners, enslaved people acted as producers and consumers in their own right.

INDEPENDENT PRODUCTION

In the formal slave economy, a staple crop was produced for the market, and when enslaved people were not needed cultivating that staple crop, countless other jobs occupied their time and kept the plantation running. Hides needed to be tanned, cows milked, butter churned, wheels mended, and wood chopped. The plantation was a hive of activity ranging from a blacksmith sharpening a hoe that had become blunt from being banged against one rock too many to women weaving on a loom late into the night so that enslaved people could receive their annual allotment of clothes. This labor occupied most of an enslaved person's day, and it was directed not for their own benefit but at increasing the profitability of the plantation. Alongside these economic activities, however, existed productive labor that enslaved people controlled. After hours, enslaved people worked for themselves and their family.

Though the supply was limited, enslaved people did have time that they could call their own, and they used their skills to produce items that could be sold or traded for consumption goods that planters did not provide. Enslaved people had garden patches, as much as two to three acres, to grow vegetables or staple crops, and they hunted, fished, and raised poultry as well. Scholars disagree

This 1825 account of a slave sale demonstrates that every enslaved person had a price based on his or her age, gender, and health. The domestic slave trade expanded in the nineteenth century as roughly three-quarters of a million people were sold from the Upper South to the Lower South. (National Archives)

about how this informal slave economy should be understood. When an enslaved person sold a commodity like a chicken or corn, is this evidence of independent economic activity? Without the permission of their owner, after all, most of this independent production would not be possible. Scholars also emphasize that some of the work performed by slaves in their own time benefited the master. Sugar planters, for instance, needed wood for the mills, but they didn't want to take time away from the staple crop to collect and chop it. By paying enslaved people a small amount of money for working on Sundays, masters were able to get the wood they needed at a small price. Similarly, planters often provided cloth, and enslaved women were expected to sew their family's clothes in their own time. In both of these instances, the work of the enslaved people cut costs, thereby increasing the profitability of a plantation. It was in a planter's interest to let slaves hunt, fish, or cultivate a vegetable garden if needed calories could be consumed without the master paying any extra for it. One Carolina overseer believed that independent production had the additional benefit of keeping slaves tied to the land. "No Negro with a well stocked poultry house, a small crop advancing, [or] a canoe partly finished . . . will ever run away" (Breeden 1980, 266). The activities performed by enslaved people on their own time existed within the slave system, not separate from it.

Yet scholars have also demonstrated that by producing for their own consumption and for sale or exchange, enslaved people improved the quality of their lives and resisted owners' domination. Planters provided rations to slaves that rarely varied, usually corn and a salted meat, and so the ability to grow vegetables, trap raccoons, or trade for goods with a shopkeeper added both nourishment and variety to their diet. In addition to growing food, enslaved people made brooms, baskets, horse collars, and other items to sell. Charles Ball has suggested that tobacco was "indispensable to comfort" and the "highest of enjoyments" (Ball 1837, 191). When enslaved people, therefore, grew or produced items to be traded for tobacco that both men and women would smoke in clay pipes, they made production and consumption decisions that reflected their own wishes and not those of their master.

Records indicate that when enslaved people grew corn, raised poultry, or made horse collars, they most often sold these items to their master. Planters kept accounts of the transactions, identifying the value of the items they purchased and what slaves received in return, and enslaved people often used the money they raised to buy items they could not produce, like sugar, tobacco, rum, or coffee. The father of Annie Parks worked a patch of land to grow cotton "so that he could make a little money to buy things for hisself and his family" (Tanner 2014, 35). Woodworking skills were used to make furniture or bowls that could be sold or exchanged for needed items, especially clothes. Planters provided slaves with clothing made of a cheap, coarse cloth, and enslaved people placed a high premium on clothing made from bright colors or fine material. In many instances, slave owners opted not to provide clothing or shoes for children under seven because they did not do any productive work. Parents, therefore, had the choice of keeping these children inside the slave cabin all winter or providing clothing for them. Animal skins could be fashioned into moccasins to protect young feet from the frost. Elizabeth Ross Hite recalled that her mother sold the corn she grew to her master and then used the proceeds to buy clothes for her family. Most of this work was performed on Sundays, the traditional day off, with the permission of owners. Yet the ability to make their own consumption and production decisions could erode the owner's power. Charles Ball argued that "the slave is a kind of freeman on Sunday all over the southern country; and it is in truth, by the exercise of his liberty on this day, that he is enabled to provide himself and his family, with many of the necessaries of life that his master refuses to supply him with" (Ball 1837, 273).

In some instances, the independent economic activity of slaves connected them to markets beyond the plantation. In Louisiana, enslaved people gathered Spanish moss from the trees, dried it, and then packed it into bales for shipment. They made contacts with agents along the Mississippi River who sold the moss, often to furniture makers who used it to make mattresses and cushions. Records from one sugar plantation reveal that in 1844, twenty-two slaves sent over 9,700 pounds of moss to St. Louis and received $162 for their labor (McDonald 1993, 287). With the money they earned, enslaved people decided to purchase livestock; ready-made clothes; or household items like candles, soap, or kettles. These independent economic activities permitted enslaved people to exert a measure of control over their daily existence and to improve the quality of their material life.

While many informal economic transactions occurred with the master's permission, some went on behind his back. Elizabeth Ross Hite's father snuck out at night to trap possum for his family but was careful not to let the master find out. Hite remembered that when they ate the possum, they "would stop up de holes to keep de scent from leakin' out" (Tanner 2014, 183). In other instances, whites participated in illicit trade with enslaved people. When Jacob Green decided to run away from his master, he raised the money he would need for his journey by stealing from neighboring plantations. Green "arranged with a Dutchman to steal small pigs, chickens, and any poultry" he could lay his hands on. In ten months, he had accumulated $124, enough for him to leave (Green 1864, 22). In addition to selling stolen goods, enslaved people traded clandestinely for alcohol, a commodity that slave owners tried to restrict. Charles Ball took advantage of the river trade to add meat to his diet without his master's knowledge. When Ball was fishing in a river to catch shad for the plantation, he made contact with a boat captain who had bacon on board. Finding that the captain was willing to make a deal, Ball exchanged 300 shad for 100 pounds of bacon. Defending the transaction, Ball acknowledged that he was selling something that "in point of law, did not belong to me; but to which, nevertheless, I felt in my conscience that I had a better right than any other person. In support of the right, which I felt to be on my side in this case, came a keen appetite for the bacon, which settled the controversy, upon the question of the morality of this traffic, in my favour" (Ball 1837, 301).

Antebellum slavery was, at its core, a system of staple crop production that allowed a small class of wealthy, white slaveholders to extract the enormous profits generated by the African American workers they had reduced to bondage. The plantation regime was deliberately structured in order to make the production of staple crops as efficient and profitable as possible but, since they were owned rather than paid wages, slaves received no direct economic benefit from the labor they performed. Indeed, the denial of compensation was itself a means of slaveholder domination as it prevented African Americans from achieving economic autonomy through accumulating savings or by acquiring property of their own. Yet even as their working lives were subjected to the economic desires of their masters, we have seen that enslaved people created an informal economy that allowed them to achieve a limited degree of economic agency. This activity is highly significant not only as a source of resistance to the system under which they lived but also because it provided a well of experience for African Americans to draw upon after emancipation. When freedom came, former slaves sought to take full control of their economic lives and were better prepared to do so than their former masters or even Northern reformers recognized.

DOCUMENT: SOLOMON NORTHUP, *TWELVE YEARS A SLAVE* (1853)

Born in New York in 1808, Solomon Northup was kidnapped and sold into slavery in 1841. He worked in the sugar and cotton fields of Louisiana, most of it for the cruel master Edwin Epps, before regaining his freedom in 1853. In this passage from his narrative, Northup describes the work performed by enslaved people to grow cotton and the techniques used by owners to force a specific pace in the fields.

The beds, or ridges, are six feet wide, that is, from water furrow to water furrow. A plough drawn by one mule is then run along the top of the ridge or center of the bed, making the drill, into which a girl usually drops the seed, which she carries in a bag hung round her neck. Behind her comes a mule and harrow, covering up the seed, so that two mules three slaves, a plough and harrow, are employed in planting a row of cotton. This is done in the months of March and April. Corn is planted in February. When there are no cold rains, the cotton usually makes its appearance in a week. In the course of eight or ten days afterwards the first hoeing is commenced. This is performed in part, also, by the aid of the plough and mule. The plough passes as near as possible to the cotton on both sides, throwing the furrow from it. Slaves follow with their hoes, cutting up the grass and cotton, leaving hills two feet and a half apart. This is called scraping cotton. In two weeks more commences the second hoeing. This time the furrow is thrown towards the cotton. Only one stalk, the largest, is now left standing in each hill. In another fortnight it is hoed the third time, throwing the furrow towards the cotton in the same manner as before, and killing all the grass between the rows. About the first of July, when it is a foot high or thereabouts, it is hoed the fourth and last time. Now the whole space between the rows is ploughed, leaving a deep water furrow in the center. During all these hoeings the overseer or driver follows the slaves on horseback with a whip, such as has been described. The fastest hoer takes the lead row. He is usually about a rod in advance of his companions. If one of them passes him, he is whipped. If one falls behind or is a moment idle, he is whipped. In fact, the lash is flying from morning until night, the whole day long. The hoeing season thus continues from April until July, a field having no sooner been finished once, than it is commenced again.

In the latter part of August begins the cotton picking season. At this time each slave is presented with a sack. A strap is fastened to it, which goes over the neck, holding the mouth of the sack breast high, while the bottom reaches nearly to the ground. Each one is also presented with a large basket that will hold about two barrels. This is to put the cotton in when the sack is filled. The baskets are carried to the field and placed at the beginning of the rows.

When a new hand, one unaccustomed to the business, is sent for the first time into the field, he is whipped up smartly, and made for that day to pick as fast as he can possibly. At night it is weighed, so that his capability in cotton picking is known. He must bring in the same weight each night following. If it falls short, it is considered evidence that he has been laggard, and a greater or less number of lashes is the penalty.

An ordinary day's work is 200 pounds. A slave who is accustomed to picking, is punished, if he or she brings in a less quantity than that. There is a great difference among them as regards this kind of labor. Some of them seem to have a natural knack, or quickness, which enables them to pick with great celerity, and with both hands, while others, with whatever practice or industry, are utterly unable to come up to the ordinary standard. Such hands are taken from the cotton field and employed in other business. . . .

Sometimes the slave picks down one side of a row, and back upon the other, but more usually, there is one on either side, gathering all that has blossomed, leaving the unopened bolls for a succeeding picking. When the sack is filled, it is emptied into the basket and trodden down. It is necessary to be extremely careful the first time going through the field, in order not to break the branches off the stalks. The cotton will not bloom upon a broken branch. Epps never failed to inflict the severest chastisement on the unlucky servant who, either carelessly or unavoidably, was guilty in the least degree in this respect.

The hands are required to be in the cotton field as soon as it is light in the morning, and, with the exception of ten or fifteen minutes, which is given them at noon to swallow their allowance of cold bacon, they are not permitted to be a moment idle until it is too dark to see, and when the moon is full, they often times labor till the middle of the night. They do not dare to stop even at dinner time, nor return to the quarters, however late it be, until the order to halt is given by the driver.

The day's work over in the field, the baskets are "toted," or in other words, carried to the gin-house, where the cotton is weighed. No matter how fatigued and weary he may be—no matter how much he longs for sleep and rest—a slave never approaches the gin-house with his basket of cotton but with fear. If it falls short in weight—if he has not performed the full task appointed him, he knows that he must suffer. And if he has exceeded it by 10 or 20 pounds, in all probability his master will measure the next day's task accordingly. So, whether he has too little or too much, his approach to the gin-house is always with fear and trembling.

Source: Solomon Northup. *Twelve Years a Slave: Narrative of Solomon Northup, a Citizen of New-York, Kidnapped in Washington City in 1841, and Rescued in 1853.* Auburn, NY: Derby and Miller, 1853, 164–168.

FURTHER READING

Ball, Charles. 1837. *Slavery in the United States: A Narrative of the Life and Adventures of Charles Ball.* New York: John S. Taylor.

Baptist, Edward. 2014. *The Half Has Never Been Told: Slavery and the Making of American Capitalism*. New York: Basic Books.

Berlin, Ira, Marc Favreau, and Steven F. Miller, eds. 1998. *Remembering Slavery: African Americans Talk about Their Personal Experiences of Slavery and Emancipation*. New York: The New Press.

Bibb, Henry. 1849. *Narrative of the Life and Adventures of Henry Bibb, an American Slave*. New York: printed by the author.

Breeden, James O., ed. 1980. *Advice among Masters*. Westport, CT: Greenwood Press.

Brown, Henry. 1851. *Narrative of the Life of Henry Box Brown*. Manchester: Lee and Glynn.

Brown, John. 1855. *Slave Life in Georgia: A Narrative of the Life, Sufferings and Escape of John Brown*. London: W. M. Watts, 1855.

Brown, William Wells. 1849. *Narrative of William W. Brown, a Fugitive Slave*. London: Charles Gilpin.

Campbell, Israel. 1861. *An Autobiography, Bond and Free*. Philadelphia: printed by the author.

Cecelski, David S. 2001. *The Waterman's Song: Slavery and Freedom in Maritime North Carolina*. Chapel Hill: University of North Carolina Press.

Daily Dispatch, Richmond, VA. November 3, 1852, p. 2.

Douglass, Frederick. 1845. *Narrative of the Life of Frederick Douglass: An American Slave, Written by Himself*. Boston, MA: Antislavery Office.

Fett, Sharla M. 2002. *Working Cures: Healing, Health, and Power on Southern Slave Plantations*. Chapel Hill: University of North Carolina Press.

Finley, Alexandra. 2017. "'Cash to Corinna': Domestic Labor and Sexual Economy in the 'Fancy Trade.'" *The Journal of American History* 104, no. 2 (September): 410–430.

Follett, Richard. 2005. "'Lives of Living Death': The Reproductive Lives of Slave Women in the Cane World of Louisiana." *Slavery and Abolition* 26, no. 2 (August): 289–304.

Glymph, Thavolia. 2008. *Out of the House of Bondage: The Transformation of the Plantation Household*. New York: Cambridge University Press.

Grandy, Moses. 1843. *Narrative of the Life of Moses Grandy, Late a Slave in the United States of America*. London: Charles Gilpin.

Green, Jacob D. 1864. *Narrative of the Life of J.D. Green, a Runaway Slave, from Kentucky, Containing an Account of His Three Escapes, in 1839, 1846, and 1848*. Huddersfield, England: Henry Fielding.

Henson, Josiah. 1849. *The Life of Josiah Henson, Formerly a Slave*. Boston: A. D. Phelps.

Hughes, Louis. 1897. *Thirty Years a Slave: From Bondage to Freedom*. Milwaukee, WI: South Side Printing Co.

Jacobs, Harriet. 1861. *Incidents in the Life of a Slave Girl*. Boston: printed by the author.

Jefferson, Thomas, to Joel Yancey. January 17, 1819. Founders Online, National Archives, accessed July 6, 2019. https://founders.archives.gov/documents/Jefferson/03-13-02-0522. (Original source: *The Papers* of Thomas Jefferson, Retirement Series, vol. 13, April 22, 1818, to January 31, 1819, ed. J. Jefferson Looney. Princeton, NJ: Princeton University Press, 2016, pp. 581–583.)

Johnson, Walter. 1999. *Soul by Soul: Life inside the Antebellum Slave Market.* Cambridge, MA: Harvard University Press.

Jones-Rogers, Stephanie E. 2019. *They Were Her Property: White Women as Slave Owners in the American South.* New Haven, CT: Yale University Press.

Joyner, Charles. 1984. *Down by the Riverside: A South Carolina Slave Community.* Urbana: University of Illinois Press.

Keckley, Elizabeth. 1868. *Behind the Scenes: Thirty Years a Slave, and Four Years in the White House.* New York: G. W. Carleton & Co.

Kemble, Frances Anne. 1863. *Journal of a Residence on a Georgian Plantation in 1838–1839.* New York: Harper & Brothers.

Loguen, Jermain. 1859. *The Rev. J.W. Loguen, as a Slave and as a Freeman.* Syracuse, NY: J.G.K. Truair & Co.

Martin, Jonathan D. 2004. *Divided Mastery: Slave Hiring in the American South.* Cambridge, MA: Harvard University Press, 2004.

McDonald, Roderick A. 1993. "Independent Economic Production by Slaves on Antebellum Louisiana Sugar Plantations." In *Cultivation and Culture: Labor and the Shaping of Slave Life in the Americas*, edited by Ira Berlin and Philip D. Morgan. Charlottesville: University Press of Virginia, 275–299.

Northup, Solomon. 1853. *Twelve Years a Slave: Narrative of Solomon Northup, a Citizen of New-York, Kidnapped in Washington City in 1841, and Rescued in 1853.* Auburn, NY: Derby and Miller.

O'Donovan, Susan Eva. 2007. *Becoming Free in the Cotton South.* Cambridge, MA: Harvard University Press.

Olmsted, Frederick Law. 1860. *A Journey in the Back Country in the Winter of 1853–1854.* New York: Mason Brothers.

Olmsted, Frederick Law. 1862. *The Cotton Kingdom: A Traveler's Observations on Cotton and Slavery in the American Slave States, Volume 1.* New York: Mason Brothers.

Pennington, James W. C. 1849. *The Fugitive Blacksmith.* London: Charles Gilpin.

Perdue, Charles L., Thomas E. Barden, and Robert K. Phillips, eds. 1976. *Weevils in the Wheat: Interviews with Virginia Ex-Slaves.* Charlottesville: University Press of Virginia.

Rawick, George P., ed. 1973. *The American Slave: A Composite Autobiography, Vol. 7: Oklahoma Narratives.* Westport, CT: Greenwood Press.

Rawick, George P., ed. 1974. *The American Slave: A Composite Autobiography, Vol. 14: North Carolina Narratives, Part 1.* Westport, CT: Greenwood Press.

Rawick, George P., ed. 1974. *The American Slave: A Composite Autobiography, Vol. 15: North Carolina Narratives, Parts 3 and 4.* Westport, CT: Greenwood Press.

Rawick, George P., ed. 1974. *The American Slave: A Composite Autobiography, Vol. 17: Florida Narratives*. Westport, CT: Greenwood Press.

Rosenthal, Caitlin. 2018. *Accounting for Slavery: Masters and Management*. Cambridge, MA: Harvard University Press.

Stevenson, Brenda. 2013. "What's Love Got to Do with It? Concubinage and Enslaved Women and Girls in the Antebellum South." *Journal of African American History* 98, no. 1 (Winter): 99–125.

Steward, Austin. 1857. *Twenty-Two Years a Slave and Forty Years a Free Man*. Rochester, NY: William Alling.

Tanner, Lynette Ater. 2014. *Chained to the Land: Voices from Cotton & Cane Plantations*. Winston-Salem, NC: John F. Blair Publishers.

2

DOMESTIC LIFE

When Agnes Hobbs expressed anguish after being separated from her husband, her mistress felt no sympathy for her loss. "There are plenty more men about here," Mrs. Burwell told the grieving Agnes, "and if you want a husband so badly, stop your crying and go and find another" (Keckley 1868, 24–25). For Mrs. Burwell, the permanent parting of a married couple was inconsequential if they happened to be enslaved. Her comments suggest that, from the perspective of owners, slave marriage was both temporary and a matter of convenience. For Burwell, enslaved people were interchangeable and a missing spouse could easily be replaced. The institution of slavery was designed to commodify people, to put a price on their bodies, and to deny their essential rights and feelings. Yet, despite the callous views of slave owners, enslaved people formed enduring bonds among family members and friends that sustained them in the face of a dehumanizing system. Peter Kolchin has argued that "families provided a crucial if fragile buffer shielding slaves from the worst rigors of slavery" (Kolchin 2003, 138). Families provided love, a sense of belonging, and material support that was a necessary bulwark against the daily abuses of the slave system. Yet it must be said that this refuge was vulnerable and could be broken. Ultimately, the master determined many intimate aspects of the domestic life of enslaved people: where they lived, what they ate, whom they married, and whether families stayed together. In antebellum America, slave families were torn apart because slave owners signed a bill of sale.

THE SLAVE TRADE

All slave families existed in what historian Walter Johnson calls the "shadow of the slave market" (Johnson 1999, 16). During the antebellum era, roughly three-quarters of a million slaves were sold from the Upper South to the Lower South, as the center of production shifted to cotton-producing areas like Georgia, Mississippi, and Louisiana. Slave owners in Maryland and Virginia responded to the decline in the agricultural productivity of their region by selling slaves to the Lower South. After losing money for several years, Virginia planter Bushrod Washington, for instance, sold over fifty slaves to a Louisiana planter in 1821. Other Virginia planters found advertisements in local papers from interstate slave traders too tempting to ignore. Franklin and Armfield, the state's largest interstate trading firm, promised cash for slaves between the ages of eight and twenty-five. The firm understood that cotton planters wanted young, strong slaves who would be able to perform exhausting physical labor, and this demand for labor created a lucrative trade. In addition to placing advertisements in newspapers, slave traders visited the homes of slave owners, making direct appeals. When the price of cotton was high, the demand for slaves increased and speculators could offer better prices to Upper South slave owners. This added inducement led many to calculate the economic value of slave sales.

For planters, the sale of slaves represented a business opportunity, to convert a commodity into cash. When one South Carolina planter decided to sell a slave, he presented his thinking in stark terms: "Give Brass a new shirt and send to Robert Blalock & Co. to be turned into money forthwith" (Baptist 2001, 1634). Brass was simply a commodity, unencumbered by feelings or family ties, to be sold when it suited his owner. In addition to the lure of making money or the need to settle debts, owners used sales as a means of disciplining willful slaves. Recounting her separation from her three brothers, Caroline Hunter explained that "if de massa couldn' rule you dey would sell you" (Perdue, Barden, and Phillips 1976, 149–150). Slaves who were deemed "incorrigible runaways" were quickly sold as punishment.

The domestic slave trade was powerfully disruptive to enslaved families in the Upper South. Historians estimate that half of all antebellum slave sales separated parents from children and one quarter separated husbands from wives. Mothers and daughters, however, had the best chance of staying together. Between 1820 and 1860, 183,000 enslaved people were sold away from Virginia, and another 366,000 were sold within the state (Dusinberre 2009, 74, 176). Barbara Fields has estimated that 12 percent of Maryland slaves were on the auction block in the 1830s. These conditions led Frederick Douglass to refer to Maryland as "a slave-breeding state—where slaves are reared for the market as horses, sheep, and swine" (Douglass 1979, 398). For enslaved people in Maryland and Virginia, the slow death of slavery on the middle ground had profound consequences. The sale of enslaved people shattered "the fragile web of family and friendship ties joining slaves to one another and to free black people" (Fields 1985, 24).

As agricultural productivity declined in the Chesapeake, it increased in areas producing staple crops like rice, cotton, and sugar. This, in turn, created a demand for labor that made slave owners in the Lower South less likely to sell slaves. The result was that enslaved people living in regions with high commodity prices had a better chance of staying together. In the rice belt of South Carolina, large planters usually bought slaves locally when they needed more labor, which often allowed family members to remain nearby. In addition, rice planters accepted that it was in their economic interest to purchase slaves in families, believing that slaves worked more efficiently when they were in family groups and that buying slaves in lots rather than single units was cheaper. When an 1819 advertisement announced the sale of "Nine valuable Negroes," it alerted potential buyers that "these negroes being one family, cannot be separated" (Pargas 2010, 186).

In addition to the interstate slave trade, family bonds were disrupted by the division of estates among heirs. While all enslaved people were vulnerable when estates were divided, the lowcountry of South Carolina, more than other regions in the slave South, tended to preserve the family unit when divisions had to be made. In contrast, the death of a master in the Upper South often meant the separation of families. When Virginia planter George Powell died in 1849, all of his slaves were sold, and the proceeds were distributed among his heirs. Unconcerned with the family separations that would follow his death, Powell did not place a request in his will "that the executers seek local buyers when they sold his slaves" (Stevenson 1996, 218). Other slave owners stipulated in their wills which slaves would be transferred in family groups and which would be sold away from family to pay off debts. In some cases, the division of an estate was simply left to chance. John Brown, for instance, recounted that the will of his Virginia master stipulated that all of the slaves should be divided into three lots of equal value, a process that paid minimal attention to family groups. The names of each slave in a lot were placed on pieces of paper, and then the three pieces of paper were put into a hat. Each heir simply picked one piece of paper out of the hat to determine his or her inheritance. Brown remembered that after the selection process had been concluded, all of the slaves gathered together, "crying and wailing," because families would be separated (Brown 1855, 8).

While the sale of slaves might represent a simple business decision for a trader or master, it was much more significant for enslaved parents and children. They experienced grief, shock, and pain at the parting that stayed with them for the rest of their lives. Charles Ball remembered that his father never recovered from his anguish after a trader purchased his wife and children, becoming "gloomy and morose" (Ball 1837, 19). When Thomas Jones saw his mother again after a thirteen-year separation, he saw the physical and emotional effects of losing her family. He found her "prematurely old, heartbroken, utterly desolate, weak and dying" (Jones 1862, 9). Often the sales came without warning, and slaves were not given the opportunity to say a proper farewell. Moses Grandy, for instance, discovered that his wife of eight months had been sold when he saw her in a gang of slaves being transported along a road. Told he would be shot if he tried to approach his wife, Grandy was given a few moments to say goodbye to the woman he loved, provided he remained at an appropriate distance. Masters often planned the sale to coincide with the absence of a loved one to avoid an emotional scene. Instead, slaves returned home to find their husband, wife, or child gone.

The sale of family members and the separation that followed had a traumatic effect on both parents and children. For some children, their separation from loved ones revealed, for the first time, the power that masters possessed over their lives. At the age of seven, Elizabeth Keckley watched as Little Joe was taken to the Big House in his Sunday best and "placed in the scales and was sold, like the hogs, at so much per pound" without his mother's knowledge (Keckley 1868, 28). For other enslaved children, their first memory was of a parent being sold. For both parents and children, separation caused a lifetime of sorrow. Over the course of her life, Charity Bowery bore sixteen children, and one by one, her North Carolina mistress sold them. "Oh, how *many* times," Charity remembered, "that woman broke my heart" (Blassingame 1977, 263; emphasis in original). The pain of separation was permanent, and memories haunted parents and children for decades after the end of slavery. When Delia Garlic was interviewed in the 1930s as part of the Federal Writers' Project interviews with former slaves, she remembered that babies were "snatched" from their mothers to be sold to speculators and children were "separated from sisters an' brothers an' never saw each other ag'in." When asked about the impact of family separation on enslaved people, Garlic offered a powerful and straightforward expression of grief: "Course dey cry; you think dey not cry when dey was sold lak cattle?" (Berlin, Favreau, and Miller 1998, 8).

This image depicts the pain caused when an enslaved man is separated from his wife and child during a slave sale. Abolitionists utilized images like this one to emphasize that slavery destroyed family bonds without warning. (Library of Congress)

Enslaved men and women hoped that they could protect their children from the shock of separation, but it could happen at any time. When Cherry Loguen found out that her master had sold two of her children to slave traders, she put her arms around them and refused to let them go. Her owner, Manasseth Logue, tried whipping her to get her to release them. When that failed, he sent two men to pry her arms open. Observing his mother's grief, Jermain Loguen remembered vividly the helplessness he felt to stop the sale of his brother and sister and the cruelty of the transaction. In some cases, enslaved people lost all contact with their family members at the point of sale, but they, nonetheless, tried to find out information.

After discovering that his mother had been taken 60 miles away, John Sella Martin entreated his master to let him visit her. When his master refused, Martin left without permission. The reunion of mother and son, however, was temporary, and both received beatings for placing familial affection above obedience to their masters.

At times, the separation of mothers and children seems arbitrary, intentionally cruel, and even contrary to the economic interests of speculators. William Wells Brown recounted the story of a new mother who had been purchased by a slave trader in Missouri and was to be sold in the New Orleans market. During the journey, the cries of the woman's infant child irritated the slave trader, and so he simply stopped a passerby and gave the child away. Parthena Rollins told an interviewer that when a slave trader found that a small child was interfering with his ability to sell the mother, he "took the baby from her, and beat it to death right before the mother's eyes" (Rawick 1973, 6: 167). This level of cruelty, however, could backfire. Rollins remembered that the buyer soon returned the woman because she was both emotionally and physically damaged after the experience. The trauma caused by separation might render an enslaved person incapable of efficiently performing the needed labor. Stories like the ones told by Brown and Rollins highlight the power of slave traders to destroy family bonds that had been carefully nurtured.

To prevent the destruction of their families, enslaved people used whatever leverage they possessed to negotiate with both owners and buyers. When speculators arrived at her master's home, the mother of Moses Grandy took her children and hid them in the woods until they left. When an enslaved man in Georgia was going to be taken away from his wife and children, he "kicked up a fuss" and convinced his owner to let him stay. This strategy worked temporarily, but if the price was right, the master made the sale. More often than not, enslaved people could not stop a sale, and once separated, they were unlikely to ever see their loved one again. In *Twelve Years a Slave*, Solomon Northup left a searing description of Eliza Berry's efforts at the New Orleans slave market to preserve her family. When a buyer selected her son Randall, she begged him to purchase the rest of the family as well. Eliza's anguished cries, however, interfered with the transactions that Theophilus Freeman, the slave trader, wanted to complete, so he threatened to whip Eliza if she didn't stop sniveling. Despite his threats, Eliza kept "begging and beseeching them, most piteously not to separate the three. Over and over again she told them how she loved her boy. A great many times she repeated her former promises—how very faithful and obedient she would be; how hard she would labor day and night, to the last moment of her life, if he would only buy them all together" (Northup 1853, 81). Nothing ultimately came of Eliza's entreaties, and the buyer took Randall away.

Soon after Eliza's separation from her son, her grief intensified when she was parted from her daughter, Emily. Northup stated that he had never seen "such an exhibition of intense, unmeasured, and unbounded grief, as when Eliza was parted from her child." Eliza begged a buyer to also purchase Emily, and this time, her love for her daughter persuaded him to agree. Freeman, however, refused to sell Emily for any price because there "were heaps and piles of money to be made of her . . . when she was a few years older." He expected to make as much as $5,000 for Emily in the fancy trade, selling her for a life as a prostitute or concubine. Northup invited all readers to imagine themselves in the shoes of Eliza and Emily as he presented the heartbreaking image of the two being torn apart, with Emily stretching out her arms and crying imploringly, "Don't leave me, mama—don't leave me." Even as Eliza was taken out of the slave pen, Emily's voice could still be heard crying for her mother to come back "until her infant voice grew faint and still more faint, and gradually died away as distance intervened, and finally was wholly lost" (Northup 1853, 85–88). Over the next months, Eliza's grief ate away at her; she lost weight and soon could not perform the work required of her.

The fact that masters could cruelly sell slaves for any reason and without warning disrupted the stability of slave families. Frederick Douglass, who was separated from his mother when he was a small child, believed that this was a customary practice in Maryland. "Frequently, before the child has reached its twelfth month," Douglass remembered, "its mother is taken from it, and hired out on some farm a considerable distance off, and the child is placed under the care of an old woman, too old for field labor." The separation hindered "the development of the child's affection toward its mother" and blunted "the natural affection of the mother for the child" (Douglass 1845, 2). While individual masters separated mothers and young children, historians believe that most slave children spent at least their early years with their mother and that the bonds of affection between mother and child were preserved to a greater degree than Douglass suggested. But the fact that sales could be made at any time meant that all enslaved families recognized the need to prepare themselves in some way for the possibility.

BONDS OF AFFECTION

While countless slaveholders made sales that separated families, many also understood that stable family units were in their material interest. They believed that enslaved people would work harder and be less likely to flee if their families were nearby. One planter advised his son to purchase slaves in family groups so they would "have ties to bind them all together." If planters instead purchased slaves without these connections, "they don't assimilate, & they ponder over former ties, of family, &c, & all goes wrong with them" (Schwalm 1997, 56). Although slave owners determined the conditions under which enslaved people lived and worked, families carved out domestic space separate from the power of the master. In the slave quarters, for example, parents expressed their love for their children, shared stories, sang songs, offered emotional support, and communicated their values. Parents worked hard to make their home a happy one, despite the ever-present fear of being separated. The love of a family counteracted efforts to dehumanize and commodify those in bondage. Social relationships helped enslaved people to improve the quality of their lives and to survive their enslavement. A variety of family structures existed under slavery, some with multiple generations living within walking distance, while many were single-parent families.

In different regions of the antebellum South, significant differences existed in the stability of family life. Enslaved families in the South Carolina lowcountry, for instance, experienced significantly more stability than other regions. Historian Charles Joyner has demonstrated that large rice plantations with hundreds of slaves allowed for the development of multigenerational families tied to the same locale. One couple lived on the same plantation for more than sixty years, and their family included children and grandchildren. Rice planters sold slaves less frequently, and when they made purchases, they favored slaves living in nearby rice plantations. Historians who have studied the records of individual rice plantations have found that 60–80 percent lived in two-parent households. Other regions did not match this level. Historian Ann Paton Malone has found that nearly half of Louisiana slaves lived in family groups comprising two parents and children. Given the steady stream of young enslaved men from the Upper South into the sugar-producing region of Louisiana, however, a significant percentage of enslaved men had no family ties. Less than 15 percent of the enslaved population lived in female-headed households,

Though the families of many enslaved African Americans were broken up by slave sales, this 1862 photograph contains five generations of a slave family in Beaufort, South Carolina. Family was a powerful buffer against the ongoing brutality of slavery. (Library of Congress)

though Malone acknowledged that this figure varied considerably over time and place. Tiger Island Plantation, for instance, had more female-headed families than two-parent families in 1842, but as the community matured, the number of female-headed, single-parent households reduced sharply (Malone 1992, 15, 261).

The domestic slave trade and the size of the slaveholding had an impact on the stability of enslaved families. Nineteenth-century Maryland slaveholders, for instance, owned fewer slaves (90 percent owned fewer than fifteen slaves) and sold slaves regularly. As a result, it was less likely that one master in Maryland would own all members of an immediate family or even a husband and wife. This demographic reality, however, did not prevent the formation of families. "Abroad" marriages, where spouses belonged to different masters, were one response to these circumstances. While families were separated for most of the week, the father's arrival on Saturday night was often a special, happy time. Charles Ball remembered his father's visits, when he would bring fruits or vegetables and tell stories. Variations based on region and time exist, but most children lived with at least one blood relative, usually the mother. When blood relatives were not present, other members of the enslaved community stepped forward to raise young children.

Understanding that families were vulnerable to separation, parents hoped to preserve these connections by naming their children after grandparents, aunts, or uncles. Marie Jenkins Schwartz has argued that parents "were less concerned that children have unique names than that they have names that connected them with other slaves" (Schwartz 2000, 168). But slave owners did not feel they needed to honor these choices, changing a slave's name to suit their own preference. If a slave had a name similar to his child, a master would change the slave's name. William Wells Brown, for instance, reclaimed the name given him by his mother once he was free, rejecting the name his master had chosen for him. Former Virginia slave David Holmes recalled that he had been called many different names while he was a slave and that he needed to answer to whatever name his master used or risk being whipped. Slave owners used the practice of naming bondpeople as another example of their power, but the enslaved found ways to preserve the naming decisions of their parents as an element of resistance.

Kinship and community ties made the day-to-day survival of enslaved people possible. The weekly ration of corn provided by slave owners needed to be ground, and so after working a long day in the fields, enslaved women used a hand mill at night to prepare food for the next day. Similarly, masters would give enslaved women fabric for clothes that they would need to sew for themselves and their children. Because slave owners often withheld basic items like shoes or blankets from children who were too young to perform productive labor, family members interceded to provide what was needed. Harriet Jacobs, for instance, recounted that as a child her grandmother gave her extra food and a pair of shoes, and Charles Ball recalled that his mother gave a portion of her food to her children so that they would not go hungry. On a daily basis, parents and grandparents helped their families to survive.

Jermain Loguen offered an extended tribute to his mother Cherry, who protected him, taught him how to do fieldwork, and nurtured his spirit and independence. Yet Cherry also wanted her son to survive, so she tempered his desire to resist the power of his enslavers. In particular, Cherry advised him not to complain that she was being mistreated, fearing that he might be sold away for insubordination. While she often counseled her son to let things go,

Cherry herself was quick to defend her children from punishment, even if that meant putting herself at risk. In one dramatic instance, Cherry set fire to some straw near the house to halt her drunken owner's vicious assault on her son. The plan succeeded, and while Manasseth Logue worked to put out the fire, Cherry went to minister to "her bruised and bleeding boy, who lay in his blood as still as a corpse" (Loguen 1859, 129). Family helped enslaved people to endure in the midst of great trials.

The desire to preserve family ties played an important role in an enslaved person's decision to run away. Numerous antebellum runaway notices, for example, included the location of family members as the probable destination for escaped slaves. After hearing the news that her son had been sold, Susan Boggs helped him escape to Canada, and she was sent to jail for three weeks as a consequence. But family could also act as a reason not to run. Mark Ramsey, for instance, informed his brother that he would not run away because he believed "it would kill their mother if he deserted her in her trouble" (Jacobs 1861, 41). William Wells Brown remembered his mother's stories of how "she had carried me upon her back to the field when I was an infant—how often she had been whipped for leaving her work to nurse me—and how happy I would appear when she would take me into her arms." His memories of her sacrifices for him when he was small made William "resolve never to leave the land of slavery without my mother. I thought that to leave her in slavery, after she had undergone and suffered so much for me, would be proving recreant to the duty which I owed to her" (Brown 1849, 30–31). After being sold to a slave trader bound for the New Orleans market, his mother encouraged William to put aside devotion to family and seek his own liberty.

Throughout the South, family survival was a priority for enslaved people, and whenever possible, they worked to raise money to free loved ones. Ann Garrison and three of her children were in jail awaiting sale when her son Robert raised the funds needed to purchase her freedom. Former bondwoman Molly Horniblow used her house as collateral to purchase her son's freedom. By working as a shoemaker at night, Isaac Hunter raised enough money to purchase his own freedom. Once freed, North Carolina law required that he leave the state and his family still enslaved. Seeking contributions in Philadelphia and New York, Hunter raised nearly $2,000 to free his wife and children in less than a year. After obtaining his own freedom, Tabb Gross worked for more than two years to earn $1,600 to purchase his wife and four children. These stories indicate the deep commitment to preserving family, even in the face of considerable obstacles (Blassingame 1977, 47–48, 216, 348–349).

While sometimes the labor of family members could lead to freedom, in more cases, it served to improve the material conditions of enslaved people. Slave families depended on the masters to provide the basic necessities of food, clothing, and shelter. Yet to have more than the bare minimum, families worked in their own time to improve conditions. Often, the weekly allotments of food provided by the master, for instance, were inadequate, and so many enslaved families supplemented their diet by hunting, fishing, raising chickens, and tending small gardens. Historian Marie Jenkins Schwartz has demonstrated that children could participate in these activities by gathering eggs, checking traps, and feeding chickens. Fish, rabbits, opossum, and squirrels provided variety and protein to a diet lacking in both. When husbands in abroad marriages would visit, they would perform tasks to help their families, like chopping the wood needed for a week. One North Carolina bondman used some of the time he could have been sleeping to work a small patch of land, and his efforts made it possible for him to purchase a cloak for his wife, a dress for each of his two daughters, and a hat and coat for his sons. In Louisiana's sugar parishes, skilled slaves like carpenters or blacksmiths could earn money working for neighboring planters. During the grinding season, however, masters would pay their own slaves if they would work on their day off. The boilers used for the sugarcane required large amounts of wood, and some enslaved men would chop it on Sunday and be paid for their overwork. Not all masters, however, allowed slaves to engage in independent economic activity. Historian Damian Pargas, for example, has demonstrated that family garden plots were not a customary right in northern Virginia because slave owners worried that gardening on their own time would interfere with a slave's productivity on the master's time. As in many aspects of life among enslaved African Americans, the daily rhythm of family life was powerfully shaped by regional circumstances and especially the demands of the staple crops that slaves were compelled to produce.

This was especially true in the lowcountry of South Carolina where enslaved people worked in the task system. Unlike the sunup to sundown gang labor system commonly used on cotton plantations, slaves in the task system were assigned specific jobs, and once they had been completed, their labor was their own. Rice planters commonly allocated slaves small plots of land, on which they grew vegetables or raised poultry and hogs. Families hunted, fished, and gardened in groups. This independent production could then be used to supplement the family's meager rations or to sell to other slaves, to neighboring plantations, and even to their master. Historian Leslie Schwalm has noted that one South Carolina planter purchased 190 chickens and ducks from his slaves in a single year. In some instances, this independent production brought in sufficient food for the family, and so they fed their weekly corn rations to the chickens. Enslaved people in South Carolina used the proceeds from their independent production to purchase numerous items that made their life more comfortable, including flour, coffee, mosquito nets, and pocket knives.

By their labor and love, families helped enslaved people to survive the deprivation and dehumanization of the slave system. Bonds of affection counteracted the calculus of the master who regarded enslaved people as simply commodities to buy, sell, and exploit. Yet despite their deep desire to create families and define their character, enslaved people could not act autonomously. Instead they confronted slave owners who sought to interfere at each stage of family development. Slave owners financially profited from slave reproduction, and so they encouraged marriage in the hopes that offspring would soon follow. Because slave owners controlled the labor of enslaved people, slave owners claimed the right to determine what accommodations would be made for the demands of family, from birth to death.

COURTSHIP AND MARRIAGE

When enslaved youth reached the age of fourteen or fifteen and began doing the work of an adult, they also began considering whom they would like to marry. Enslaved people faced numerous challenges finding a partner, ranging from the availability of potential spouses to getting the necessary consent to marry. Historian Larry Hudson has demonstrated that courtship could be competitive, and a woman might have a number of suitors vying for her attention. This was especially the case in the sugar-producing parishes of Louisiana, where men outnumbered women. Enslaved people openly socialized at parties and arranged covert meetings away from the prying eyes of parents or masters. Flirting, of course, could occur anywhere—in the fields, while completing an errand in town, or on a neighboring plantation, as well as during leisure time.

Dances provided one opportunity for young people to dress in their best clothes, have fun, and attract attention. Young women used honeysuckle and rose petals as perfume and wore hoops in their dresses made out of grape vines. Some borrowed jewelry from their mistress, and others fashioned beads out of dried chinaberries. Young men might dress up in their master's cast-off clothes, and shoes, in particular, were a sign of status. Young couples would hold hands; dance; and drink coffee, corn whiskey, or apple brandy. Dances occurred for a variety of reasons; the Christmas holidays were a time for socialization, but work could also be the spur. Corn shuckings, for instance, often brought together slaves from neighboring plantations, and after the work was finished, the festivities would begin. Hattie Clayton told an interviewer in Opelika, Alabama, that they had dances almost every Saturday night, and the raucous fun "made the rafters shake" (Rawick 1973, 6: 76). Remembering simpler affairs as well, Nancy Williams described courting couples dancing at a cabin in the woods to fiddle and banjo music. Sometimes dancing became highly competitive as rivals vied for the attention of an especially attractive young woman. Solomon Northup described one dance when three young men competed for Miss Lively's attention. After supper she favored Sam Roberts with her hand, and the two began dancing, with Sam's legs flying "like drum-sticks down the outside and up the middle, by the side of his bewitching partner." Spurred on by the applause he received, Sam danced harder, forgetting temporarily about his partner. Sam's rivals stepped in, and one after the other, each tried to win Miss Lively's affections through their dancing prowess, but she exhausted each of them, earning the reputation as "the 'fastest gal' on the bayou" (Northup 1853, 219). While beauty, finery, and dancing might attract suitors, young men and women also considered whether a prospective spouse had the skills, strength, and health to survive bondage. The evidence suggests that young men and women attempted to retain control over who, when, and if they married.

Henry Bibb offers an example of how slavery interfered with and complicated the natural human desire to love, marry, and have children. When Bibb was eighteen, he became interested in Malinda, a young woman from a nearby plantation. Though she had a number of suitors, Malinda encouraged Bibb with her smiles, warm greetings, and the touch of her hand. Like many young couples, Henry and Malinda confronted disapproving parents. Bibb's mother thought he was too young to marry, and her mother thought she should marry someone else. Henry Bibb, however, understood that marriage might tie him to a life in slavery that he was desperate to escape. As he was falling in love with Malinda, Bibb acknowledged courting her "would greatly obstruct my way to the land of liberty" (Bibb 1849, 34). For Bibb, like all enslaved people, the natural desire to form familial relations was fraught with complexity because all ties could be severed by the will of the master, and the love of family members could itself be used by slaveholders to control or manipulate those they owned. Bibb's narrative brilliantly explained that slavery corrupted the natural relations that white Americans took for granted.

Bibb ultimately resolved the tension between love and his desire to escape by sharing both feelings with Malinda. Once he discovered that they were in agreement about the two biggest issues—religion and liberty—he proposed marriage. Bibb's marriage to Malinda and the subsequent birth of their daughter presented challenges and regrets. He recalled having to watch, unable to help, as her master violently abused her. Because slavery undercut the traditional role of a husband and father, Bibb could offer no protection to his loved ones. This fact caused him sorrow, and he even lamented that he had become "a father and a husband of slaves." While Malinda worked in the field, their daughter Frances was mistreated by her owner and both parents were powerless to do anything about it. In one instance, Frances cried because she missed her mother, and the white mistress struck her so hard that the young child's face was bruised for over a week. Why, Bibb wondered, should enslaved people have children if they were to be the "victims of this kind of torture and cruelty" (Bibb 1849, 35, 44)?

As young people like Henry Bibb made choices about whom they wanted to court or marry, they needed permission from both parents and owners. If a bondman wanted to court a woman from the same plantation, he would first need to seek his owner's permission. If the woman in question was owned by a neighbor, then the bondman's owner would write to the woman's owner, asking permission. If the girl, her parents, and the owner agreed, then formal courting could begin. Slave owners did not simply acquiesce to the wishes of enslaved people, however, and they often involved themselves in the selection process. William Wells Brown remembered that his owner wanted him to marry and offered to purchase an enslaved woman from a neighboring plantation whom they believed he cared for. Other slave owners criticized women for their preferences, warning that "if you cannot pick a mate better than that I'll do the picking for you" (Hudson 1997, 159). In some cases, masters did more than threaten, and they intervened, often selecting partners for their slaves based on breeding possibilities. Masters believed that strong, healthy slaves were more likely to produce strong, healthy offspring and selected partners based on these criteria. Rose Williams remembered that at age sixteen her master ordered her to live with another slave "'gainst my wants." Initially Rose misunderstood her master's order, thinking she was only supposed to cook and clean for Rufus and the other slaves who lived in the cabin. Rose disliked Rufus, calling him a bully who liked to order people around. After performing the household chores, Rose retired to what she thought was *her* bunk. When Rufus joined her, Rose told him he was "teched in the head" and ordered him out (Berlin, Favreau, and Miller 1998, 129). Angry that Rufus refused to leave, she shoved him out of bed and struck him in the head with a poker. While Rose defied her master for one night, she was soon given an ultimatum: either accept Rufus as her partner or else she would be whipped.

Whatever level of involvement owners played in selecting a partner, they did encourage enslaved people to marry. James Henry Hammond promoted slave marriage by offering financial incentives to slaves, giving newly married couples $5 after he conducted the ceremony. Before a marriage could occur, enslaved men needed permission from their owner, and, if different, the bondwoman's owner. Sometimes permission was not granted, but neighboring owners who got along were more likely to agree. Arnold Gragston remembered that his Kentucky master, Mr. Tabb, accommodated slaves who wanted to marry someone who lived on another plantation, even trading slaves with a neighbor or family member so that the couple could live together. In contrast to Tabb, some owners denied permission if marriage would mean losing a prized domestic servant from the Big House. The master's own physical attraction toward an enslaved woman might also induce him to refuse permission. Harriet Jacobs, for instance, bitterly remembered that she was not permitted to marry the man of her choosing because her master had sexual designs on her. Owners were also concerned that abroad marriages would shift the husband's loyalty and labor to his wife's home, thereby interfering with the economic profitability of slavery. Henry Bibb's owner initially opposed his marriage to Malinda, a woman from another plantation, because "he feared my taking off from his farm some of the fruits of my own labor for Malinda to eat, in the shape of pigs, chickens, or turkeys" (Bibb 1849, 40).

Slave marriages could involve both formal and informal ceremonies. One common way to celebrate marriage was known as "jumping the broom," a ritual that involved two people holding the ends of a broom off the floor and the couple jumping or stepping over it. Recalling her marriage, Mary Reynolds explained that her master and mistress stood inside the house and held "a broom crosswise of the door," and Mary and her intended stepped over the broom into the house. In contrast to a formal ceremony, Reynolds noted "that's all they was to the marryin'" (Tanner 2014, 11–12). When Ophelia Whitley described the ritual in North Carolina, she emphasized that the enslaved couple stepped over the broom twice and then sealed their marriage with a kiss. In contrast to Whitley and Reynolds, Tempie Herndon Durham recounted a much more involved ceremony at the Big House that included a wedding cake, flowers, a white dress for the bride, and a wedding ring made by the groom out of a red button. Tempie explained that Exeter, her husband, had cut out the center of the button with his pocket knife and then polished it. Their wedding ceremony was officiated by a black preacher, and afterward the master urged Tempie and Exeter to jump backward over the broomstick to see who was going to be the boss of the household. While Tempie easily cleared the broom, Exeter, perhaps having had too much to drink, got his feet tangled and fell over the broom. The master laughed uproariously at Exeter, informing him that he would "be bossed 'twell he skeered to speak" without Tempie's permission (Berlin, Favreau, and Miller 1998, 125).

When an enslaved couple married, the service might be conducted by a minister, or the couple could simply declare their love for each other publicly. In either case, the sanctity of slave marriage was not recognized in law, and consequently slave marriages did not have the same permanence as marriages between free people. Descriptions of slave marriages often emphasize that Southerners chose to remove the phrase "let no man put asunder" from the ceremony because sales could easily rupture the bonds between an enslaved couple. Historian Tera Hunter has argued that "marriage for them was not an inviolable union between two people but an institution defined and controlled by the superior relationship of master to slave" (Hunter 2017, 6). Masters wanted slaves to marry, but they would also buy and sell people based on their economic value without regard for the emotional and social bonds that connected enslaved people together. This reality led former slave Harriet Jacobs to argue that a slave marriage "was a mere form, without any legal value" because slave owners "could annul it any day they pleased" (Jacobs 1861, 217). Jacobs understood that because enslaved people were considered property in law, they could not legally enter into contracts. Regardless of the ability of a slave owner to annul a marriage, enslaved couples decided for themselves if the marriage was real and binding. Thomas Jones, for instance, remarked, "We called it and we considered it a true marriage" (Jones 1862, 30). Similarly, Henry Bibb believed that his marriage to Malinda was "honorable before God" (Bibb 1849, 41). An enslaved woman on St. Simons Island in Georgia informed Fanny Kemble Butler that Tony, the man known on the island as her husband, was in fact "not her *real* husband" (Kemble 1863, 205; emphasis in original). The man she continued to call her real husband had been sold away many years before as an incorrigible runaway.

In addition to ending because of the arbitrary decisions of owners, slave marriages dissolved because of the preferences of the couple. Unlike antebellum white women, enslaved women were not economically dependent on their husbands for their food and shelter, thereby making separation easier. In addition, many slave owners refused to force couples to remain in abusive or conflict-ridden marriages. Some overseers found divorce an effective response to marital disagreements. If an enslaved couple was fighting, one Georgia overseer, for instance, would break up the marriage and create a new one, "whether they chose it or not" (Kemble 1863, 167).

Beyond approving potential spouses or deciding to separate husbands and wives, masters found additional ways to interfere with slave marriages. Enslaved men could not protect their wives from a master's abuse, whether in the form of a whip or sexual exploitation. In some instances, enslaved men were forced to watch as their wife was beaten, powerless to stop it. Some chose to run away rather than remain in such an untenable situation. White slave owners and overseers believed it was their prerogative to have sexual relations with their bondwomen, whether they were married or not. South Carolinian Mary Chesnut confirmed not only that white Southern men fathered children with their slaves but also that it was common knowledge. Chesnut argued that white Southern women could identify "who is the father of all the Mulatto children in everybody's household" except those in her own home, where she was oblivious (Chesnut 1981, 29). The presence of mixed-race children who resembled white men startled Fanny Butler when she first encountered it on her husband's Georgia plantation. When she asked her husband about the likeness between a white overseer and a slave, his nonchalant reply that he was "very likely his brother" convinced Fanny that the practice was widespread and unremarkable to many white families in the area (Kemble 1863, 162).

PREGNANCY AND CHILDBIRTH

Enslaved women had value to slaveholders because of the work they performed and their ability to reproduce. Plantation manuals and Southern periodicals offered recommendations about questions of workload, nursing, and weaning. Yet the goals of production and reproduction were often in conflict with each other. Edward De Buiew recounted that his mother died one hour after giving birth to him because she had been worked too hard during her pregnancy. The driver had forced her to continue hoeing even though she complained to him about feeling ill. Harriet Jacobs detailed the story of her aunt Nancy who experienced numerous miscarriages and stillbirths because of the demands her mistress placed on her. Every night her mistress expected Nancy to sleep in her doorway of her room, in case she woke in the night and needed a drink of water or one of the children needed attention. Working all day and being denied adequate sleep, Nancy's constitution "completely broke down," and she was never able to carry a baby to term. Testifying to the prevalence of miscarriages and premature babies, Josephine Bacchus succinctly stated, "I haven't never had a nine months child" (Rawick 1973, 2: 20). While slave owners did not unduly concern themselves with the emotional pain that slaves experienced as a result of miscarriages or infant mortality, they did attempt to balance the demands of work and the needs of pregnant women.

Arduous physical labor could interfere with fertility and increase the risks of miscarriages, still births, and infant mortality. In his work on the reproductive lives of slave women in Louisiana, Richard Follett has found that the demands of sugar production interfered with both conception and carrying babies to term, resulting in high rates of child mortality and lower fertility rates. Louisiana sugar planters, Follett found, "favored labor over leave" and kept pregnant women working in the fields until just before they gave birth (Follett 2005, 73–75). Other slave owners believed it was in their interest to prevent miscarriages by putting new work rules in place. Because it was in their interest that enslaved women reproduce, most slave owners lightened the workload of pregnant women; some left fieldwork toward the end of their pregnancy and were instead tasked with sewing, spinning, and weaving. In the lowcountry of South Carolina where health risks existed because of the heat, humidity, and malaria, pregnant women's work was reduced as soon as they informed the overseer that they were pregnant. In other regions, owners waited to the final trimester to make any alteration in the workload of expectant mothers.

Yet the decision about what kind of work a pregnant woman should or should not perform was left to individual masters, and so a wide range of conditions existed. Some planters, for instance, determined that pregnant women should not work in the fields, while others decided that specific tasks like hoeing and picking cotton were acceptable but pulling fodder was too onerous. Some owners created a "trash gang" composed of pregnant women and nursing mothers as well as elderly and young slaves and assigned them lighter tasks, including raking stubble, pulling weeds, and light hoeing. Owners had a material interest in reproduction, and so they balanced their immediate interest in enslaved women performing productive labor with their longer-term interest in reproductive labor. Reducing the workload of a pregnant woman would increase the odds of a successful birth but also reduce the efficiency of a cotton or rice plantation. Research has demonstrated that owners were less likely to remove women from fieldwork when the price of the staple crop was high.

Recognizing the economic value that owners placed on reproduction, some expectant mothers believed that their condition gave them the opportunity to negotiate with overseers, masters, and mistresses for a reduction in the workload. When a group of pregnant women approached Fanny Kemble Butler, asking her to intercede on their behalf, the overseer expressed great annoyance that the women had raised the issue, claiming "their work was not a bit too much for them" (Kemble 1863, 135–136). After Fanny brought one complaint too many to her husband, Pierce Butler, he angrily informed her that he would not listen to any more of the complaints and that she should not be taken in by their lies either. While Butler refused any further reduction in their workload, enslaved women generally understood that if pregnant, they might, in fact, receive better treatment. Some owners offered rewards, extra food, clothing, or a silver dollar to women who were pregnant or had just given birth. One Virginia planter even promised an enslaved woman that he would set her free once she bore five children. Placing an economic value, a price, on the body of enslaved women, owners rewarded fertile bondwomen and often sold those who did not conceive a child after an extended period of time.

In addition to offering incentives and rewards to pregnant women, slave owners determined how quickly new mothers would return to work. The length of the lying-in period varied but rarely exceeded a month. In the lowcountry of South Carolina where the child mortality rate was substantially higher than the Southern average, planters granted new mothers four weeks lying-in and two additional weeks of light work. In other areas of the South where a new mother's labor was needed, they might be exempt from heavy chores only for two weeks, before having to return to the fields. Some feared that rushing women back to exhausting work would damage not only their own health but also the life of their newborn. Brenda Stevenson found in her study of northern Virginia that a two-week lying-in period did not increase child mortality, noting that the mortality rates among white and black children were comparable in the antebellum era. While bondwomen could not autonomously make crucial decisions about their private life, they did attempt to negotiate better terms. Two enslaved women in Georgia, Charlotte and Judy, approached their mistress expressing concerns about gynecological problems like a prolapsed uterus caused by "sending women to labor in the fields in the third week after their confinement." Another group of enslaved women on St. Simons Island hoped that they would not have "to resume their labor of hoeing in the fields three weeks after their confinement" and would instead receive a month's respite (Kemble 1863, 174, 182). Despite the fact that enslaved women often could not convince their owners to make significant concessions, they attempted to establish a place for themselves to make parenting decisions.

PARENTING ENSLAVED CHILDREN

Though antebellum America was full of advice about a mother's responsibilities in childrearing, enslaved women had to balance their desire to care for their children with the necessity of complying with the labor demands their owners placed upon them. On larger plantations, an older woman was often charged with caring for all the small children while their mothers worked in the field or in the Big House. Historian Damian Pargas, however, has estimated that at most one-third of the enslaved children in Fairfax County, Virginia, could have been supervised by an elderly woman because many of the region's small holdings simply did not include one.

When a day nursery was not an option, other arrangements were devised. Fanny Kemble, for instance, remarked that on her husband's Georgia plantation, the older children cared for the infants, while the mothers labored in the fields. Former slave John Brown remembered that as a young child his job was to nurse his younger brother, but he sometimes did not watch him carefully and his brother paid the price. When he wanted to go play or take a nap, Brown would first lay his brother in the shade of a tree. His brother would wake up screaming because he was "covered with ants, or musquitos [sic], or blistered from the heat of the sun" (Brown 1855, 325). When young children were left unsupervised, accidents could occur. A Virginia slave owner returned home to find that the servants' hall, barn, and stables had burned after an unsupervised child had set fire to a straw bed.

Once new mothers returned to work, owners sought efficient means for them to feed their children without unduly interrupting the workday. The time it would take a new mother to walk from the field to her baby needed to be reduced, either by having enslaved women work nearby or by having older children bring the infants to the fields two or three times a day for breastfeeding. In other instances, new mothers would bring their infants to the fields, often suspending them in a swing from a tree limb to keep them away from the ants while they performed fieldwork. In contrast to the gang system where feedings were at a scheduled time, slave women under the task system had more leeway to determine when to feed their offspring. Fathers and others in the slave community often helped new mothers complete their assigned work so that they could spend more time nurturing their child.

Enslaved women who worked in the plantation house often kept their children with them during the day, nursing as needed. Mothers, however, could not respond to the needs of unhappy children. When Harriet Jacobs could not give her daughter the attention she needed because of her work, the young girl cried herself sick under the window where her mother was working. Finally exhausting herself, the child crawled under the house to sleep. While the tears of her daughter were heartrending to Harriet, the incident became even more disturbing when she found out that a large snake was under the house at the same time as her daughter. Mothers like Harriet Jacobs could not protect their children as they would like because their owner controlled their time.

The long hours spent working in the fields or in the Big House limited the time parents could devote to their children. Once young children were weaned, quick and efficient means to feed them were devised. Nannie Williams observed the feeding of fourteen babies, noting that Aunt Hannah "po' dat trough full of milk an' drag dem chillun up to it. Chillun slop up dat milk jus like pigs" (Schwartz 2000, 68). As a child, Frederick Douglass remembered being fed boiled cornmeal in a similar fashion. The food "was put into a large wooden tray or trough, and set down upon the ground. The children were then called, like so many pigs, and like so many pigs they would come and devour the mush; some with oyster-shells, others with pieces of shingle, some with naked hands, and none with spoons. He that ate the fastest got most; he that was strongest secured the best place; and few left the trough satisfied" (Douglass 1845, 27).

Like all parents, enslaved people wanted to spend more time with their children, feeding, nurturing, and supervising their development, but they struggled against the relentless demands that the slave system placed upon their time. The task system offered parents greater opportunities to nurture their children after they had completed the day's labor. Yet the demands of the gang system meant that their day from sunup to sundown was controlled by the slave owner. Given the early bedtime of young children, enslaved parents might see very little of their children except on Sundays. That fact, however, did not prevent slave owners from criticizing their parenting skills. Each Sunday morning inspections were made at the Big House, and mothers were expected to have their children present, clean, and in their best clothes. Plantation mistresses did not hesitate to blame mothers for their perceived shortcomings.

In some cases, slave owners decided they would supervise enslaved children, bringing them to the Big House at age six or eight to perform specific jobs for the family, like fetching needed items, minding the master's children, or fanning the family. Austin Steward was removed from his family's quarters at age eight and brought to the master's home to be an errand boy and to stand behind his master's chair until he was needed. At night Austin slept in the same room as his master and mistress, fanning them when necessary. He slept on the floor like a dog, without any pillow or blanket. Enslaved people created family ties that were vulnerable to the whims of slave owners, who routinely intruded into their domestic lives.

For enslaved children, experiences were marked by distinct stages of development. Before age ten, enslaved children exercised more freedom than older slaves. Until Jermain Loguen was ten, he was able to spend much of his day hunting or fishing. Recalling his own childhood, Frederick Douglass stated: "I had a great deal of leisure time. The most I had to do was to drive up the cows at the evening, keep the fowls out of the garden, keep the front yard clean, and run errands for my old master's daughter. . . . The most of my leisure time I spent in helping Master Daniel Lloyd in finding his birds, after he had shot them" (Douglass 1845, 27). As a young girl, Harriet Jacobs remembered that she was allowed to run and jump or to gather berries and flowers. After this stage, leisure was replaced by the productive labor a master required. Once enslaved children started working, they were also more vulnerable to sale and separation from family. If children below age eight were sold, they were likely to remain with their family. This circumstance altered as they grew because planters in slave-importing regions like Alabama and Louisiana needed to purchase young slaves who would grow cotton or sugar. Wilma King has argued that "the majority of slaves sold in the Upper South traffic in the antebellum era were teenagers and young adults" (King 2011, 233). Unlike the youngest children who generally remained with their mothers, enslaved youths were separated from their family. After these ties were disrupted, enslaved people experienced deep pain and loneliness, but they endured. Ultimately, new family bonds would replace the ones that had been severed. In their domestic life, enslaved people resisted the logic of the market that defined human beings as property and by the labor they could perform.

DOCUMENT: HENRY BROWN, *NARRATIVE OF THE LIFE OF HENRY BOX BROWN* (1851)

This excerpt focuses on Henry Brown's efforts in Richmond, Virginia, to create a home for his wife, Nancy, and their children in the midst of slavery. His wife's owner, Mr. Colquitt, arranged to sell Nancy to Samuel Cottrell, who then approached Brown with an offer that would allow the Browns to live as a family. This passage demonstrates the importance of family, the vulnerability of enslaved people within a system that offered them no protection from a duplicitous individual, and the power of slave sales to separate families. After Brown's family was sold away from Virginia, he devised a risky but dramatic escape route. Brown was mailed from Virginia to Pennsylvania in a wooden crate, earning him the name, Henry "Box" Brown.

This man came to me one day and told me that Mr. Colquitt was going to sell my wife, . . . but he said her master asked 650 dollars

Domestic Life

for her and her children, and he had only 600 that he could conveniently spare but if I would let him have fifty, to make up the price, he would prevent her from being sold away from me. I was, however, a little suspicious about being fooled out of my money, and I asked him if I did advance the money what security I could have that he would not sell my wife as the others had done; but he said to me "do you think if you allow me to have that money, that I could have the heart to sell your wife to any other person but yourself, and particularly knowing that your wife is my sister and you my brother in the Lord; while all of us are members of the church? Oh! no, I never could have the heart to do such a deed as that." After he had shown off his religion in this manner, and lavished it upon me, I thought I would let him have the money, not that I had implicit faith in his promise, but that I knew he could purchase her if he wished whether I were to assist him or not, and I thought by thus bringing him under an obligation to me it might at least be somewhat to the advantage of my wife and to me; so I gave him the 50 dollars and he went off and bought my wife and children:—and that very same day he came to me and told me, that my wife and children were now his property, and that I must hire a house for them and he would allow them to live there if I would furnish them with everything they wanted, and pay him 50 dollars, a year; "if you don't do this," he said, "I will sell her as soon as I can get a buyer for her." I was struck with astonishment to think that this man, in one day, could exhibit himself in two such different characters. A few hours ago filled with expressions of love and kindness, and now a monster tyrant, making light of the most social ties and imposing such terms as he chose on those whom, but a little before, had begged to conform to his will. . . .

I paid him the hire of my wife regularly, whenever he called for it—whether it was due or not—but he seemed still bent on robbing me more thoroughly than he had the previous day; for one pleasant morning, in the month of August, 1848, when my wife and children, and myself, were sitting at table, about to eat our breakfast, Mr. Cottrell called, and said, he wanted some money to day, as he had a demand for a large amount. I said to him, you know I have no money to spare, because it takes nearly all that I make for myself, to pay my wife's hire, the rent of my house, my own ties to my master, and to keep ourselves in meat and clothes; and if at any time, I have made anything more than that, I have paid it to you in advance, and what more can I do? Mr. Cottrell, however said, "I want money, and money I will have." I could make him no answer; he then went away. I then said to my wife, "I wonder what Mr. Cottrell means by saying I want money and money I will have," my poor wife burst into tears and said perhaps he will sell one of our little children, and our hearts were so full that neither of us could eat any breakfast, and after mutually embracing each other, as it might be our last meeting, and fondly pressing our little darlings to our bosoms, I left the house and went off to my daily labour followed by my little children who called after me to come back soon. . . . I had not been many hours at my work, when I was informed that my wife and children were taken from their home, sent to the auction mart and sold, and then lay in prison ready to start away the next day for North Carolina with the man who had purchased them. . . .

My agony was now complete, she with whom I had travelled the journey of life in chains, for the space of twelve years, and the dear little pledges God had given us I could see plainly must now be separated from me for ever, and I must continue, desolate and alone, to drag my chains through the world. O dear, I thought shall my wife and children no more greet my sight with their cheerful looks and happy smiles! for far away in the North Carolina swamps are they henceforth to toil beneath the scorching rays of a hot sun deprived of a husband's and a father's care! . . .

While I was thus musing I received a message, that if I wished to see my wife and children, and bid them the last farewell, I could do so, by taking my stand on the street where they were all to pass on their way for North Carolina. I . . . placed myself by the side of a street, and soon had the melancholy satisfaction of witnessing the approach of a gang of slaves, amounting to three hundred and fifty in number, marching under the direction of a Methodist minister, by whom they were purchased, and amongst which slaves were my wife and children. I stood in the midst of many who, like myself, were mourning the loss of friends and relations and had come there to obtain one parting look at those whose company they but a short time before had imagined they should always enjoy, but who were, without any regard to their own wills, now driven by the tyrant's voice and the smart of the whip on their way to another scene of toil, and, to them, another land of sorrow in a far off southern country.

Source: Henry Brown. *Narrative of the Life of Henry Box Brown*. Manchester: Lee and Glynn, 1851, 36–46.

FURTHER READING

Ball, Charles. 1837. *Slavery in the United States: A Narrative of the Life and Adventures of Charles Ball*. New York: John S. Taylor.

Baptist, Edward E. 2001. "'Cuffy,' 'Fancy Maids,' and 'One-Eyed Men': Rape, Commodification and the Domestic Slave Trade in the United States." *American Historical Review* 106, no. 5 (December): 1619–1650.

Berlin, Ira, Marc Favreau, and Steven F. Miller, eds. 1998. *Remembering Slavery: African Americans Talk about Their Personal Experiences of Slavery and Emancipation*. New York: The New Press.

Bibb, Henry. 1849. *Narrative of the Life and Adventures of Henry Bibb, an American Slave*. New York: printed by the author.

Blassingame, John W., ed. 1977. *Slave Testimony: Two Centuries of Letters, Speeches, Interviews, and Autobiographies*. Baton Rouge: Louisiana State University Press.

Brown, John. 1855. *Slave Life in Georgia: A Narrative of the Life, Sufferings and Escape of John Brown*. London: W. M. Watts.

Brown, William Wells. 1849. *Narrative of William W. Brown, a Fugitive Slave*. London: Charles Gilpin.

Chesnut, Mary Boykin. 1981. *Mary Chesnut's Civil War*, edited by C. Vann Woodward. New Haven, CT: Yale University Press.

Douglass, Frederick. 1845. *Narrative of the Life of Frederick Douglass: An American Slave, Written by Himself*. Boston, MA: Antislavery Office.

Douglass, Frederick. 1979. "A Simple Tale of American Slavery: An Address Delivered in Sheffield, England, on September 11, 1846." In *The Frederick Douglass Papers*, edited by John Blassingame, John R. McKivigan, and Peter P. Hinks, vol. 1. New Haven, CT: Yale University Press.

Dusinberre, William. 2009. *Strategies for Survival: Recollections of Bondage in Antebellum Virginia*. Charlottesville: University of Virginia Press.

Fields, Barbara Jeanne. 1985. *Slavery and Freedom on the Middle Ground: Maryland during the Nineteenth Century*. New Haven, CT: Yale University Press.

Follett, Richard. 2005. *The Sugar Masters: Planters and Slaves in Louisiana's Cane World, 1820–1860*. Baton Rouge: Louisiana State University Press.

Hudson, Larry. 1997. *To Have and to Hold: Slave Work and Family Life in Antebellum South Carolina*. Athens: University of Georgia Press.

Hunter, Tera. 2017. *Bound in Wedlock: Slave and Free Black Marriage in the Nineteenth Century*. Cambridge, MA: Harvard University Press.

Jacobs, Harriet. 1861. *Incidents in the Life of a Slave Girl*. Boston: printed by the author.

Johnson, Walter. 1999. *Soul by Soul: Life inside the Antebellum Slave Market*. Cambridge, MA: Harvard University Press.

Jones, Thomas H. 1862. *The Experience of Thomas H. Jones, Who Was a Slave for Forty-Three Years*. Boston: Bazin & Chandler.

Keckley, Elizabeth. 1868. *Behind the Scenes: Thirty Years a Slave, and Four Years in the White House.* New York: G. W. Carleton & Co.

Kemble, Frances Anne. 1863. *Journal of a Residence on a Georgian Plantation in 1838–1839.* New York: Harper & Brothers.

King, Wilma. 2011. *Stolen Childhood: Slave Youth in Nineteenth-Century America*, 2nd ed. Bloomington: Indiana University Press.

Kolchin, Peter. 2003. *American Slavery, 1619–1877.* New York: Hill and Wang.

Loguen, Jermain. 1859. *The Rev. J.W. Loguen, as a Slave and as a Freeman.* Syracuse, NY: J.G.K. Truair & Co.

Malone, Ann Paton. 1992. *Sweet Chariot: Slave Family and Household Structure in Nineteenth-Century Louisiana.* Chapel Hill: University of North Carolina Press.

Northup, Solomon. 1853. *Twelve Years a Slave: Narrative of Solomon Northup, a Citizen of New-York, Kidnapped in Washington City in 1841, and Rescued in 1853.* Auburn, NY: Derby and Miller.

Pargas, Damian Alan. 2010. *The Quarters and the Field: Slave Families in the Non-Cotton South.* Gainesville: University Press of Florida.

Perdue, Charles L., Thomas E. Barden, and Robert K. Phillips, eds. 1976. *Weevils in the Wheat: Interviews with Virginia Ex-Slaves.* Charlottesville: University Press of Virginia.

Rawick, George P., ed. 1973. *The American Slave: A Composite Autobiography, v. 2: South Carolina Narratives, Part 1.* Westport, CT: Greenwood Press.

Rawick, George P., ed. 1973. *The American Slave: A Composite Autobiography, v. 6: Alabama and Indiana Narratives.* Westport, CT: Greenwood Press.

Schwalm, Leslie A. 1997. *A Hard Fight for We: Women's Transition from Slavery to Freedom in South Carolina.* Urbana: University of Illinois Press.

Schwartz, Marie Jenkins. 2000. *Born in Bondage: Growing Up Enslaved in the Antebellum South.* Cambridge, MA: Harvard University Press.

Stevenson, Brenda. 1996. *Life in Black and White: Family and Community in the Slave South.* New York: Oxford University Press.

Tanner, Lynette Ater. 2014. *Chained to the Land: Voices from Cotton & Cane Plantations.* Winston-Salem, NC: John F. Blair Publishers.

3

MATERIAL LIFE

When Jennie Hill described her material life as a slave in Missouri, she emphasized that she had received enough food and clothing. Even though the provisions were adequate, Hill keenly felt the restrictions on her material life. "It was hard to work all day, day in and day out," Hill remembered, "and never have anything we could call our own" (Blassingame 1977, 591). Understanding the quality of an enslaved person's material life requires investigation into what slave owners provided and what enslaved people acquired for themselves. The system of slavery meant that enslaved people depended upon their masters for material necessities like food, clothing, and shelter. Although slave owners had an interest in keeping their slaves alive, they also wanted to keep their costs as low as possible. Skimping on the quality or the amount of the food and clothing was one way of reducing costs, and as a result, individual masters, whether because of their disposition or wealth, provided more than others. In the end, however, the material life of slaves was, like other aspects of their daily lives, a balance between the control exercised by masters and the agency of the slaves themselves.

The material life of enslaved people was also influenced by structural factors—like whether enslaved people performed domestic or fieldwork and whether they lived in rural or urban areas. In his autobiography, Frederick Douglass compared city and plantation slaves, concluding that a city slave was "much better fed and clothed, and enjoys privileges altogether unknown to the slave on the plantation." Douglass was not arguing that urban slave owners cared more for their slaves but rather that their concern for their own reputations influenced what material goods, especially food, they provided. He suggested that few city slave owners were "willing to incur the odium attaching to the reputation of being a cruel master; and above all things, they would not be known as not giving a slave enough to eat" (Douglass 1845, 35). Instead, they were anxious to be known as owners who fed their slaves well, which was implicitly a mechanism to display their own wealth and social status. Rural slave owners, on the other hand, were removed from the prying and judgmental eyes of their neighbors and could restrict the food and clothing provided to enslaved people without fear for their reputation.

Despite these differences, all slave owners understood that material goods could be used to express their power over slaves on a variety of levels. Some slave owners dispensed food, clothing, or other material possessions as rewards for those they favored, and they often used these rewards to make slaves work at a faster pace. One Louisiana slave owner, for example, provided a new suit of clothes to the highest cotton picker, a production incentive that reflected the value that slaves placed on clothing. But the enormous gap between the material goods of slave owners and those of their slaves was also meant to convey an unmistakable difference in status, and enslaved people were constantly reminded that the master lived far better than they did. Slaves lived in hovels, ate a monotonous diet of corn, and wore clothes made of the cheapest fabrics, while the material goods of their owners were of a significantly higher quality. Not only did white planters consume more food, but also they ate items that were almost never a part of a slave's weekly rations. Their dinner tables were full of fish; poultry or beef; a range of fruits and vegetables; and butter, cheese, tea, and coffee. Their houses were not tiny one-room cabins with dirt floors and only the crudest furniture but, instead, large multiroom homes with elegant furniture. The chasm that existed between the material life of slaves and that of slave owners was used to reinforce the message of inferiority and subordination that comprised the very foundation of the slave system.

While slave owners sought to control slaves in all of these ways, enslaved people found a variety of means to resist. Perhaps the most basic level of such resistance was their refusal to accept that, because of race or social status, whites somehow deserved to live better than they did. They rejected the idea that they deserved to be cold, hungry, and half-dressed, and to live in substandard housing, eat poor food, and wear cheap clothing. Enslaved people implicitly recognized that wealthy white Southerners had appropriated the products of slave labor to achieve material abundance. Power, not racial inferiority, had made whites rich and deprived slaves of a decent standard of living. In response to the radically unequal distribution of resources, enslaved people combined skill and ingenuity to improve the quality of their own material life. They planted gardens, fished, and stole to supplement the food provided by slave owners. They made baskets, brooms, and bowls to trade for necessities and luxuries. They bought clothing and made furniture for their home. These efforts could not transform their material life from scarcity to abundance, but they did assert their identity through the goods they acquired.

FOOD

What slaves ate varied from region to region and from farm to farm. Within a single farm, enslaved people consumed different food, depending upon the season, their age, and what work they did. Some owners dispensed more food as a reward or because the work performed was especially onerous. Unlike field hands, domestic workers had access to the leftovers from the master's table, which often included better-quality meat. In broad strokes, masters provided weekly rations that were supplemented by enslaved people, through hunting, trapping, fishing, and tending gardens. In addition, some chose the risky path of procuring food without the master's permission. To have more food than the bare minimum, however, required hard work, resourcefulness, and a willingness to take advantage of the slightest opportunity. It was also essential for enslaved people to acquire and shepherd their food resources collectively and to work hand in hand with other members of the slave community to provide each person what he or she needed on a daily basis.

The autobiography of former slave Charles Ball provides essential insights into these themes as Ball regularly discussed his material life as a slave, paying careful attention to food. After being sold from Maryland to a planter in South Carolina, Ball arrived on the plantation without anything but the threadbare clothes on his back and a blanket. He had no food, nothing to cook with, and no basket in which to place his weekly food allotment. Other enslaved people helped Ball through the transition period, and they soon created a community in which all benefited. He was placed in a slave cabin with a family who willingly shared their meager food with him, in particular their molasses. In response to their kindness, Ball proposed that he contribute his rations and all the animals he trapped to the family allotment, and they would share food and live as a family (Ball 1837, 192).

Ball learned to fish in the Patuxent River in Maryland, and this experience combined with his ability to construct fishing equipment, in particular his ability to knit a seine, or large net, created an opportunity for him to obtain additional food. When his master heard about his skills, he made Ball the head of a fishing party to supply fish for the plantation. In two weeks Ball had completed the seine made from rope and twine, and then he and three other enslaved men began clearing old trees and brush from the riverbed that might interfere with the nets. An overseer was hired to make sure that they performed the required work and that all of the shad they took out of the Congaree River went to the master. The enslaved men were permitted to eat any "common fish," like pike or perch, that they caught. Ball concluded that "a broiled freshwater fish is not very good, at best, without salt or oil; and after we had eaten them every day, for a week, we cared very little for them" (Ball 1837, 295). When the operation commenced, they worked in the daytime, but since night was the best time for taking shad, they switched their schedule. The overseer, however, did not want to lose sleep and, without the slave owner's knowledge, turned the supervision of the fishing over to Ball. Taking advantage of this system, Ball and the others "cooked as many shad as we could all eat" while the overseer slept and disposed of the scales from the stolen fish "far out in the river" (Ball 1837, 298).

Although Charles Ball enjoyed the shad, he craved bacon, something that was missing from his diet since he arrived in South Carolina. Out in his small fishing boat one night, he came in contact with the captain of a commercial vessel traveling along the Congaree River. While the overseer slept, Ball and the boat captain devised a plan to exchange shad for bacon. Though the captain made sure that the bargain greatly benefited him, Ball received 100 pounds of bacon for 300 shad. To avoid detection, he placed the bacon in an old barrel and buried it in a hole in his cabin floor. Ball emphasized that he would not steal anything but food from his master, and his hunger justified his actions. For two weeks, the four men feasted on bacon and fried shad, barely touching their ration of bland corn bread and unseasoned broiled fish. The improved diet made visible changes to his body, and a white neighbor noticed his healthy appearance. The neighbor, certain that Ball's appearance resulted from meat and not from his approved diet of river fish, stated that no one "could look as fat, and sleek, . . . and greasy, as you if he had nothing to eat but corn bread and river chubs" (Ball 1837, 314). Ball's ability to catch fish translated into an opportunity to improve his diet by manipulating an overseer, resisting his master's control, and negotiating a deal. But his actions were not without risks, and he would have been severely whipped if his master had learned of his actions. Ball made changes to his diet because he deemed that the food provided by his master was inadequate for the work he was required to perform. Finally, Ball's experience demonstrates that the quality and quantity of slave food had visible effects on the appearance and health of enslaved people.

Weekly Rations

Enslaved people most commonly received rations of corn and fat pork. Edwin Epps, for example, provided all slaves on his Louisiana plantation with a weekly ration of "three and a half pounds of bacon, and corn enough to make a peck of meal" (Northup 1853, 168). Epps's rations conformed to the average in the antebellum South, but some masters were more or less generous with their allotments. Austin Steward stated that on his plantation all enslaved people received a peck of corn or cornmeal per week. If they received their ration as corn, then they needed to grind it using a mortar after they had finished the day's labor. This pattern was fairly typical throughout the South, but unlike many slaves, Steward was "provided with very little meat" (Steward 1857, 14). Besides the corn, they received a small amount of salt, molasses, and a few herrings, but any additional food, they needed to provide for themselves. Some masters added to the rations seasonally, allowing enslaved people to substitute sweet potatoes for corn or to pick apples or peaches. Basic items like butter, coffee, tea, and sugar were not provided as part of the weekly rations.

Not all of the weekly rations of pork and corn, however, could be consumed. In some instances, the master included bone when providing pork, without altering the weight of the allowance. In addition, though the pork was smoked, it still might be infested with worms, and Solomon Northup found that the warmth of the Louisiana climate made it so that he and other slaves on Epps's plantation on some occasions received their weekly allowance of bacon "full of these disgusting vermin" (Northup 1853, 173). John Brown agreed that the food he received was of "bad quality," and he suggested that the corn was usually shriveled up and the bacon was old and "generally alive" with maggots (Brown 1855, 191–192). Frederick Douglass wrote that the pork provided by Colonel Lloyd was "often tainted" and the herring "was of the poorest quality." The quality of the corn, Douglass argued, was poor and roughly 15 percent was fit only for pigs (Douglass 1855, 100).

During his tour of Southern states in the 1820s, Scottish traveler Basil Hall observed that every slave above fourteen years on Cannon's Point plantation in Georgia received nine quarts (just over a peck) of Indian corn weekly and a one-quart monthly salt allotment. In some instances, they received salt beef, but Hall emphasized that it could "never be claimed as a right" (Hall 1829, 223). Carlyle Stewart, a former slave from Louisiana, received the usual ration of cornmeal, but he emphasized that they rarely had meat (Tanner 2014, 97). In contrast, slaves doing the physically demanding work of digging canals often received more than the average allotment of meat. Moses Grandy, for instance, stated that he received a peck of cornmeal and six pounds of cheap-quality pork each week when he was digging a canal near the Great Dismal Swamp. The amount of meat that slaves received clearly varied depending upon the owner and the work performed.

At certain times of the year, masters provided their slaves with larger amounts of food. During the rigorous sugarcane harvest, slave owners gave those working in the refinery a calorie-rich drink known as cane juice (Follett 2005, 161). Slave owners also provided extra food at special occasions like Christmas and harvest time. For some, Christmas dinner represented only a modest improvement from their normal fare, with the addition of molasses and sweetmeats, but in other cases, holidays were memorable because of the amount and variety of food that was available. Solomon Northup described Christmas dinner on Epps's Louisiana plantation containing "varieties of meat and piles of vegetables" but none of the corn bread and fatty bacon that made up their diet the rest of the year. Chickens, ducks, turkeys, pigs, and occasionally a wild ox were roasted, and they ate biscuits, peach tarts, and pies. After listing the delicacies available at Christmas, Northup concluded that "only the slave who has lived all the years on his scanty allowance of meal and bacon, can appreciate such suppers" (Northup 1853, 215). Louis Hughes described the festive Fourth of July barbeque as an exciting time when pigs and sheep were roasted in a trench in the ground and basted with butter, pepper, salt, and vinegar. The favorite foods of young and old alike, however, were sweet, and the peach cobbler and apple dumpling were "relished by all the slaves" (Hughes 1897, 48–49). Charles Ball described an elaborate meal celebrating the cotton harvest that included soup made with beef, bacon, and vegetables, plus bread, black-eyed peas, fruit, and a pudding made of cornmeal, lard, and molasses. In another instance, Ball's master divided two hogs between his slaves. Ball's share meant that the family ate their fill of stewed pork and sweet potatoes and still saved some of their pork to eat at another meal (Ball 1837, 262). These events were memorable to Northup, Hughes, and Ball because they stood in stark contrast to the food provided by the master during the rest of the year.

Food Preparation and Consumption

Cornmeal, the staple food provided by slave owners across the South, could be used in a stew with vegetables and meat, or it could be served as corn bread, hoecake, or ashcake. These cakes were a common part of an enslaved person's diet and could be easily taken to the field or made for supper at the end of the workday. Susan Kelly remembered that her mother made ashcake by mixing cornmeal, water, and salt together and shaping it into round cakes. When available, pork fat was also added. Initially, the cakes were placed on hot bricks in the fireplace until the edges browned and then covered with ashes until they were fully cooked (Perdue, Barden, and Phillips 1976, 189). Because ashes could get mixed into the dough, some enslaved people preferred, when possible, to wrap the cake in cabbage leaves before covering it with ashes. For Austin Steward, this method resulted in bread that was "sweet and very good" (Steward 1857, 16). A hoecake was a variant of an ashcake, with the cornmeal cake being placed on a hoe in the bottom of the fireplace and covered with ashes. It took about five minutes for the small cake to be fully cooked and then the ashes were washed off. One enslaved person emphasized that the hoecake should be eaten quickly because it tasted "like nothin' if you let it get cold" (Perdue, Barden, and Phillips 1976, 269).

While pork and cornmeal were the staple foods for Southern slaves, different patterns of food preparation emerged. In many instances, individual slaves were responsible for cooking their own food and bringing it to the fields with them in the morning for their noon meal. As a slave in Louisiana, Solomon Northup, for instance, described his process of filling one gourd with water and a second one with his cold bacon and corn cake (Northup 1853, 171). In other instances, slave owners decided that it was more efficient to have a plantation cook prepare the meal for all slaves and cart it out to the field. Elderly enslaved men and women who could not perform much fieldwork were often selected to bake corn bread for the whole gang and then distribute it at the appointed time. On Benjamin Johnson's Georgia plantation, all seventy-five field hands received their meal of potatoes, greens, corn bread, and meat in a tin pan. The noon meal was the big meal of the day, but supper and the next day's breakfast would have to be prepared after the long, tiring workday. In some instances, the food was unseasoned and therefore almost tasteless. One master, for instance, provided corn bread made without any salt as breakfast for his slaves who had been working for more than two hours in the fields.

Slave owners utilized any opportunity to communicate to enslaved people that their status was no better than that of an animal. As a child, Frederick Douglass was given mush, boiled cornmeal, to eat from either a wooden tray or trough that was placed on the ground. "The children were then called, like so many pigs, and like so many pigs they would come and devour the mush; some with oyster-shells, others with pieces of shingle, some with naked hands, and none with spoons." The hungry children were pitted against one another, and "he that ate the fastest got most" but "few left the trough satisfied" (Douglass 1845, 27). Masters often did not provide a separate ration for enslaved children, preferring to provide food communally from the plantation kitchen, and the trough was a common mechanism to easily feed a large group. Besides Douglass's mush, other masters dispensed sour milk or buttermilk in a trough. One former slave from Georgia, Tom Hawkins, remembered, for example, that "grown folks and chilluns" used wooden spoons to eat crumbled corn bread and buttermilk from a trough (Rawick 1974, 12: 128).

Supplying Their Own Food

The weekly rations were limited and repetitive, and week after week, enslaved people consumed the same monotonous diet. But they did not simply depend on their master for food. Beyond what the master provided, enslaved people varied their diet by raising chickens, cultivating gardens, and trapping and fishing. Wild food remains found in slave quarters indicate that enslaved people consumed possums, rabbits, and raccoons but not deer, ducks, or wild birds. The distinction is probably explained by the fact that the latter were hunted with guns, and slaves in most cases did not have access to them. Streams, rivers, and the ocean provided additional sources of food, including fish, crabs, clams, oysters, mullet, and turtles (Singleton 1991, 172).

Some masters provided a plot of land for slaves to grow their own vegetables. Tending the garden occurred only after the work dictated by the master had been completed, and thus it usually had to be performed at night. Slaves who worked in the task system in South Carolina had more time to supplement their diet, while those working in the gang system found that since their master controlled their time from sunup to sundown, these activities were restricted to nighttime. Provision gardens supplied vegetables like potatoes, peas, and beans that enriched their diet, and Charles Ball remembered that he added raw vegetables grown in his garden to his simple breakfast of corn bread. In addition to consuming what they produced, enslaved people sold vegetables, chickens, and eggs to their master or a third party. This money and the money earned by working on Sunday were then used to buy food, salt, tobacco, alcohol, or other needed material goods.

To add meat to their diet, many enslaved people fished or trapped, catching possum and raccoons at night, often without permission from their master. James Bolton, an ex-slave from Georgia, recalled that his master never asked too many questions about where the possums came from, and he supplied dogs to help them catch rabbits (Berlin, Favreau, and Miller 1998, 186). Masters often allowed slaves to hunt because it might make them less likely to steal from the smokehouse and because raccoons got into the corn in the fields. Charles Ball became adept at trapping raccoons, possums, and rabbits, and these animals provided him with two or three meals a week, including his Sunday dinner. Former slave Simon Stokes remembered that his mother would roast possum with sweet potatoes, while Will Sheets preferred fried rabbit. During his twelve years as a slave in Louisiana, Solomon Northup supplemented his inadequate diet of cornmeal and wormy bacon with possum and raccoons. Northup found raccoon edible but stated that "there is nothing . . . so delicious as a roasted possum" (Northup 1853, 201).

Hunger drove enslaved people to trap animals, but it decreased the amount of time they could sleep. Charles Ball went out three nights a week to check the traps he had laid three miles from home. Not all enslaved people wanted to lose that much precious sleep time. To preserve his sleep, Northup, who lived near the Bayou Boeuf in Louisiana, chose fish over animals. Northup constructed a fish trap and baited it with wet cornmeal rolled in cotton. When fish swam through the trap, they knocked over small sticks that he had placed in the trap, thereby closing the door and trapping the fish inside the frame (Northup 1853, 202–203). Bricks and stones were used as weights in fish traps, and grape vines secured them to overhanging tree branches. Enslaved people constructed their fishing gear from available materials. Nets in coastal North Carolina and Virginia, for instance, were made from jute or twine. Fish bones or dress pins were repurposed as hooks, cane served as fishing poles, and gourds could be used as floats (Cecelski 2001, 69). Recalling his time as a slave in Missouri, Henry Bruce stated, "We made lines of hemp grown on the farm and hooks of bent pins" (Bruce 1895, 17).

Slaves in coastal regions of the South had access to a variety of fish and shellfish. Evidence from a plantation on St. Simons Island in Georgia has revealed that slave owners saved on the purchase of pork and instead encouraged slaves to supplement their diet with fish, which amounted to nearly three-quarters of the meat consumed on the plantation (Cecelski 2001, 75). Julia Rush stated that her Georgia master provided no meat and instead expected "slaves to catch fish, oysters and other sea food for their meat supply" (Rawick 1974, 13: 229). Archaeological evidence from coastal plantations has revealed that enslaved people at times ate a greater variety of seafood and fish than white people, who preferred herring and shad. Enslaved people would consume, for example, gar fish, something whites termed "trash fish" (Cecelski 2001, 72). Charles Ball remembered that as a slave near the Patuxent River in Maryland, bacon was often in short supply, and so the slave community supplemented their diet with herring. Along the river, Ball learned how to fish and to make fishing gear, skills that would serve him well after he was sold to an owner in South Carolina. When possum and raccoons were in short supply, Ball drew on his fishing skills and made a weir (or enclosure) "of pine sticks, lashed together with white oak splits," and used the flow of the Congaree River in South Carolina to trap fish (Ball 1837, 276–277). Within five days, Ball had collected a half bushel of fish.

Stealing Food

Beyond seeking more protein, enslaved people also wanted more taste in their diet, and obtaining salt, a scarce item often in short supply on plantations, required creative solutions. When one group of enslaved people in Florida needed salt, they went into the smokehouse and removed the floorboards that were beneath the smoked hams hanging from the rafters. Because the wood had become saturated with salt and grease that had dripped off the meat, they simply put the boards into their soup to add needed flavor (Berlin, Favreau, and Miller 1998, 187). In addition to growing vegetables, trapping animals, and catching fish, therefore, some slaves resorted to taking the items they needed, with the smokehouse, millhouse, and orchards being common targets.

Inadequate provisions induced some enslaved people to steal from their masters, even though they risked whipping if they were caught. Some forms of theft, like taking apples or peaches from the orchard, were quite common. Children often took food from the Big House, and cooks brought home what their master's family did not finish. Some enslaved people devised more elaborate plans to get food when their rations ran out. George Womble described slaves sneaking into the millhouse and using an auger to bore a hole in a barrel containing cornmeal. They filled their bags with the free-flowing meal and then stopped up the hole. Meat, however, was more precious than meal, and so slaves sought ways to raid the smokehouse or steal pigs and chickens without getting caught. In particular, they needed to dispose of all parts of the animals that they would not eat, usually by burying them or throwing them in a river, and to cook the meat without being detected.

While some enslaved people were successful, others faced serious consequences when their actions were discovered. Marrinda Jane Singleton accepted that stealing was wrong but pragmatically stated: "Hunger will make you do a lot of things." She devised an ambitious "pig plan" that involved stealing a pig, killing it in the swamp, and then dividing it among her co-conspirators. The weakness in her plan, however, was keeping the children from broadcasting that their bellies were full of stolen meat. Despite all Singleton's efforts, the master found out that she had stolen a pig, and she was whipped as a consequence (Perdue, Barden, and Phillips 1976, 266). Proximity to chickens, pigs, and sheep was a daily temptation to people who were chronically hungry. After working especially hard and not having eaten meat in more than six months, an enslaved man gave into temptation and caught one of his master's sheep. He hoped that cooking the meat during the night would allow him to avoid detection, but his master was still up and discovered the purloined sheep in the kettle. As punishment, this enslaved man was tied to a post for the rest of the night before receiving 250 lashes in the morning.

Because necessity drove their decision to take food, enslaved people felt that their actions were justified as a result. John Brown argued that the theft of food was commonplace on Southern plantations and that if slaves did not steal, then they "could scarcely live" (Brown 1855, 192). Hunger drove them to take food, and the fear of what would happen to them if they got caught was not a deterrent. Former slave Arthur Greene agreed pragmatically that "if dey had give 'em nough to eat dey wouldn have no cause to steal" (Perdue, Barden, and Phillips 1976, 124). Since slave owners expected slaves to work in the fields, they should have provided enough food. As one former slave assured his interviewer, no one liked "to work with his belly groanin'" (Berlin, Favreau, and Miller 1998, 193). In many slave narratives and interviews with former slaves, they remembered bitterly that while slaves went hungry, white families ate well. Alice Marshall emphasized that her owner had plenty of food, but she gave little of it to the slaves who did all the work. Because the mistress never gave them enough to eat, Marshall's mother "had to git food de bes' way she could." Waiting until the mistress was distracted by a visit from the local minister, Marshall's mother snuck into the smokehouse and took meat, being careful to cover the tracks she had made in the sawdust on the floor (Perdue, Barden, and Phillips 1976, 201). Benjamin Johnson similarly recalled the unfairness of his diet when compared to the ham and sausages that white families consumed. He stated that the only way for an enslaved person to eat chicken was to steal it, preferably at night while the white family was sleeping. To be safe, Johnson said that they always buried the feathers because if they burned them, "white folks would smell 'em" (Rawick 1974, 12: 322).

When enslaved people "stole" food, they often understood the morality of their actions in light of the larger system of slavery which was, in essence, based on the theft of human bodies and their capacity to labor. Former slave William Wells Brown stated this idea explicitly at the very beginning of his narrative: "The man who stole me as soon as I was born recorded the births of all the infants which he claimed to be born his property" (Brown 1849, 13). But perhaps the most powerful rejection of the slaveholders' condemnation of enslaved people's stealing came from escaped slave Jermain Loguen, whose former mistress accused him of stealing the white family's horse as he fled North and demanded money for it. "You say I am a thief, because I took the old mare along with me," he responded. "Is it a greater sin for me to steal his horse, than it was for him to rob my mother's cradle and steal me?" (Loguen 1859, 454). Enslaved people understood that their treatment as objects rather than as human beings exempted them from moral condemnation by those who robbed them of their liberty and their dignity on a daily basis.

Because they knew that stealing food was a common occurrence, some owners developed their own strategies to prevent it. Frederick Douglass explained that Colonel Lloyd put tar on the fence surrounding the garden to stop slaves from stealing fruit. If anyone had tar on their clothes, they received a whipping for being in the garden without permission (Douglass 1845, 16). After the food had been dished out for the family, Harriet Jacobs's mistress would spit in the pans "to prevent the cook and her children from eking out their meagre fare with the remains of the gravy and other scrapings" (Jacobs 1861, 22). In these instances, slave owners claimed the right to control what slaves ate and to punish anyone who resisted their authority. In *They Were Her Property*, historian Stephanie Jones-Rogers uncovered examples of white mistresses limiting the food a slave received and then responding to any transgression with extreme cruelty. The story of one young girl, Harriet King, is especially disturbing. As a young child, King was responsible for emptying the chamber pots in the house, and on one occasion she found a piece of candy left by her mistress to tempt her. After seeing it for several days, the hungry young child ate the candy. For this act, she was brutally punished. The mistress placed Harriet's head under a rocking chair and rocked back and forth, crushing her jaw on one side. Harriet King's face was permanently disfigured, and she could not chew for the rest of her life (Jones-Rogers 2019, 11).

Nutrition and Health

In his proslavery novel, *Swallow Barn*, John Pendleton Kennedy created an image of slave owners providing an abundant supply of food, ranging from poultry to cucumbers, sweet potatoes, and cabbages. Despite Kennedy's rosy picture of abundant food, conflicting accounts exist in the available evidence. In the Federal Writers'

Project interviews with former slaves, some emphasized that they had plenty of food, while others, like Benjamin Johnson from Georgia, noted that "we boys in de fiel' used to be so hungry 'till we didn't know what to do" (Rawick 1974, 12: 322). Frederick Douglass at times was well fed, but he emphasized that "the painful gnawings of hunger" he experienced on the plantation were hard to cope with after receiving ample food while living in Baltimore (Douglass 1845, 51). Meat was often in short supply for many slaves. Frances Kemble recorded that on her husband's Georgia plantation, "animal food is only allowed to certain of the harder working men, hedgers and ditchers, and to them only occasionally, and in very moderate rations" (Kemble 1863, 134). The scarcity induced some young children to beg her for meat. Charles Ball stated that as many as thirty slave children would surround his South Carolina cabin when they smelled a possum or raccoon roasting, begging for a piece. As Mary Reynolds remembered, there "never was as much as we needed" (Tanner 2014, 6). While there has been extensive debate regarding whether slaves received a sufficient diet, the consensus among scholars is that while most slaves received an adequate amount of calories, their diet was often nutritionally deficient.

Unless supplemented by foods that enslaved people provided, the diet was unvarying and low in protein and needed vitamins. A diet that relied on corn for most calories would not have supplied all the amino acids needed for complete protein. Similarly, most of the pork slaves received was fatty, and so it yielded half the protein found in lean meat. Deborah Gray White has argued that slaves "were plagued by sickness," to a large extent because the diet of slaves was low in foods like fruits, vegetables, eggs, milk, and poultry that helped the immune system to fight disease and infection (White 1999, 83). Slaves experienced illnesses like scurvy, pellagra, and anemia that resulted from diets that did not contain sufficient vitamins and minerals. Scurvy, often associated with sailors, occurs because of a deficiency in vitamin C and causes weakness, tiredness, pain in the joints, and swollen gums. Because vitamin C cannot be stored in the body, people need a year-round source of the vitamin, but the evidence indicates that foods rich in vitamin C, like sweet potatoes, were available to enslaved people only seasonally. A Louisiana doctor concluded that a diet composed "mostly of salt pork, cornbread, and molasses" and lacking in fresh vegetables produced a condition "closely allied to scurvy" (Follett 2005, 295). Pellagra, another disease that plagued slaves, resulted from a niacin deficiency, and symptoms include skin rashes, diarrhea, and dementia. Corn and fat pork supply only a small amount of the needed niacin, and as a result, the diet of enslaved people was often deficient. Kenneth Kiple and Virginia King have argued that "the absence of sufficient niacin in turn suggests that the slaves were unable to properly metabolize the carbohydrates, fats, and proteins in the diet, which means they could not possibly have received the full benefit of those nutrients" (Kiple and King 1981, 91). In addition to a diet deficient in protein, vitamin C, and niacin, enslaved people did not consume enough calcium, which had an impact on growth and bone health.

As with most aspects of slave life, conditions varied across the South. In *Down by the Riverside*, Charles Joyner found no evidence in All Saints Parish, South Carolina, of niacin deficiency leading to pellagra, and he emphasized that the natural increase in the slave population suggests that the diet was adequate (Joyner 1984, 104–105). But Louisiana stands in marked contrast to the data from the lowcountry of South Carolina. Historian Richard Follett has found that female slaves working on sugar-producing plantations in Louisiana had low fertility rates and high infant mortality rates. Their inadequate diet limited fertility and increased the risk of miscarriages or the birth of underweight babies who lived only a short time. Follett concluded that "the evidence thus leads to the overwhelming conclusion that inadequate food and poor nutrition, when combined with heavy labor duties, compromised fertility" (Follett 2005, 298). Scholars have studied the precise nutritional effects of the slave diet, but the personal appearance of slaves provided ample evidence at the time that they were poorly fed. Charles Ball reported that "a half-starved negro is a miserable looking creature. His skin becomes dry, and appears to be sprinkled over with whitish husks, or scales; the glossiness of his face vanishes, his hair loses its color, becomes dry, and when stricken with a rod, the dust flies from it" (Ball 1837, 44).

SLAVE QUARTERS

As with food, living conditions for slaves varied widely across the South, but they were consistently inferior to the living conditions of slave owners. Overall, slave quarters were small, crowded, and rudimentary. Most cabins were a single story and made from logs or hewn wood. When the floor of the cabins was dirt, the rooms remained damp, and so some slave owners preferred using wood flooring as a healthier option. They was often only one room, ranging from 10′ × 10′ feet to 16′ × 20′ feet. Another common structure was the double pen, a cabin containing two rooms with a central fireplace separating them. One family lived in each room that measured roughly 16′ × 16′ feet, and this arrangement, in some cases, allowed extended family to live together. The fireplace, usually located at the back of the cabin, was also a simple design of brick or even cheaper materials. Allen Parker described a 6-foot-long fireplace built of logs with a wooden chimney that was plastered with wet clay that hardened with the heat of the fire. Parker stated that this form of masonry was both cheap and easily repaired since "the material cost nothing as was always at hand" (Parker 1895, 13). While Parker emphasized their cheapness, chimneys constructed of sticks and mud were also dangerous, and they could easily catch on fire. As one former slave reported, "Many the time we have to get up at midnight and push the chimney away from the house to keep the house from burnin' up" (Joyner 1991, 88).

In his autobiography, Solomon Northup described his living conditions as "comfortless and extremely disagreeable" (Northup 1853, 170). His poorly constructed cabin had a dirt floor and a door

This double-pen slave cabin was built in the 1840s on Andrew Jackson's plantation, The Hermitage. This design, often referred to as the saddlebag form, contained two rooms around a central chimney and usually housed two families. (Library of Congress)

but no windows, and there were gaps between the logs that let in light and rain. Jourden Banks also stated that his cabin in Alabama had large, unfilled gaps between the logs and openings in the roof, through which he could see the stars (Pennington 1861, 50–51). Though absent in the cabins inhabited by Northup and Banks, mud or clay was often used to fill the gaps between the logs. Along with the wind and rain that came *into* the cabin, John Brown disliked that "the smoke will not go out" (Brown 1855, 191). These cabins were cold in the winter and hot in the summer. Charley Williams remembered that the slave cabins on his plantation in northern Louisiana were "good and warm" in the summer, and so they slept in an open shed at the side of the cabin to keep cool (Tanner 2014, 45). After observing slave quarters in South Carolina, Frederick Law Olmsted expressed surprise that humans lived in the buildings. If it weren't for the chimneys, he said, he would have "conjectured that it had been built for a powder-house, or perhaps an ice house—never for an animal to sleep in" (Vlach 1993, 156).

This slave cabin was built between 1830 and 1850 at Sotterley Plantation in St. Mary's County, Maryland. The single-room cabin measures 16′ × 18′, and prior to renovation, it contained a brick or stone chimney, a loft for sleeping, and a hard-packed dirt floor. (Library of Congress)

Overcrowding was a serious problem and, as Ceceil George stated, the cabins were "packed wid' people" (Tanner 2014, 168). The slave narratives reveal, however, that the extent of the overcrowding varied in slave quarters across the South. When he was sold to a planter in South Carolina, Charles Ball was assigned to a 16' × 16' cabin made from hewn wood, with a shingled roof and a pine floor. As a single man, he joined a household comprising two parents and five children, ranging in age from one to twelve. The 38 cabins on the plantation were built in a row, and they housed 250 people—an average of 6.7 people per cabin (Ball 1837, 139). In contrast, Henry Watson stated that his master housed 100 slaves in 27 cabins, or 3.7 people per cabin (Watson 1848, 14). William Green's living accommodations lacked the privacy that separate cabins offered. His master housed roughly thirty slaves in a single building with a central chimney and exposed beams. Whenever enslaved people could find any spare wood or old blankets, they would partition separate living spaces for their family, but the master offered no assistance (Green 1853, 8–9).

Because cheaply constructed cabins with leaking rooves and dirt floors increased the likelihood of illness, antebellum slave owners began arguing for changes in their design. Some focused on the need to construct a better roof, while others emphasized that cabins should be raised off the ground. In the nineteenth century, planters pointed to health concerns as their main reason for changing how slave cabins were constructed. Historical archaeologists have excavated root cellars filled with tools, ceramics, and food remains in a number of eighteenth-century slave cabins, but they have noted that these cellars became less common in the nineteenth century. Convinced that root cellars became filled with garbage that was unhealthy for the occupants, one planter argued in 1850 that slave cabins should be elevated so that "if there should be any filth under them, the master or overseer, in passing, can see it and have it removed" (Breeden 1980, 120–121). Cabins were raised two feet off the ground, ostensibly to promote a healthy flow of air, but this change also prevented slaves from digging cellars in which they could hide items from the master. Charles Grandy remembered stealing chickens and needing to hide them from patrollers: "We always had a trap in de floor . . . to hide dese chickens in" (Singleton 1991, 167). Planters blended their concern for healthy living quarters with their desire to enforce discipline by elevating slave cabins, eliminating the possibility of root cellars, and denying enslaved people a convenient place to conceal any items they did not want the master to see.

When a couple married, some masters permitted them to establish their own household by providing them a cabin to live in. If not, multiple generations of family members lived together in the same cabin. To set up housekeeping, a couple needed basic items like bedding, a table and chairs, and an iron pot for cooking. These items had to be purchased or constructed by skilled carpenters on the plantation. Historian Marie Jenkins Schwartz has calculated that one Virginia planter paid roughly $50 for each female slave who set up housekeeping in the 1820s (Schwartz 2000, 51). When a cabin needed to be built for a couple, most slave owners waited until work on the staple crop was slow before authorizing it. Winter, for instance, was a time when work slowed on a rice plantation, and owners would approve the construction of a new cabin. In other regions, planters preferred that cabins be built in the summer, after the crop had been planted, but needed little attention (Schwartz 2000, 51). Most cabins were built by enslaved men following the specifications of the white landowner. James Curry, for instance, stated that his stepfather felled trees and then built a "commodious" log cabin for his family to live in (Blassingame 1977, 132). Along with the cabin itself, most of the furniture in a cabin was made by enslaved men. Thomas Jones fondly remembered the cabin that he lived in for the first nine years of his life when his family was together. His parents made the cabin a happy home, and they "worked late into the night many and many a time to get a little simple furniture for their home" (Jones 1862, 5). Many enslaved people had at least a few basic pieces of furniture, like a small bed, a bench, and a pine table, usually made by hand. The addition of items they crafted themselves or flowers planted out front, in some cases, made the rudimentary cabins more pleasant.

The quality of sleeping arrangements varied from a bare spot on the floor to a bedstead. Planter Edwin Epps provided little to the slaves who toiled all day on his plantation, and thus, Solomon Northup slept on a plank with only a coarse blanket to keep him warm (Northup 1853, 170). Other slaves reported that they slept on corded beds—cords were threaded through holes in the head, foot, and sides of the wooden bedframe. Henry Baker described a bunk in which two holes were made in the wall, pieces of wood were stuck in the holes, and then two posts supported the other side. He suggested that the bed would be crowded with as many adults and children as could fit (Blassingame 1977, 669). Enslaved people stuffed mattresses and pillows made from coarse linen with straw, corn shuck, pine needles, and, in rare cases, feathers. For those whose masters would not provide even the basic material goods, enslaved people slept on a bed of straw. When Moses Grandy was hired out to build canals, he found out how rudimentary his living conditions could become. Though a canal might take years to complete, only temporary shelter or huts were built. Though Grandy was engaged in arduous labor cutting roots and hauling mud for hours every day, his employer did not provide blankets, insisting that one could be obtained only if a slave completed not only his assigned tasks but also extra work (Grandy 1843, 35).

Some masters provided the basic items for cooking; others felt they had only minimal responsibility to provide any material goods beyond food and clothing. James Smith stated that on his Virginia plantation, enslaved people had only the bare minimum for housekeeping: a water pail, a cooking pot, and a few gourds. At mealtime they simply squatted around the fire and ate directly out of the pot using oyster shells for spoons. For cooking, William Green recalled that enslaved people had only a few utensils and a long-handled shallow iron skillet used to fry salt pork or bacon. Northup remarked that when his master purchased a new slave, he provided "neither knife, nor fork, nor dish, nor kettle, nor any other thing in the shape of crockery, or furniture of any nature or description" (Northup 1853, 195). If slaves wanted any of these items, they needed to use money earned from working on Sundays to buy them. Northup preferred to make do with items that were readily available. He used a gourd to store his cornmeal, a small wooden box to hold his corn, and the axe from the woodpile to cut his bacon. Enslaved people with woodworking skills were in a position to improve their material life beyond meager possessions that Northup possessed. Whenever he had spare time, Charles Ball would make wooden bowls, ladles, and trays that he sold to a local storekeeper, and he bought food and blankets with the proceeds. Given that slave owners often provided only minimal material goods, enslaved people either had to do without or had to use their own skills to improve their living conditions.

Making up 10 percent of the total slave population, urban slaves had distinct work experiences that led to different living arrangements from slaves on a plantation. Employers who needed labor, but wanted a flexible system, hired slaves for the year instead of purchasing them. Slaves hired out to work in Richmond's tobacco factories, flour mills, and iron foundries experienced significantly different living conditions than slaves on rural plantations. Employers did not provide housing, and so slaves who were hired to work in these jobs lived in boarding houses or rented a room in a house. Hired slaves usually lived in racially segregated sections of the city, near the waterfront, for example, that offered cheap housing (Takagi 1999, 96–97). While their accommodations might have been dingy and dirty, living out offered enslaved people the opportunity to make decisions about their material life usually reserved for slave owners.

Living out made it possible for enslaved people who had different owners to inhabit the same household. Henry Brown, who worked at a tobacco factory, had a wife and children owned by a different master in Richmond, and their owner, Mr. Cottrell, offered Brown what appeared to be an excellent opportunity to live with his wife and children. Cottrell asked Brown to pay him $50 a year and to take responsibility for providing food and lodging for his family. The arrangement offered the Brown family a chance to live together without any oversight by an owner, but it was risky. Understanding that Henry Brown loved his family and wanted to live with them, Cottrell used that information to his advantage and was soon making new demands. One day Cottrell arrived while the family was eating their breakfast and demanded that Brown pay him a large sum of money or else, he implied, they would be sold away. Henry Brown did not have the money because he had the expenses for rent, furniture, and food. After Brown left for work, Cottrell sold his wife and children and all Brown's material possessions as well. While he was able to recover his possessions, Brown lost his family forever. Working in Richmond offered Brown a chance to have more autonomy over his material life; he lived apart from his master and purchased food and furniture on his own. Yet Brown had no power to force Cottrell to honor the bargain they had struck, and Brown's carefully constructed world collapsed when Cottrell exercised the right of the master and sold his property.

CLOTHING

Masters provided clothing for their slaves, but in most cases it was made from cheap, coarse fabric, simply referred to as "Negro cloth." James Lowry, for example, described Richard's clothing as consisting of a black coat, a hat, and "common negro cloth pants" (*Sumter Banner* 1853, 3). In the antebellum period, New England textile mills produced inexpensive fabric specifically for the slave market. Slave owners purchased yards of the plain white fabric and either distributed it to enslaved people who sewed their clothes in their own time or tasked a group of slaves with making clothes for all the field hands. Some masters dispensed clothes annually, but many provided separate summer and winter allotments. Slave owners were more concerned with the price of the cloth and its durability than how it felt to wear, and so they most commonly selected a coarse cotton blend for summer clothes and "plains," a woolen material, for the winter. Masters preferred to purchase coarse, cheap cloth that was made to last, even if it was uncomfortable to wear. After Pierce Butler distributed heavy plains to slaves, his wife believed they resembled a carpet and were completely ill suited for the Georgia climate, even in winter (Kemble 1863, 61).

When providing clothing, slave owners made distinctions based on the work performed. Slaves who worked in the Big House received better-quality clothes made from fine fabrics to reflect the master's status. The mistress often donated old dresses to her lady's maid, and the master gave old suits or boots to his valet. In contrast, male field hands received two shirts and two pairs of pants twice a year, with a jacket made of coarse wool added in the winter. Women received two dresses or long skirts and blouses in summer and winter, and by the end of the season, these clothes were often ragged and tattered. As undergarments, women usually wore a shift, a shapeless smock worn next to the skin, or "pantalets," which came to the knee and were tied at the waist. Pregnant women did not have any maternity clothes; they simply wore loose shirts and skirts. A drawstring allowed them to adjust the waistline as their pregnancy progressed.

When a baby was born, some owners distributed flannel to new mothers to use for the infant's clothing. This supply was not replenished, and when new clothing was needed, slave mothers often had to beg the plantation mistress for cloth (Schwartz 2000, 54). As part of their clothing allotment, field hands received a hat and a pair of shoes with wooden soles and a thick leather upper, called brogans by many slaves. Children went barefoot—even in winter—until they began doing fieldwork. Like the weekly food rations, the clothing allotment for field hands was uniform and unvarying. Since children did little or no productive labor, slave owners provided only a minimal clothing allowance for them, and they wanted to communicate the message that clothing had to be earned. Both girls and boys wore a long shirt when they were young, and many commented that enslaved children were often half-dressed or even naked. In winter, some parents had to keep their children inside, while others cut up blankets to sew warm clothing for their children. When children went to work in the fields or in their owner's house, the change in their life was marked by the receipt of their first pants or dress.

The quality and the amount of clothing distinguished enslaved people from their white owners. Deborah Gray White has argued that the bodies of enslaved women were exposed in ways that distinguished them from "respectable" white women, who wore multiple layers of clothing and kept their arms and legs covered. In specific instances—on the auction block or while being whipped—enslaved women could be stripped naked or to the waist. Yet on a daily basis, some women wore thin, tattered clothing that exposed their bodies. Former slave Delia Garlic, for instance, stated, "I never had a undershirt until jest befo' my first chil' was borned. I never had nothin' but a shimmy an' a slip for a dress" (Rawick 1973, 6: 131). In addition, to perform fieldwork and domestic chores, enslaved women often had to pin up their skirt to make the work easier. These circumstances contributed to the tendency of whites to associate black women with promiscuity (White 1999, 31–33). When Frederick Law Olmsted observed a group of women working in the mud on a South Carolina plantation, he commented that they "reefed up" their skirts and tied them around their waist, thereby exposing legs covered only in loose leggings. He remarked that the women in the group had "sly, sensual, and shameless" expressions (Olmsted 1862, 208).

While slave owners provided only minimal clothing, enslaved people wanted to look their best and devised a number of strategies to enhance their clothing. One option was to designate a set of the clothing for special occasions and holidays and reserve the other for work. In addition, some slave owners allowed their slaves to borrow a dress or boots for parties or other special occasions. Mary Wyatt, however, decided not to wait for an offer and took one of her mistress's dresses without permission to wear to a dance (Perdue, Barden, and Phillips 1976, 333). To look stylish at a dance, Nancy Williams dyed her shoes yellow to match her dress and knitted stockings and bought ribbons to wear in her hair. Enslaved people were connected to the local economy and sold items like baskets, chickens, eggs, or vegetables to buy material goods of their own choosing. In addition to clothes, enslaved people purchased items of personal adornment—ribbons, combs, jewelry, and glass beads. Women wore ribbons in their hair and beads around their neck or attached beads to their clothes to enhance their personal appearance. These transactions could occur clandestinely or openly with local shopkeepers, but in either case, whites who traded with enslaved people often took advantage of slaves. When an enslaved man exchanged eggs for fabric so that his wife could have a new dress, a Darien, Georgia, shopkeeper gave him poor-quality cotton cloth that ripped as soon as it was worn (Kemble 1863, 299). Masters who prohibited trade off the plantation instead purchased the items that slaves produced and regularly exchanged vegetables, fish, or poultry for fabric or ready-made clothing. Historian Betty Wood has noted that slaves bought items from their master with cash or on credit. Wood demonstrated that in 1830, "a bondman named Jeffrey made a down payment of $.94 . . . toward the purchase of 'twilled homespun'" and Nancy "bought 'Calico and an apron' valued at $1.37" (Wood 1995, 67).

Instead of purchasing ready-made cloth, some masters chose to have a group of enslaved women spin and weave. They became skilled at designing patterns, weaving stripes and checks into the cloth, and dying thread. They crafted an assortment of natural dyes made from tree bark or moss to make brown, red, purple, or yellow thread. As a result of their use of dyes, enslaved women could make "two an' three color'd cloth by putting diff'rent color'd thread on de shuttles" (White and White 1998, 22). Historians Shane White and Graham White have concluded that a significant difference existed between slaves' clothing Monday to Saturday and their attire on Sunday. On this day, when their master had less control over their time, they dressed to please themselves and express their individuality. One South Carolina observer commented that slaves were "a'mos' naked, wen deys at work," but on "Sundays dey is mighty well clothed" (Olmsted 1862, 211).

When enslaved people designed clothes for themselves, they expressed both their individual taste and their African heritage. While the master offered only drab clothing, they preferred bright, contrasting colors. Former slave Lizzie Norfleet remembered that women made dresses that alternated dark and bright stripes and concluded that "folks them days knowed how to mix pretty colors" (White and White 1998, 22). In contrast, Fanny Kemble called the Sunday apparel of the slaves on her husband's plantation "grotesque" and "ludicrous." She noted that the son of their cook wore a "magnificent black satin waistcoat" but no shoes or stockings on his feet. The fabric worn by enslaved women was brighter than that she was accustomed to, and Kemble found their combination of elements unsettling. Enslaved women wore patterns and chintzes together; they wore brightly hued kerchiefs around their head, and "beads, bugles, flaring sashes, and above all, little fanciful aprons" (Kemble 1863, 68–69). While white Southerners expressed disgust at the fashion choices, enslaved people made the purchase of clothing that reflected their own identity a priority.

The material lives of enslaved people were shaped profoundly by a system designed to maximize the productivity of their labor and to minimize the cost of their upkeep. Without compromising their slaves' ability to work, owners reduced the allotments and the quality of food, clothing, and housing as much as possible. At the same time, they sought to preserve their immense social power by maintaining sharp differences between their lifestyle and that of the people they owned. One side of the story of the slave's material life, therefore, is one of scarcity, deprivation, and utter dependency upon the will of their owners. But as in other aspects of their daily lives, enslaved people used their own labor, creativity, and traditions to forge a much richer material culture than the one their owners attempted to force upon them. Working within, outside, and around the system that was designed to trap and define them, slaves developed ways to produce or acquire food, augment their allotments of clothing, improve their dwellings, and humanize the material circumstances of their lives.

DOCUMENTS: INTERVIEW WITH TEMPIE CUMMINS (1937) AND CHARLES BALL, *SLAVERY IN THE UNITED STATES* (1837)

This section contains two short documents that address the food, clothing, and cabins of enslaved people. The first one is from a collection of interviews with former slaves conducted by the Federal Writers' Project in the 1930s. Tempie Cummins was born before the Civil War in Brookeland, Texas. The second source is from Charles Ball's 1837 narrative. The excerpt begins as Ball arrived on a cotton plantation in South Carolina after being sold from his home in Maryland. He provided rich details about the material conditions under which he lived. Both sources speak to the scarcity of their material resources.

Interview with Former Slave Tempie Cummins, Texas, 1937

I slep' on a pallet on the floor. They give me a home-spun dress once a year at Christmas time. When company come I had to run and slip on that dress. At other time I wore white chillens' cast-off clothes so wore they was ready to throw away. I had to pin them up with red horse thorns to hide my nakedness. My dress was usually split from hem to neck and I had to wear them till they was strings. Went barefoot summer and winter till the feets crack open.

Source: Born in Slavery: Slave Narratives from the Federal Writers' Project, 1936 to 1938, vol. 16, Texas, Part 1, Adams-Duhon, 263. https://www.loc.gov/collections/slave-narratives-from-the-federal-writers-project-1936-to-1938/about-this-collection/

Charles Ball, *Slavery in the United States*, 1837

I followed my new friend to his cabin, which I found to be the habitation of himself, his wife, and five children. The only furniture in this cabin, consisted of a few blocks of wood for seats; a short bench, made of a pine board, which served as a table; and a small bed in one corner composed of a mat, made of common rushes, spread upon some corn husks, pulled and split into fine pieces, and kept together by a narrow slip of wood, confined to the floor by wooden pins. There was a common iron pot, standing beside the chimney; and several wooden spoons and dishes hung against the wall. Several blankets also hung against the wall upon wooden pins. An old box, made of pine boards, without either lock or binges, occupied one corner.

At the time I entered this humble abode the mistress was not at home. She had not yet returned from the field; having been sent, as the husband informed me, with some other people late in the evening, to do some work in a field about two miles distant. I found a child, about a year old, lying on the mat-bed, and a little girl about four years old beside it.

These children were entirely naked, and when we came to the door, the elder rose from its place and ran to its father, and clasping him round one of his knees, said, "Now we shall get good supper." The father laid his hand upon the head of his naked child, and stood silently looking in its face—which was turned upwards toward his own for a moment. . . .

The mother wore an old ragged shift; but the children, the eldest of whom appeared to be about twelve, and the youngest six years old, were quite naked. When she came in, the husband told her that the overseer had sent me to live with them; and she and her oldest child, who was a boy, immediately set about preparing their supper, by boiling some of the leaves of the weed called lamb's-quarter, in the pot. This, together with some cakes of cold corn bread, formed their supper. My supper was brought to me from the house of the overseer by a small girl, his daughter. It was about half a pound of bread, cut from a loaf made of corn meal. My companions gave me a part of their boiled greens, and we all sat down together to my first meal in my new habitation.

I had no other bed than the blanket which I had brought with me from Maryland; and I went to sleep in the loft of the cabin which was assigned to me as my sleeping room; and in which I continued to lodge as long as I remained on this plantation. . . .

On Monday morning I heard the sound of the horn, at the usual hour, and repairing to the front of the overseer's house, found that he had already gone to the corn crib, for the purpose of distributing corn amongst the people, for the bread of the week; or rather, for the week's subsistence; for this corn was all the provision that our master, or his overseer, usually made for us;—I say usually, for whatever was given to us beyond the corn, which we received on Sunday evening, was considered in the light of a bounty bestowed upon us, over and beyond what we were entitled to, or had a right to expect to receive.

When I arrived at the crib, the door was unlocked and open, and the distribution had already commenced. Each person was entitled to half a bushel of ears of corn, which was measured out by several of the men who were in the crib. Every child above six months old drew this weekly allowance of corn; and in this way, women who had several small children, had more corn than they could consume, and sometimes bartered small quantities with the other people, for such things as they needed, and were not able to procure.

The people received their corn in baskets, old bags, or any thing with which they could most conveniently provide themselves. I had not been able since I came here, to procure a basket, or any thing else to put my corn in, and desired the man with whom I lived to take my portion in his basket, with that of his family. This he readily agreed to do, and as soon as we had received our share we left the crib.

Source: Charles Ball. *Slavery in the United States: A Narrative of the Life and Adventures of Charles Ball.* New York: John S. Taylor, 1837, 142–145, 188–189.

FURTHER READING

Ball, Charles. 1837. *Slavery in the United States: A Narrative of the Life and Adventures of Charles Ball.* New York: John S. Taylor.

Berlin, Ira, Marc Favreau, and Steven F. Miller, eds. 1998. *Remembering Slavery: African Americans Talk about Their Personal Experiences of Slavery and Emancipation*. New York: The New Press.

Blassingame, John W., ed. 1977. *Slave Testimony: Two Centuries of Letters, Speeches, Interviews, and Autobiographies*. Baton Rouge: Louisiana State University Press.

Breeden, James O., ed. 1980. *Advice among Masters*. Westport, CT: Greenwood Press.

Brown, Henry. 1851. *Narrative of the Life of Henry Box Brown*. Manchester: Lee and Glynn.

Brown, John. 1855. *Slave Life in Georgia: A Narrative of the Life, Sufferings and Escape of John Brown*. London: W. M. Watts.

Brown, William Wells. 1849. *Narrative of William W. Brown, a Fugitive Slave*. London: Charles Gilpin.

Bruce, Henry. 1895. *The New Man: Twenty-Two Years a Slave, Twenty-Nine Years a Free Man*. York, PA: P. Anstadt & Sons.

Cecelski, David S. 2001. *The Waterman's Song: Slavery and Freedom in Maritime North Carolina*. Chapel Hill: University of North Carolina Press.

Douglass, Frederick. 1845. *Narrative of the Life of Frederick Douglass, an American Slave, Written by Himself*. Boston, MA: Antislavery Office.

Douglass, Frederick. 1855. *My Bondage, My Freedom*. New York: Miller, Orton & Mulligan.

Follett, Richard. 2005. "'Lives of Living Death': The Reproductive Lives of Slave Women in the Cane World of Louisiana." *Slavery and Abolition* 26, no. 2 (August): 289–304.

Grandy, Moses. 1843. *Narrative of the Life of Moses Grandy, Late a Slave in the United States of America*. London: Charles Gilpin.

Green, William. 1853. *Narrative of Events in the Life of William Green*. Springfield, MA: L. M. Guernsey.

Hall, Basil. 1829. *Travels in North America in the Years 1827 and 1829*, volume 3. Edinburgh: Cadell and Co.

Hughes, Louis. 1897. *Thirty Years a Slave: From Bondage to Freedom*. Milwaukee, WI: South Side Printing Co.

Jacobs, Harriet. 1861. *Incidents in the Life of a Slave Girl*. Boston: printed by the author.

Jones, Thomas H. 1862. *The Experience of Thomas H. Jones, Who Was a Slave for Forty-Three Years*. Boston: Bazin & Chandler.

Jones-Rogers, Stephanie E. 2019. *They Were Her Property: White Women as Slave Owners in the American South*. New Haven, CT: Yale University Press.

Joyner, Charles. 1984. *Down by the Riverside: A South Carolina Slave Community*. Urbana: University of Illinois Press.

Joyner, Charles. 1991. "The World of the Plantation Slaves." In *Before Freedom Came: African-American Life in the Antebellum South*, edited

by Edward D. C. Campbell, Jr. Charlottesville: University Press of Virginia.
Kemble, Frances Anne. 1863. *Journal of a Residence on a Georgian Plantation in 1838–1839*. New York: Harper & Brothers.
Kennedy, John Pendleton. 1832. *Swallow Barn, or a Sojourn in the Old Dominion*. Philadelphia, PA: Carey & Lea.
Kiple, Kenneth F., and Virginia King. 1981. *Another Dimension to the Black Diaspora*. New York: Cambridge University Press.
Loguen, Jermain. 1859. *The Rev. J.W. Loguen, as a Slave and as a Freeman*. Syracuse, NY: J.G.K. Truair & Co.
Northup, Solomon. 1853. *Twelve Years a Slave: Narrative of Solomon Northup, a Citizen of New-York, Kidnapped in Washington City in 1841, and Rescued in 1853*. Auburn, NY: Derby and Miller.
Olmsted, Frederick Law. 1862. *The Cotton Kingdom: A Traveler's Observations on Cotton and Slavery in the American Slave States, Volume 1*. New York: Mason Brothers.
Parker, Allen. 1895. *Recollections of Slavery Times*. Worcester, MA: Chas. W. Burbank & Co.
Pennington, J.W.C. 1861. *A Narrative of Events of the Life of J.H. Banks, an Escaped Slave, from the Cotton State, Alabama, in America*. Liverpool, England: M. Rourke.
Perdue, Charles L., Thomas E. Barden, and Robert K. Phillips, eds. 1976. *Weevils in the Wheat: Interviews with Virginia Ex-Slaves*. Charlottesville: University Press of Virginia.
Rawick, George P., ed. 1973. *The American Slave: A Composite Autobiography, v. 6: Alabama and Indiana Narratives*. Westport, CT: Greenwood Press.
Rawick, George P., ed. 1974. *The American Slave: A Composite Autobiography, v. 12: Georgia Narratives, Parts 1 and 2*. Westport, CT: Greenwood Press.
Rawick, George P., ed. 1974. *The American Slave: A Composite Autobiography, v. 13: Georgia Narratives, Parts 3 and 4*. Westport, CT: Greenwood Press.
Schwartz, Marie Jenkins. 2000. *Born in Bondage: Growing Up Enslaved in the Antebellum South*. Cambridge, MA: Harvard University Press.
Singleton, Theresa A. 1991. "The Archaeology of Slave Life." In *Before Freedom Came: African-American Life in the Antebellum South*, edited by Edward D. C. Campbell, Jr. Charlottesville: University Press of Virginia.
Smith, James Lindsay. 1881. *Autobiography of James L. Smith*. Norwich, CT: The Bulletin.
Steward, Austin. 1857. *Twenty-Two Years a Slave and Forty Years a Free Man*. Rochester, NY: William Alling.
Sumter Banner, South Carolina, May 10, 1853.

Takagi, Midori. 1999. *"Rearing Wolves to Our Own Destruction": Slavery in Richmond, Virginia, 1782–1865.* Charlottesville: University Press of Virginia.

Tanner, Lynette Ater. 2014. *Chained to the Land: Voices from Cotton & Cane Plantations.* Winston-Salem, NC: John F. Blair Publishers.

Vlach, John Michael. 1993. *Back of the Big House: The Architecture of Plantation Slavery.* Chapel Hill: University of North Carolina Press.

Watson, Henry. 1848. *Narrative of Henry Watson, a Fugitive Slave.* Boston, MA: Bela Marsh.

White, Deborah Gray. 1999. *Ar'n't I a Woman? Female Slaves in the Plantation South.* New York: W. W. Norton.

White, Shane, and Graham White. 1998. *Stylin': African American Expressive Culture from Its Beginnings to the Zoot Suit.* Ithaca, NY: Cornell University Press.

Wood, Betty. 1995. *Women's Work, Men's Work: The Informal Slave Economies of Lowcountry Georgia.* Athens: University of Georgia Press.

4

RELIGIOUS LIFE

In 1855, former slave Peter Randolph published a thirty-five-page antislavery pamphlet entitled *Sketches of Slave Life: Or Illustrations of the "Peculiar Institution,"* which, in addition to its scathing indictment of slavery, described the centrality of religion in the daily experiences of enslaved African Americans. He paid special attention to the "religious exercises" that occurred among slaves on the Sabbath day, either with or without the permission of the master. Gathering covertly in an "old log cabin" on the edge of the plantations or "in the swamps, out of reach of the patrols," black worshippers reinforced deep communal bonds by sharing stories of their recent sufferings and by offering emotional support to those in special need of comfort. Soon, however, the gathered congregation began a round of "praying and singing all round" that generated intense spiritual excitement before slave preachers began to move the people toward a passionate recommitment to their faith. "The speaker usually commences by calling himself unworthy, and talks very slowly," Randolph remembered, "until, feeling the spirit, he grows excited and in a short time, there fall to the ground twenty or thirty men and women under its influence." As the service ended, he recalled, slaves passed "from one to another, shaking hands, and bidding each other farewell, promising, should they meet no more on earth, to strive and meet in heaven, where all is joy, happiness and liberty" (Randolph 1855, 30–31).

In contrast to the sincerity and devotion of the slave worshippers, Randolph described the religion of the masters as insincere and utterly corrupted by their commitment to slavery. Traders, for example, would often cite the religious faith of slaves on the auction block as a device to drive up the price, arguing that religious devotion made them more docile and obedient. He remembered one weeping slave mother named Jenny who was sold away from "all her little children" by a slave trader who told prospective buyers that "her master says he believes her to be a Christian, a very pious old woman" who, so long as she was allowed to pray, "would never lie nor steal." At the same time however, Randolph suggested that other masters feared that the religion of the slaves could become a source of moral and physical resistance to slavery and as a result attempted to suppress it. "In some places," he wrote, "if the slaves are caught praying to God, they are whipped more than if they had committed a great crime." Eager to establish the legitimacy of their physical power over enslaved people, some masters forbade their slaves from calling upon God or Jesus for comfort when they were being beaten or abused. "Sometimes, when a slave, on being whipped, calls upon God, he is forbidden to do so, under threat of having his throat cut, or brains blown out." When masters did allow their slaves to hear preaching or attend worship, Randolph reported, they hired ministers who offered grotesquely truncated form of Christianity that contained little more than pointed admonitions to work hard and obey authority. He remembered one Baptist preacher who told the slaves that "it is the devil who tells you to try and be free" and that the whipping of disobedient slaves was highly pleasing to God. "After such preaching," Randolph concluded, "let no one say that the slaves have the Gospel of Jesus preached to them" by white pastors (Randolph 1855, 31–32).

Peter Randolph's descriptions of religion in the daily lives of enslaved people conform to larger patterns that historians of American slavery have observed more generally. These include the role of religious faith in strengthening slave communities, the distinctive forms of spiritual expression that existed in those communities, the solace that religious conviction offered to the oppressed, the ways in which slave Christianity undermined the authority of masters, and the emergence of a powerful critique of proslavery religion among the enslaved. At the same time, however, the role of religion among African American slaves is more complex than any single description can capture, and Randolph's picture needs both greater explanation and significant addition. This chapter will explore the varied dimensions of spiritual life among slaves, beginning with the African roots of their beliefs and practices and then exploring the dynamic interaction between African religious traditions and the evangelical Christianity to which increasing numbers of African Americans adhered during the years before the Civil War. In general, the chapter will continually return to the ways in which the religion of the slaves shaped their strategies to survive the brutality of slavery, to resist its dehumanizing logic, and in some cases to foment outright rebellion against the system itself.

THE AFRICAN SPIRITUAL LEGACY

Historians Sylvia Frey and Betty Wood have argued that the adoption of Christianity among enslaved people was "arguably the most significant event in African American history" (Frey and Wood 1998, 1). By this they mean that Christian beliefs and practices, especially the evangelical form of American Protestant Christianity, created the basis for a stronger, more unified slave community with shared values and a common language of resistance. At the same time, however, they acknowledge that the slaves' conversion to Christianity did not eliminate their continued practice of, and adherence to, traditional African religions that existed side by side with Christianity on the plantations of the American South. Indeed, the distinctive qualities of slave Christianity, which arose partly out the experience of slavery and oppression, reflected the blending of these two traditions in ways that many whites found confusing or even threatening. As early as 1777, whites in Richmond, Virginia, fled in fear from a revival meeting because of the emotional intensity of black converts who expressed their devotion through loud shouts, dances, and tearful cries for divine mercy. Unaware of the central roles that sound, physical movement, and emotional expression played in African spiritual traditions which enslaved people had inherited, these white observers feared that "the great deep was going to overwhelm them" (Frey and Wood 1998, 123).

The African spiritual traditions that enslaved people preserved despite the horrific experience of the Middle Passage and the harsh conditions of plantation slavery defy easy description. The vast regions of West Africa from which slaves were taken were home to an array of complex spiritual forms that included the monotheistic religions of Islam and Christianity, as well as a wide variety of animistic traditions that conceived of the physical world as permeated by spiritual presences and magical power. The latter were enormously influential among African peoples, even those who also practiced monotheistic faiths, because of the ways in which they structured daily life and gave meaning to key moments in the life cycle, especially childbirth, illness, marriage, and death. Among many West African peoples, moreover, the worship and propitiation of ancestor spirits was a central part of religious life and created a powerful bond between the living and the dead. Rituals of protection and healing, practices surrounding the naming and raising of children, and proper attention to the bodies of the dead were all associated with respect for ancestor spirits who possessed power over the lives and well-being of their descendants. Like peoples from many other parts of the world, West Africans also believed in the potential magical power of herbs, plants, or other natural objects. Often referred to as "conjure" in the American South, herb or root magic became a powerful tool by which enslaved people sought control over their lives in the midst of an oppressive institution designed to render them powerless. And finally, the African spiritual heritage that shaped the lives of antebellum slaves also celebrated the power of spirits to take possession of the minds and bodies of living people, most often in moments of emotional ecstasy.

Perhaps the most powerful evidence for the survival of African traditions into the antebellum slave experience is that of conjure, which historian Albert Raboteau calls "a system of magic, divination and herbalism" linked to both the voodoo cult of the black Caribbean and to the larger system of African folk beliefs (Raboteau 1978, 80). Many slave communities in the United States included those who specialized in the uses of root magic and, for a small price, would offer what they insisted were powerful antidotes to an array of problems that enslaved people faced in their daily lives. Escaped slave Henry Bibb, for example, wrote that during his youth in Kentucky he had "great faith in conjuration and witchcraft" and frequented the home of several conjurers who offered him mixtures of plants, powders, hair, and even cow dung to prevent his master from flogging him. But masters were not the only targets of such practices, and Bibb also used conjure to make one of the young women in his community fall in love with him. Assured by one local conjurer that scratching the bare skin of his beloved with a dried frog bone was a sure-fire way to obtain her permanent and total devotion, he "fetched her a tremendous rasp across the neck with this bone, which made her jump." Unfortunately for Bibb, however, the effect was the opposite of what he intended, and he found that "she felt more like running after me to retaliate on me for thus abusing her, than she felt like loving me" (Bibb 1849, 26–27).

Although a few historians have argued that African spiritual traditions failed to survive the physical and cultural dislocations of the Middle Passage, the persistence of root magic in the daily lives of enslaved people in the American South is a powerful argument in favor of cultural persistence. Belief in the power of such magic was a significant psychological weapon in the hands of slaves during times of crisis. At a time when Frederick Douglass was experiencing almost constant beatings at the hands of the brutal "slave breaker" Edward Covey, for example, he sought spiritual advice from a "genuine African" named Sandy who told him "he had inherited some of the so-called magical powers said to be possessed by the eastern nations." Although Douglass said that Sandy believed in and practiced a system "for which I have no name," the herb lore and root magic Sandy offered were consistent with common West African folk traditions. Claiming that he had never been beaten by a white man while carrying a certain root with him, Sandy instructed Douglass to do the same. Although Douglass later came to see Sandy's advice as "superstition" or even "sinful," he was deeply affected by it at the time and approached his white "tormentor" with a renewed sense of confidence and willingness to resist. Just a few days later, when Covey mercilessly assaulted him during his daily work, Douglass suddenly found the courage to fight back and soundly thrashed the white man. Though his later conversion to progressive, antislavery forms of Christianity led him to reject African root magic, its role in what Douglass called "the turning-point in my 'life as a slave' " seems clear enough (Douglass 1881, 133–134).

Other key examples that point to the persistence of West African religion in the American South include funeral practices and ideas of the afterlife among enslaved people. In Africa, funerals for the dead typically took place in two phases, with the first focusing on the preparation of the deceased's body and its burial along with objects deemed necessary for life in the next world. The graves of the deceased were often heavily decorated with personal objects including cooking pots, utensils, and other items, which, if not made available, might delay the soul's progress to the afterlife and cause the departed spirit to haunt the living. At times, these objects might be deliberately cracked in order to "free their spirits" and "enable them to follow the deceased" (Raboteau 1978, 85). The second phase celebrated the completion of the journey from life to death, from the physical to the spiritual world, and the arrival of the soul among the spirits of its ancestors. This latter ritual was accompanied by feasts, ritual dances, and animal sacrifices and could last "from several days to several weeks" (Frey and Wood 1998, 25). Rather than renewed expressions of grief, which were appropriate for the interment of the corpse, these events brought a sense of completion and satisfaction that all appropriate ritual requirements had been performed.

Although life under slavery did not permit enslaved African Americans to observe all of these customary funeral practices, the evidence strongly suggests that key aspects of them persisted, especially the notion that death was the beginning of a journey that the living could assist the dead in completing. During his life as a slave in Maryland, for example, Charles Ball helped a grieving slave couple to bury their dead infant with a variety of items they believed he would need when he returned to his ancestors in Africa. Among other things, the child's father provided him with a "miniature canoe, about a foot long" and a strip of "white muslin, with several curious and strange figures painted on it . . . by which . . . his relations would know the infant was his son" (Ball 1837, 265). The African practice of multiple funeral rites seems to have persisted even after large numbers of enslaved people had converted to Christianity as Christian funeral sermons were often preached well after the burial of the dead. Antislavery Methodist pastor John Dixon Long, who preached to slaves in Maryland, remembered that "a negro funeral is different from the 'burying'" and noted that the funeral sermon was given "several weeks after burial." With a mixture of confusion and disapproval, he noted that the second event was accompanied by a "frolic" rather than with outpourings of grief (Long 1857, 20).

African spiritual traditions shaped daily life and provided the basis for individual acts of resistance, but there is also significant evidence that those traditions motivated collective forms of slave rebellion. In 1822, for example, white leaders in Charleston, South Carolina, executed over thirty blacks for participation in which they alleged was a widespread conspiracy to overthrow slavery through violent rebellion. Led by Denmark Vesey, a free black carpenter who was likely born in the Caribbean, large numbers of enslaved people in and around the Charleston area planned to arm themselves, burn the city to the ground, and then lead a slave exodus out of the lowcountry with the help of ships from the Republic of Haiti. Vesey and his rebels were inspired by a variety of personal and ideological factors, but conjure played a key role as well. As the plot moved toward fruition, "a little man" whom anxious rebels called "Gullah Jack" told them that he possessed charms that could make them immune to the weapons of white people as well as special powders that could be used to poison the slaveholders. Jack had warned the rebels that the defensive charms they wore would injure them if they betrayed their friends and the fear of such retributive magic remained powerful even after the conspiracy was discovered and the leaders put on trial. One slave, who was eventually forced to testify against Gullah Jack, begged the court to send him away from Charleston out of fear that Jack's power would pursue him. "I consider my life as in great danger," he pleaded, "Jack [is] a conjurer" (Egerton and Paquette 2017, 199).

A somewhat different but equally important connection between African spiritual traditions and slave rebellion can be found in Nat Turner's revolt of 1831 in Southampton County, Virginia. As will be discussed later in the chapter, Nat Turner was an enslaved Baptist preacher whose vision of an apocalyptic battle between white people and enslaved blacks was drawn from the book of Revelation in the Christian New Testament. But Turner's Christianity was also practiced in conjunction with West African ways of seeing and knowing that had been passed from one generation to another. Historian Makungu Akinyela has argued, for example, that Turner's claims to secret knowledge of the natural world, especially the meanings of planetary orbits or shifts in the tides, were "all in the tradition of the African priest who must know these things in order to divine the will and activities of the spirit world." In his famous *Confessions* taken down by a white lawyer, Turner also speaks of seeing visions that solidified his identity as a black messiah and the necessity of violent confrontation with white Virginia slaveholders. "I saw white spirits and Black spirits engaged in battle, and the sun was darkened," he remembered, "the thunder rolled in the heavens, and blood flowed in streams" (Greenberg 1996, 46). Since these visions occurred outside the biblical revelations that were so important to Turner's Christianity, his interpretation of them was informed by aspects of West African cosmology in which "deity is expressed through nature rather than outside it" (Akinyela 2003, 275). The ultimate failure of the Turner and Vesey rebellions should not detract from the evidence they provide for the influence of African spiritual traditions on slave rebellions.

Although it is impossible to know with any precision the numbers of Muslim slaves who were brought to the United States during the years of the Atlantic slave trade, historians have been also able to document the existence of Islamic beliefs and practices among a significant portion of the slave population. Well represented in the regions of West Africa from which so many enslaved people were taken, Islam was a powerful economic, political, and cultural influence over the region, which likely spread beyond those who were formal adherents of the faith. For a variety of reasons, moreover, it appears that American slaveholders sometimes exercised a preference for Muslim slaves, and eighteenth-century advertisements for the return of runaway slaves included names and ethnic descriptions that point directly to the Islamic origins of the fugitives. Describing their runaways as "Moorish" or from the "Fullah Country" and identifying their names as "Ahmad" or "Mahomet," the authors of the advertisements provided indirect but, nevertheless, clear evidence of an Islamic presence in the colonies of South Carolina and Georgia (Gomez 1998, 70). These colonies, with their heavy emphasis on rice planting, had imported a disproportionate number of slaves from rice-producing Senegambia and Sierra Leone, regions where Muslims represented a significant percentage of the population.

While Muslim slaves faced many challenges to practicing their faith in antebellum America, particularly the requirement to pray five times a day, the records indicate that many persisted despite the obstacles. Former slave Charles Ball, who spent several years in South Carolina, observed several slaves performing their daily prayers, although he did not understand what they were doing at the time. "I knew several, who must have been, from what I have since learned, must have been Mohomedans," he recalled. "There was one man of this plantation who prayed five times a day, always turning his face to the east, when in the performance of his devotions" (Ball 1837, 165). A former slave interviewed by the Federal Writers' Project during the 1930s remembered a man simply known as "Old Israel" who prayed at sunup and sundown with the help of a prayer mat and a special book that he otherwise kept secret. The old man also covered his head with a special white cloth he kept for the purpose, which is consistent with the Islamic taqiya worn by men during prayer (Turner 1994, 33).

Such practices were somewhat easier to preserve in regions like the South Carolina and Georgia Sea Islands. The black population in those areas was significantly larger, a task system of labor was the norm, and white intervention in the daily lives of slaves was somewhat less frequent. On Sappelo and St. Simons Islands, Georgia, in fact, there appear to have been an unusually large number of practicing Muslims among the slave population. One white observer claimed that there was a large family, known by the name of Bilali, who openly and proudly practiced their Islamic faith. "They conversed with us in English," she wrote, "but in talking among themselves used a foreign tongue that no one else understood" (Turner 1994, 30). The formidable patriarch of the family, known simply as "Bilali," gave Islamic names to his many children and grandchildren and led them in the cycle of daily prayer. Though their numbers were relatively small, the communities of practicing Muslims among the slave population left a strong legacy of faith and cultural resistance to their descendants.

CHRISTIANITY AND CONVERSION

While African traditions, including Islam, remained a key element in the daily spiritual experiences of enslaved people, Christianity played an increasingly important role as well. Beginning with intense revival movements of the mid-1700s, what later generations called the First Great Awakening, evangelical forms of Protestant Christianity spread quickly among African American slaves and became a critical element of Southern black culture by the beginning of the antebellum period. During much of the colonial era, white planters had resisted the attempts of missionaries to preach to their slaves, concerned that it would be difficult to justify the enslavement of fellow Christians. For their part, slaves had been reluctant to abandon their own African spiritual traditions, and they found the catechisms and formal liturgical practices of the

Church of England unappealing. Evangelical preaching, however, with its emphasis on the equally sinful character of all people and the necessity for everyone to undergo a miraculous "conversion" experience proved far more compelling. The physical, emotionally charged nature of evangelical conversions, which was consistent in some ways with West African traditions, not only spoke to the needs of oppressed people but also encouraged them to form new, tight-knit communities of like-minded believers.

As it was for white evangelicals, slaves regarded conversion as a powerful, transformative experience that involved more than just an acceptance of basic Christian doctrines. Enslaved Virginian Peter Randolph, for example, remembered his own youthful conversion as an agonizing emotional ordeal that began with despair over the sinful condition of his life. "I prayed that [God] would kill me, for I did not want to live to sin against him anymore," he recalled. But in the moment of his deepest anguish, he recalled, "I felt my guilt give way, and thought that I was a new being . . . the eyes of my mind were open, and I saw things as I never did before" (Randolph 1855, 25–26). An enslaved Maryland woman named Elizabeth told of an even more intense experience that occurred when she was just thirteen years old. Told by her mother that she "had none in the world to look to but God," she spent nearly six months in abject misery about the state of her soul, stealing away to lonely places in order to pray and to beseech God for mercy. In ways that would have been at least partially recognizable to her West African ancestors whose spiritual experiences included trances, visions, and spirit possessions, Elizabeth explained that her religious conversion resulted from a direct interaction with the risen Christ. "He led me down a long journey to a fiery gulf and left me standing upon the brink of this awful pit," she recalled more than half a century later. "I began to scream for mercy, thinking I was about to sink to endless ruin," but rather than condemn her, in the vision Christ offered his hand as a sign "that my sins were forgiven me, and the time of my deliverance was at hand" (Elizabeth 1889, 3–4).

One striking consequence of many slave conversions, including those of Peter Randolph and Elizabeth, is the impetus they provided for converts to become literate. The authority of the Bible and the necessity for individual Christians to work out their salvation through direct engagement with the scriptures, doctrines that evangelicals were especially eager to uphold, meant that converted slaves went to great lengths to acquire Bibles and to read them. In Peter Randolph's case, both conversion and his determination to lead others to conversion created a "great desire to read easily this book," which he referred to as "the great book of God—the source of all knowledge." Despite a rudimentary knowledge of the alphabet, Randolph slowly and painstakingly educated himself by comparing the readings he heard in church with the copy of the Bible he possessed at home. "I used to go to the church to hear the white preacher," he reported. "When I heard him read his text, I would read mine when I got home . . . this is the way . . . I learned to read the Word of God when I was a slave" (Randolph 1855, 26). Elizabeth, who also sought to become a religious teacher despite the even greater obstacles she faced as a black woman, struggled against the self-doubt resulting from her illiteracy. "I could read but little," she remembered, and "I questioned within myself how it would be possible for me to deliver the message, when I did not understand the Scriptures." In her case, the doubts were resolved only when she accepted that direct revelations from God, the sort her own conversion had included, were just as important as scripture as sources of teaching. When one white preacher insisted that there had been no direct revelation from God since "Christ's ascension," Elizabeth asked him quite pointedly "where the apostle John got his revelation while he was in the Isle of Patmos" (Elizabeth 1889, 6). Perhaps she was not quite as ignorant of scripture as she sometimes feared.

The conversions of Peter Randolph and Elizabeth were intensely individual experiences, but many enslaved people, indeed many white evangelicals, experienced such spiritual transformations in the context of revivals or camp meetings that occurred throughout the South in the period between the American Revolution and the Civil War. Methodist, Baptist, and Disciples of Christ preachers led the way, followed closely by Presbyterians and Congregationalists in pioneering new ways of converting masses of Americans, including the slaves, to the Christian Gospel. Those attending revival meetings, like the one at Cane Ridge, Kentucky, in 1801, heard round-the-clock preaching from itinerant ministers whose emotional appeals, vivid storytelling, and folksy language proved highly effective in reaching poor, rural, and largely uneducated people. Although Southern evangelical churches were not always diligent about keeping accurate counts of their black members, the existing statistics suggest that revivals brought a large number of

African Americans into the ranks. During the first two decades of the nineteenth century, for example, the number of African American Methodists more than doubled, with similar increases to be found among Baptists. Camp meetings proved enormously appealing to enslaved people, not only because of the style of worship they encountered there but also because such meetings provided a respite from plantation labor and an opportunity to reaffirm family and community bonds. "By no class is a camp-meeting hailed with more unmixed delight than by the poor slaves," wrote antislavery Methodist pastor John Dixon Long in 1857. "Here they get to see their mothers, their brothers, and their sisters from neighboring plantations" (Long 1857, 159).

Yet if all who attended such meetings heard the same messages about sin and the need for repentance, slaves experienced camp meeting revivals in ways that were significantly different from their white counterparts. First, while whites sat facing the preaching stands that were erected on one side of the large circle of tents and wagons, slaves and free blacks were strictly segregated behind the preachers and largely beyond the sight lines of their white counterparts. This arrangement clearly reinforced the racial hierarchy in the South, but it also provided enslaved people with space to develop distinctive approaches to conversion, worship, and spiritual community that were "at once Christian and African" (Frey and Wood 1998, 143). In these segregated worship spaces on the physical margins of the camp meeting, black worshippers refashioned and adapted West African musical and dance styles to encourage Christian conversion. Perhaps the most distinctive and widespread of these techniques was the "ring shout" in which worshippers formed a moving circle and sang, shouted, clapped, and stomped their feet in rhythmic patterns. Similar in many ways to ring dances in West Africa that were meant to honor ancestors, the ring shout was adapted by African American slaves in ways that blended their cultural roots and their embrace of Christianity. When one slave worshipper was told that the shout was "a heathenish way to worship and disgraceful," he responded that at least among slaves "at a camp meeting there must be a ring here, a ring there, a ring over yonder, or sinners will not get converted." The critics of the ring shout may have been right in that its origins are African rather than European, but black Christians insisted that "the spirit of God works upon people in different ways" (Raboteau 1978, 68–69).

ORIGINS OF THE BLACK CHURCH

For enslaved people who had experienced conversion, whether in solitary places or in the hurly-burly of the camp-meeting revival, participation in regular communal worship was the next logical step in their spiritual lives. One possibility was for converts to join one of the white-controlled evangelical churches that included enslaved people in the membership rolls. Christian masters often preferred this arrangement because it enabled them to fulfill their spiritual responsibilities toward the slaves while ensuring that only proslavery understandings of the faith were preached on Sunday mornings. But slaves whose only option was to attend such churches were required to sit in the galleries or in the very back of the church and to remain silent except during communal prayers or hymn singing. Even when blacks made up a majority of the membership in these congregations, moreover, church offices were controlled by whites and the weddings and funerals of black members were often performed in the basements or backrooms rather than in the sanctuary. Harriet Jacobs, before her escape from slavery in Edenton, North Carolina, attended one such church in her hometown where she endured long, repetitive sermons by a white clergyman named Pike who insisted that God required slaves to obey the authority of masters. "I went home with the feeling that I had heard the Reverend Mr. Pike for the last time," she wrote later with disgust. She was convinced that the slaves who sat in the galleries of such churches were "nearer to the gate of heaven than sanctimonious Mr. Pike, and other long-faced Christians, who see wounded Samaritans, and pass by on the other side" (Jacobs 1861, 107).

Because such churches humiliated black members and failed to address their spiritual needs, many enslaved Christians preferred to join a growing number of separate black congregations founded after the American Revolution. These churches were most heavily concentrated in the Upper and Border South as well as in urban areas, and they were largely created by black Methodists and Baptists who were dissatisfied by their treatment in biracial churches. The African Methodist Episcopal (AME) Church, which had been founded in Philadelphia in 1816 by former slave Richard Allen, offered black Methodists, both free and enslaved, an opportunity to express their religious convictions through an independent organization in which all church offices were held by African American

Praise houses like this one on Sapelo Island, Georgia, were built on some plantations as places where enslaved people could gather for Christian worship. It was here that a highly distinctive form of slave Christianity, including the "ring shout," emerged. (Library of Congress)

leaders. But independent black churches in the slaveholding South always generated hostility and suspicion from whites, who feared that they might become breeding grounds for slave rebellion. In Charleston, South Carolina, for example, the Emanuel AME Church was identified by state and local authorities as the epicenter of Denmark Vesey's conspiracy of 1822, and several members, including Vesey himself, were arrested and executed for their role in the conspiracy. The church building itself was attacked by violent white mobs who burned it to the ground, a fate that it shared with other independent black churches that whites believed harbored antislavery sentiments.

For most enslaved people in the antebellum South, religious life was centered less on formal church buildings than in and around the plantations where they lived and worked. Eager to control the physical mobility of the men, women, and children they owned, some masters permitted the construction of small, crude buildings away from the main plantation house where slave worship could take place. These "praise houses" became central to the slave community, serving as gathering places for prayer, singing, and religious dancing, as well as the revival preaching that often resulted in the conversion experiences discussed earlier. Their relative physical isolation from areas where masters and overseers resided meant that it was possible for black people to practice their faith without the constant oversight of whites and to develop their own distinctive approaches to church practice and structure. Because of the distinctive, African-derived forms of worship that characterized slave Christianity, for example, slaves generally preferred that praise houses contain no seats or benches that would inhibit the physical movement of the worshippers. Since the ring shout had become so important in the conversion experiences of many enslaved Christians, it was critical that the praise house be set up in ways that permitted worshippers to practice and develop that tradition without physical impediments. A somewhat-bemused Northern traveler to the antebellum South was told that slaves had petitioned one slaveholder to remove the benches he had supplied for the praise house because "it did not leave *them room enough to pray*" (Young 2008, 187; emphasis in original). As movement through space was not a characteristic or requirement of prayer in most white churches, it was difficult for white observers to understand such requests.

The building of praise houses occurred in the early years of the nineteenth century, a period in which many slaveholders were tolerant of informal religious meetings of their slaves, especially if they had themselves experienced conversions. In the aftermath of Nat Turner's Rebellion in 1831, however, many slaveholders prohibited their slaves from congregating on or near the plantation for fear that their religious exercises would result in flight or rebellion. The fact that Turner had developed a radically antislavery understanding of Baptist Christianity convinced the slaveholding class that tighter controls over the spiritual lives of black people were required to maintain the racial order. As a result, many states passed laws prohibiting slaves from gathering publicly in groups of any size and forbidding religious meetings that were not supervised by whites, and blacks who violated these strictures faced dire consequences. Moses Grandy, who grew up near the Great Dismal Swamp in northeastern North Carolina, remembered the fury and vindictiveness of slaveholders who found that their orders against attending prayer and worship meetings had been violated. "A number of slaves went privately into the wood to hold meetings [and] when they were found out, they were flogged, and each was forced to tell who else was there," he recalled. Grandy's brother-in-law Isaac, who had led the prohibited meeting, was whipped multiple times for his offense, and not long after "his wife was sold away with an infant at her breast" (Grandy 1843, 57).

Slaves continued to hold covert religious meetings despite threats from anxious and potentially violent masters. To do so, however, slaves needed clandestine strategies by which to alert the community that a meeting was to be held and to prevent the sounds of praise and worship from reaching the ears of suspicious masters. William Robinson reported that songs were often used to convey the message that a meeting was to take place. "White people would think they were only singing for amusement," he remembered, but spirituals like "There a Meeting Here Tonight" had a very specific meaning when sung by slaves on Saturday or Sunday evenings. He also recalled that as a child he had wondered why enslaved worshippers placed pots and kettles along the fence rails where religious meetings took place. Just before the Civil War, he learned that these devices were used to conceal the sounds of praise and worship, "the kettles catching the sound [and] in this way they were not detected" (Robinson 1913, 79–80). Referring to the secrecy with which many worshippers were forced to conduct their prayer meetings or worship services, one elderly ex-slave believed that the words of the hymn "Steal Away to Jesus" constituted a sort of anthem of the plantation church. Those who "were once slaves," he insisted, could not help but remember that religious slaves "sang and prayed almost in a whisper for fear of being heard" (Johnson 1909, 18–19).

Along with the clandestine forms of worship in what were sometimes called "hush harbor" churches were more open celebrations of Christian holidays, especially Christmas. For many slaves, the Christmas period was less a religious celebration and more a time of rest as many masters gave them several days off as well as extra supplies of food and drink. In some areas of the South, slaves could see family members who lived on nearby plantations, while others engaged in athletic contests, singing, dancing, and the consumption of alcohol supplied by the master. Many former slaves, especially those who had themselves experienced religious conversions, believed that duplicitous masters encouraged drunkenness during the Christmas holidays in order to prove that slaves inherently lacked self-control and were thus incapable of living as free people. "Thus, by an artfully-contrived plan," wrote escaped slave Francis Fedric, "the slaves themselves are made to put the seal upon their own servitude" (Fedric 1863, 28). Indeed, on some plantations, the opposition to drinking and dancing among evangelical converts created tensions and even division among the slaves. "A great many of the strict members of the church who did not dance would be forced to do it to please their masters," recalled Jacob Stroyer.

"No one can describe the intense emotion of the negro's heart," when they are required to violate their convictions to "please their masters and mistresses" (Stroyer 1879, 35).

RELIGION AND DAILY LIFE

The debate among enslaved people about the celebration of Christmas raises important questions about the relationship between religious life and the daily experiences of slaves. Did religion, especially Christianity, make slaves easier to control as some slaveholders hoped, or were slaveholders right to be concerned that slave Christianity fostered rebellion? Historians have debated these issues for years, and they continue to be central questions in the literature on slave religion. On one level, the religion of the slaves clearly enabled them to cope with the brutal realities of their daily lives, which included unremitting labor, the constant threat of white violence, the searing losses of family members through slave sales, and countless other horrors endemic to the system of human bondage that prevailed in the South. This was one of the key functions of the slave spirituals that, along with the ring shout, were among the most distinctive and original characteristics of slave religion. These songs not only were sung in connection with religious meetings but also constituted part of the daily "lived religion" of enslaved people as they worked in the fields, barns, and plantation houses of the antebellum South. One elderly former slave named Bob Ledbetter remembered that a slave would sing "to nearly everything he did . . . he sings as he cuts the logs and keeps time with his axe." Slave women "sing as dey bend over de washtub, de cotton pickers sing as he chops cotton." Ledbetter believed that spirituals provided a way to cope with the brutal realities of life on plantations, a way to relieve sadness by imagining a better world where slavery was ended. It gave them the "mos' joy, an mos' comfort w'en he needs all these things" (Berlin, Favreau, and Miller 1998, 185).

Bob Ledbetter's belief that the spirituals offered mainly comfort could support the idea that religion encouraged slaves to accept their lot in this life in exchange for the promise of freedom in the next. But a closer look at these songs suggests that they were highly adaptable to different contexts and contained a distinctive theology that could modulate between resignation and resistance depending on circumstances. Concepts like heaven, hell, damnation, and salvation appeared regularly in slave songs, but their meanings spoke to both the spiritual and earthly needs of slave communities. For example, when enslaved people sang of a heaven in which slavery and racial oppression were absent and where all had abundant food, clothing, and shelter, they not only made it easier to bear the sorrows of the world they inhabited but also offered a searing critique of that world. Thus, unlike the plantation where mobility was severely restricted and the threat of losing family members to the slave trade loomed large, the heaven of the slave songs was a place for people to "walk easy," where there was "plenty good room" and where "there is parting no more" (Raboteau 1978, 262–263). White slaveholding Christians were eager to make a sharp distinction between the spiritual freedom that slaves might achieve in heaven and the permanence of slavery on earth, but slave songs suggest that enslaved people were unwilling to accept such a dichotomy. Fountain Hughes, a former slave from Virginia, remembered an enslaved preacher who, when considering whether "we'll ever be free," led his little hush harbor congregation in the songs "One Day Shall I Ever Reach Heaven and One Day Shall I Fly" (Berlin, Favreau, and Miller 1998, 199). Heaven and slave flight merged seamlessly in the minds of enslaved Christians as such songs were sung and performed in the clandestine meetings of plantation churches.

One other important effect of the slave songs is the way in which they encouraged enslaved people to forge a powerful sense of identification with the biblical characters and stories that appeared and reappeared in the words of the spirituals. Since few enslaved people could read the Bible for themselves, it was often through the songs that they developed vivid images of Moses, David, Jesus, and Paul. Perhaps the most powerful connection they drew was with the story of the exodus of the Israelite slaves from bondage in Egypt, a narrative that spoke directly to their condition as oppressed people and that offered the possibility of earthly redemption. In identifying themselves with the ancient Hebrew slaves, moreover, African American slaves claimed a status as God's chosen people and conversely identified their masters as cruel Pharaohs whose stiff-necked defense of slavery placed them in direct conflict with God's decrees. One historian has argued that when slaves asked, "Did not old Pharaoh get lost, get lost, . . . get lost in the Red Sea?" they were holding out the possibility that their dire oppression might be altered in the same dramatic and immediate way as that of the Israelites who had seen the armies of Pharaoh drowned at God's command (Levine 1997, 76, 78). One former slave from Virginia described the brutal whipping of his mother and recalled that her hatred of white people had been expressed in distinctly biblical terms. Certain that God would punish slaveholders as he had chastised the cruel Egyptians, she had predicted that "the flood waters gwine drown some mo'" (Perdue, Barden, and Phillips 1976, 93).

The ability of Old Testament stories to speak so powerfully to the hopes and fears of enslaved people shaped the way in which they viewed Christianity more broadly. Concepts of personal sin and redemption remained central to the experience of individual enslaved Christians, but their strong identification with the children of Israel led them to think in collective terms as well, associating sin with the social injustice of slavery and understanding salvation as deliverance from its horrors. Black abolitionist David Walker, who had grown up among enslaved people in Wilmington, North Carolina, expressed this in his famous *Appeal to the Colored Citizens of the World*, when he insisted that black people of America would be delivered as a group from the sinful whites who had enslaved them. "I assure you that God will accomplish it," he predicted, "he will hurl tyrants and devils into atoms and make way for his people" (Harding 1981, 91). In this theological revision, born in the daily struggles of slaves, Jesus was an earthly liberator as well as a personal friend and savior. Sometimes sounding more like King David or Moses than the Jesus of the New Testament, the Christ of the slave songs was sometimes a conquering king or a warrior mounted on horseback who would mete out divine justice on the side of the oppressed. "Ride in King Jesus, no man can hinder me," said one spiritual, while another proclaimed that Christ's Second Coming would set the world on fire and separate the sheep and the goats (Raboteau 1978, 260). Once again using biblical typology, slaves regarded themselves as Christ's sheep and regarded their masters as the goats who would suffer torment in the last days.

In comparing their owners to cruel Pharaohs, duplicitous Pharisees, or crucifying Romans, enslaved people forged a powerful critique of slavery and of the religion of their masters. Indeed, one of the most common arguments in narratives written by former slaves who had escaped to the North was that slaveholding had utterly corrupted Southern white Christianity. Perhaps the most powerful indictment came from Harriet Jacobs, a former house slave from North Carolina who had suffered unremitting sexual harassment from her owner, James Norcum, from the age of twelve. Jacobs recalled her hopes that Norcum's behavior would change after he joined the local Episcopal Church but came to see that the church simply did not judge the morality of white men by their treatment of black people. "The worst persecutions I endured from him were after he was a communicant," she remembered with disgust. Jacobs reported that white ministers who committed adultery with white women were dismissed by their congregations but that if the women "is colored it does not hinder his continuing to be their good shepherd" (Jacobs 1861, 115). Louis Hughes reported that his Mississippi owner regularly required his slaves to attend Sunday services at a white church wearing their best clothes, even those who were suffering from the physical effects of whipping and having salt water poured on their wounds. "My boss took pride in having all his slaves look clean and tidy at the Sabbath service," he wrote later, "but how would he have liked to have the slaves, with backs lacerated with the lash, appear in those assemblies with their wounds uncovered?" (Hughes 1897, 90–91).

When enslaved Christians condemned their white counterparts for sinful hypocrisy, they asserted their own moral authority and claimed the right to formulate ethical standards that were different and at times antithetical to those of the slaveholders. For example, when slaves supplemented their meager and monotonous allowance of food by purloining supplies from their masters' stores, they utterly rejected the notion that such actions constituted theft. "When you don't git 'lowanced right, you has to keep right on workin' in the field," one elderly ex-slave told an interviewer in the 1930s. "No ma'am, the good Lord won't call that stealin', now will he?" Although white preachers were constantly pointing out that the Bible contained a commandment against all forms of theft, slaves implicitly countered whites' abuse of scriptural authority with their own deeply felt sense of justice. "Dey talks a heap 'bout de niggers stealin," another former slave complained. "Well you know what was de fust stealin done? Hit was in Afriky, when de white folks stole de niggers jes' like you'd go get a drove o' hosses and sell 'em." While illiteracy prevented many slaves from quoting scripture in their own defense, slave preachers were sometimes in a position to use the authority of the Bible in ways that masters found frustrating to say the least. One such plantation preacher was accused of stealing from a patch of collard greens he tended for his mistress, and, when confronted by the master, he openly confessed to the act. But after listening to a long lecture about the evils of stealing, which included reading the commandment against stealing, the preacher rejected the charge of theft on the basis of the scriptural verse saying that "whatsoever a man soweth, that shall he also reap" (Berlin, Favreau, and Miller 1998, 193–194).

RELIGION AND REBELLION

Religious belief and practice also played a significant role in the most prominent slave rebellions during the first half of the nineteenth century. Although the Virginia slave rebel Gabriel Prosser was motivated by concepts of liberty and equality derived from secular republican ideas, his planned revolt in 1800 had religious roots as well. During discussions among key rebel leaders, for example, it appears that the Bible was cited several times to bolter Gabriel's leadership and to provide support for his decisions about the timing of the revolt. When some doubted the ability of the rebellion to succeed, for example, one of Gabriel's most trusted followers reminded fellow conspirators of the passage in Leviticus which stated that "five of you shall conquer an hundred of an hundred, a thousand of our enemies" (Sidbury 2003, 122). A similar but even more comprehensive use of the Bible, and of the identification of enslaved people with the ancient Israelites, can be seen in Denmark Vesey's rebellion two decades later in Charleston, South Carolina. Because many of the key figures in the rebellion were leaders in the AME Church, they were deeply immersed in scripture and appear to have developed a distinctive approach to Old Testament passages that justified and directed their plans for the uprising. Witnesses later testified that Vesey used scripture to demonstrate the sinfulness of slavery and to show his followers that God intended his followers to punish those who remained mired in idolatry and wrongdoing. Turning slaveholders' self-serving use of Christian textual and moral authority against them, Prosser and Vesey forged revolutionary movements from a radically alternative reading of their religious environment.

Yet it is in Nat Turner's 1831 rebellion in Southampton Country, Virginia, where the revolutionary potential of slave Christianity was revealed most dramatically. The "rising," as it was called at the time, resulted in the bloody execution of over fifty white men, women, and children, and its leader was inspired by intense religious zeal. Born at the turn of the nineteenth century, Turner was raised during a time of accelerating evangelical activity among both free and enslaved people, and his rebellion was informed by aspects of evangelical belief and practice. First, like many early converts in what became known as the Second Great Awakening,

Nat Turner (1800–1831) and his fellow insurgents, shown in this 1863 engraving, led a violent rebellion against slavery in southeastern Virginia in 1831. Though the rebellion was suppressed and the leaders, including Turner, were executed, the fear of slave insurrections haunted the slaveholding class of the antebellum South. (New York Public Library)

Turner's personal religious experience included what he believed were direct revelations from God, through dreams and visions, many of which clarified the meaning of scripture. At one point he reported seeing black and white spirits fighting in the heavens and drops of blood on the corn in the fields near his home, both of which he interpreted as signs that God was intending to complete some important work through him. Second, Turner was clearly influenced by the Christian concept of millennialism. This belief, rooted in the book of Revelation, held that Christ's Second Coming would usher in a period of divine rule at the end of which a final, decisive battle between good and evil would take place. The visions and auditory revelations he experienced convinced him that just such a time had arrived, that "the great day of judgement had arrived," and that he must now "fight against the Serpent, for the time was fast approaching when the first should be last and the last should be first" (Greenberg 1996, 47). Indeed, it was Turner's ability to draw on personal revelations, scriptural authority, and millennial prophecies that convinced his fellow rebels to take the enormous risks of following him into battle with white slaveholders.

If Nat Turner's Christianity contained concepts and practices that were shared more widely among Southern evangelicals, its distinctive radicalism resulted from a potent admixture of African spirituality and of the tradition of American slave resistance. As noted earlier, Turner's visions included an ability to read signs, omens, and portents in the natural world, a common practice among West African peoples. For example, alongside the scripturally based millennial prophecies he communicated to his followers was his reading of the solar eclipse of February 1831 as a sign to begin the rebellion and the knowledge he claimed to understand the movement of tides, revolutions of the planet, and the changes of the seasons. Turner fused these deeply rooted African spiritual continuities with explosive images of enslaved blacks as God's chosen people whose cruel bondage at the hands of white pharaohs would be avenged and redeemed in a dramatic reversal of all earthly power relations. The "children of darkness" in Turner's vision were white slaveholders, and the "Serpent" against which God directed him to wage bloody battle was slavery itself. Like Moses, who had been chosen to lead the people of Israel out of their bondage to cruel Egyptians, Turner believed that the signs had directed him to "arise and prepare myself, and slay my enemies with their own weapons." Although the weapons Turner spoke of were knives, axes, and clubs, he might easily have spoken of religion itself, which he and other slave rebels wielded in their struggles against the horrors of American slavery (Greenberg 1996, 48).

Religion played a significant role in the daily lives of enslaved African Americans as it did for nearly all Americans during the nineteenth century. It provided them with answers to central questions about the meaning and purpose of their lives, instilled a strong moral and ethical system by which to judge their own and others' actions, and offered reassurance that suffering and death would not have the final word. But as an oppressed people, slaves also used their religious beliefs as an antidote to the dehumanizing effects of living under a system that defined them most fundamentally as property. As we have seen, slaves refused to surrender their African religious heritage, even as more and more of them adopted Christianity, and throughout the period African traditions remained central to the ways in which they approached issues of birth, death, and suffering. Yet in their conversions to Christianity, the formation of African American churches, and the development of a distinctive form of Christian thought and practice, enslaved African Americans forged a new, hybrid identity; nurtured a strong sense of community; and developed tools of personal and collective resistance to slavery. While slave rebels like Denmark Vesey and Nat Turner were unusual in the scale of their confrontations with the power of slaveholders, the antislavery religious vision that nurtured and propelled their rebellions existed throughout the South and manifested itself in smaller, less dramatic acts of resistance. Thus, when the great upheavals of the Civil War era finally ended the system of chattel slavery in the United States, it is perhaps not surprising that so many enslaved people understood it as the year of jubilee, when God released the prisoners and set the captives free.

DOCUMENT: PETER RANDOLPH, *SKETCHES OF SLAVE LIFE: OR, ILLUSTRATIONS OF THE "PECULIAR INSTITUTION"* (1855)

Peter Randolph, born a slave in eastern Virginia, began preaching around the age of ten. After a protracted legal battle over his deceased master's will, Randolph was freed, traveled North, and became a full-time Baptist minister. A chaplain to an African American regiment during the Civil War, he went on to a long and highly successful career as a Baptist leader. This excerpt from Randolph's narrative provides a powerful description of the ways in which enslaved people created their own religious culture despite the sometimes-violent opposition of slaveholders and the proslavery version of Christianity they heard from white preachers.

After doing their morning work, and breakfast over, (such as it is,) that portion of them belonging to the church ask of the overseer permission to attend meeting. If he is in the mood to grant their request, he writes them a pass. . . . Should a pass not be granted, the slave lies down, and sleeps for the day—the only way to drown his sorrow and disappointment. Others of the slaves, who do not belong to the church, spend their Sabbath in playing with marbles, and other games, for each other's food, &c. Some occupy the time in dancing to the music of a banjo, made out of a large gourd. This is continued till the after part of the day, when they separate, and gather wood for their log-cabin fires the ensuing week.

Not being allowed to hold meetings on the plantation, the slaves assemble in the swamps, out of reach of the patrols. They have an understanding among themselves as to the time and place of getting together. This is often done by the first one arriving breaking boughs from the trees, and bending them in the direction of the selected spot. Arrangements are then made for conducting the exercises. They first ask each other how they feel, the state of their minds, &c. The male members then select a certain space, in separate groups, for their division of the meeting. Preaching in order, by the brethren; then praying and singing all round, until they generally feel quite happy. The speaker usually commences by calling himself unworthy, and talks very slowly, until, feeling the spirit, he grows excited, and in a short time, there fall to the ground twenty or thirty men and women under its influence. Enlightened people call it excitement; but I wish the same was felt by everybody, so far as they are sincere.

The slave forgets all his sufferings, except to remind others of the trials during the past week, exclaiming: "Thank God, I shall not live here always!" Then they pass from one to another, shaking hands, and bidding each other farewell, promising, should they meet no more on earth, to strive and meet in heaven, where all is joy, happiness and liberty. As they separate, they sing a parting hymn of praise.

Sometimes the slaves meet in an old log-cabin, when they find it necessary to keep a watch. If discovered, they escape, if possible; but those who are caught often get whipped. Some are willing to be punished thus for Jesus' sake. Most of the songs used in worship are composed by the slaves themselves and describe their own sufferings. Thus:—

"O, that I had a bosom friend,
To tell my secrets to,
One always to depend upon
In everything I do!"
"How I do wander, up and down;
I seem a stranger, quite undone;
None to lend an ear to my complaint,
No one to cheer me, though I faint."

Some of the slaves sing—

"No more rain, no more snow,
No more cowskin on my back";

then they change it by singing—

"Glory be to God that rules on high."

In some places, if the slaves are caught praying to God, they are whipped more than if they had committed a great crime. The slaveholders will allow the slaves to dance, but do not want them to pray to God. Sometimes, when a slave, on being whipped, calls upon God, he is forbidden to do so, under threat of having his throat cut, or brains blown out. O, reader! this seems very hard,— that slaves cannot call on their Maker, when the case most needs it. Sometimes the poor slave takes courage to ask his master to let him pray, and is driven away with the answer, that if discovered praying, his back will pay the bill.

I did not know of any other denomination where I lived in Virginia, than the Baptists and Presbyterians. Most of the colored people, and many of the poorer class of whites, are Baptists.

The slaves talk much of the sufferings of Christ; and oftentimes, when they are called to suffer at the hands of their cruel overseers, they think of what he endured, and derive patience and consolation from his example. Their ideas of him, however, are not very clear. They think that He is standing somewhere, looking at them with pitying eyes, and He knows all about what is going on. They conceive of God as a very large man, with feet and hands, and eyes and ears, whose house is somewhere in the skies, and that He has books, and is always writing down what takes place on the earth. They expect to see Him as a man; and that He will talk to them, if they will look for Him. They think Jesus to be inferior to God in size; and that the reason why He is so small is, that He once dwelt in the flesh, and was so badly treated as to hinder his growing large!

Source: Peter Randolph. *Sketches of Slave Life: Or, Illustrations of the "Peculiar Institution."* Boston: printed by the author, 1855, 30–34.

FURTHER READING

Akinyela, Makungu. 2003. "Battling the Serpent: Nat Turner, Africanized Christianity, and a Black Ethos." *Journal of Black Studies* 33, no. 3 (January): 255–280.

Ball, Charles. 1837. *Slavery in the United States: A Narrative of the Life and Adventures of Charles Ball.* New York: John S. Taylor.

Berlin, Ira, Marc Favreau, and Steven F. Miller, ed. 1998. *Remembering Slavery: African Americans Talk about Their Personal Experiences of Slavery and Emancipation.* New York: The New Press.

Bibb, Henry. 1849. *Narrative of the Life and Adventures of Henry Bibb: An American Slave, Written by Himself.* New York: printed by the author.

Douglass, Frederick. 1881. *Life and Times of Frederick Douglass, His Early Life as a Slave, His Escape from Bondage, and His Complete History to the Present Time.* Hartford, CT: Park Publishing Co.

Egerton, Douglas R., and Robert L. Paquette, eds. 2017. *The Denmark Vesey Affair: A Documentary History*. Gainesville: University Press of Florida.

Elizabeth. 1889. *Elizabeth: A Colored Minister of the Gospel, Born in Slavery*. Philadelphia, PA: The Tract Association of Friends.

Fedric, Francis. 1863. *Slave Life in Virginia and Kentucky, or Fifty Years of Slavery in the Southern States of America*. London: Wertheim, Macintosh, and Hunt.

Frey, Sylvia, and Betty Wood. 1998. *Come Shouting to Zion: African American Protestantism in the American South and the British Caribbean to 1830*. Chapel Hill: University of North Carolina Press.

Gomez, Michael A. 1997. *Exchanging Our Country Marks: The Transformation of African Identities in the Colonial and Antebellum South*. Chapel Hill: University of North Carolina Press.

Grandy, Moses. 1843. *Narrative of the Life of Moses Grandy; Late a Slave in the United States of America*. London: Charles Gilpin.

Greenberg, Kenneth, ed. 1996. *The Confessions of Nat Turner and Related Documents*. New York: Bedford/St. Martins.

Harding, Vincent. 1981. *There Is a River: The Black Struggle for Freedom in America*. New York: Harcourt Brace.

Hughes, Louis. 1897. *Thirty Years a Slave: From Bondage to Freedom: The Institution of Slavery as Seen on the Plantation and in the Home of the Planter*. Milwaukee, WI: South Side Printing Co.

Jacobs, Harriet. 1861. *Incidents in the Life of a Slave Girl, Written by Herself*. Boston: printed by the author.

Johnson, Thomas L. 1909. *Twenty-Eight Years a Slave: Or The Story of My Life in Three Continents*. Bournemouth, England: W. Mate & Sons.

Levine, Lawrence. 1997. "Slave Songs and Slave Consciousness: An Exploration in Neglected Sources." In *African-American Religion: Interpretive Essays in History and Culture*, edited by Timothy Earl Fulop and Albert J. Raboteau. New York: Routledge, 57–88.

Long, John Dixon. 1857. *Pictures of Slavery in Church and State; Including Personal Reminiscences, Biographical Sketches, Anecdotes, etc. etc. with an Appendix, Containing the Views of John Wesley and Richard Watson on Slavery*. Philadelphia, PA: printed by the author.

Perdue, Charles, Jr., Thomas E. Barden, and Robert K. Phillips, eds. 1976. *Weevils in the Wheat: Interviews with Virginia Ex-Slaves*. Charlottesville: University Press of Virginia.

Raboteau, Albert. 1978. *Slave Religion: The "Invisible Institution" in the Antebellum South*. New York: Oxford University Press.

Randolph, Peter. 1855. *Sketches of Slave Life: Or Illustrations of the Peculiar Institution*. Boston: printed by the author.

Robinson, William H. 1913. *From Log Cabin to the Pulpit, or, Fifteen Years in Slavery*. Eau Claire, WI: Publishing Printer.

Sidbury, James. 2003. "Reading, Revelation and Rebellion: The Textual Communities of Gabriel, Denmark Vesey, and Nat Turner." In *Nat*

Turner: A Slave Rebellion in History and Memory*, edited by Kenneth R. Greenburg. New York: Oxford University Press, 119–133.
Stroyer, Jacob. 1879. *Sketches of My Life in the South, Part I*. Salem, MA: Salem Press.
Thompson, Katrina D. 2014. *Ring Shout, Wheel About: The Racial Politics of Music and Dance in North American Slavery*. Urbana: University of Illinois Press.
Turner, Richard Brent. 1994. "What Shall We Call Him: Islam and African American Identity." *Journal of Religious Thought* 51, no. 1 (Summer/Fall): 25–52.
Young, Jason R. 2008. "Spirituality and Socialization in the Slave Community." In *A Companion to African American History*, edited by Alton Hornsby, Jr. Malden, MA: Blackwell, 176–198.

5

POLITICAL LIFE

Understanding the political life of enslaved people requires a broader definition of politics than is used in common speech and writing. In formal terms, of course, slaves had no political rights and thus were barred from voting, office holding, or openly expressing their political views. But if we think about politics as relating to the distribution of power between people or groups of people within a defined sphere of human activity, the political dimensions of slave life come into view. The rules that governed plantation life were established by white planters and often enforced by overseers, but enslaved people constantly negotiated with their masters and overseers about the rules and conditions under which they lived and worked. Moreover, if antebellum plantations were most fundamentally units of economic production, they were also, in a real sense, systems of government with hierarchies, assumptions about legitimate and illegitimate uses of violence, and sites where informal debates over the distribution of power took place.

But without rights, how can enslaved people be said to exercise power? The answer lies in the very humanity of the slaves themselves, people whose minds and bodies were essential to the economic and social status of the men and women who owned them. Unable to extract everything they wanted from their enslaved workers through brute force alone, slaveholders often lamented the fact that they had to negotiate with slaves or modify their demands based on opposition or resistance from them. Masters engaged in such negotiations from positions of enormous power, but historians have shown that such power was not absolute, thus creating a limited sphere in which the political life of Southern plantations emerged. As one recent historian has argued, the politics of the Southern plantation was "a daily tug of war over labor, culture and power" in which slaves constantly contested the authority of their masters in "day to day acts of resistance" rather than in "formal institutions such as courtrooms or political organizations" (Camp 2004, 2–3). As we will see, the slaveholders themselves often failed to recognize the disobedience of their slaves as resistance, preferring to call it laziness or ingratitude. But the pattern of daily resistance to slavery is unmistakable and constitutes the hidden politics of daily life in the plantation South.

PATERNALISM: THE IDEOLOGY OF PLANTATION GOVERNMENT

Southern planters liked to think of themselves as patriarchal figures, men whose vast authority over their dependents, both white and black, was sanctioned by both nature and biblical truth. The rhetoric of proslavery paternalism insisted that the existence of inequality was written fundamentally into the law of nature, so that the strong would always rule over the weak and that insistence upon ideals of equality not only was unnatural but also would result in social disintegration. In the face of the increasingly democratic rhetoric of American political life in the antebellum period, Southern planters argued that order, not equality, was the highest social goal and that the authority of men over women and children, the power of whites over blacks, and the rule of wealthy educated men over poorer folk ensured the smooth functioning of society. "In all social systems there must be a class to do the menial duties, to perform the drudgery of life," argued James Henry Hammond of South Carolina in a speech before the U.S. Senate in 1858. "Fortunately for the South, she found a race adapted to that purpose to her hand. A race inferior to her own, but eminently qualified in temper, in vigor, in docility, in capacity to stand the climate, to answer all her purposes. We use them for our purpose, and call them slaves" (Hammond 1858, 962).

Southern ministers provided a strong biblical foundation for such views, pointing out that the scriptures nowhere sanctioned race, gender, or class equality but rather demanded that those entrusted by God to occupy positions of power do so benevolently and with the best interests of their dependents in mind. "The South did not seek or desire the responsibility, and the onerous burden, of civilizing and Christianizing these degraded savages," wrote slaveholder and Baptist minister Thornton Stringfellow, "but God, in his mysterious providence, brought it about" (Stringfellow 1856, 144). Preachers like Stringfellow instructed women, children, and enslaved people to submit to the authority of wealthy white men and to carry out their assigned social roles loyally and cheerfully. Although they argued that violent punishment should be a last resort, paternalism contained within it the notion that correction or chastisement could legitimately be meted out to those who failed to defer to their betters or who resisted the imposition of legitimate authority. Antebellum planters imagined that, unlike the North with its raucous and at times conflicted social and ideological landscape, their own society conformed to the decrees of nature and nature's God.

At the core of this notion of an ordered, well-governed society based on a divinely sanctioned hierarchy was, of course, the plantation itself, which proslavery rhetoric depicted as a microcosm of ideal social and political relations. The pinnacle of the plantation political hierarchy was occupied by the white planter, whose ownership of the land and slaves as well as the incredibly lucrative staple crops they yielded was protected by the majestic power of the law. Indeed, one historian has recently observed that on antebellum Southern plantations "elite slaveholders had many of the powers later ascribed to the state" (Camp 2004, 2). On many larger holdings, however, planters preferred to employ their power through the intermediary of the overseer, often a white relative or neighbor, who was paid to govern the slaves on a day-to-day basis and to mete out punishment for insubordination, poor work, or other infractions against plantation discipline. The ability of overseers to exert such power resulted from the authority conferred upon them by masters and, of course, by the fact that they were white men whose race placed them in position of superiority over all of the black men, women, and children who resided on the plantation.

Yet the politics of plantation life existed within the planter's household as well as in and around the fields that produced his crops. House slaves also inhabited a space in which the authority of masters was delegated to others, in this case the plantation mistress, whose responsibility for household management mirrored her husband's larger control over the plantation complex as a whole. Although subject to her husband's ultimate authority, the plantation mistress exercised considerable power over slaves who cooked, cleaned, sewed, and cared for the personal needs of the white family. Like the planter himself, the plantation mistress ruled by virtue of her class and race, and she was charged with maintaining the same ideals of order and legitimate authority that the larger paternalist ideology prescribed. The ideal plantation mistress was a perfect combination of mother, disciplinarian, domestic manager, and hostess, all of which depended on her ability to manage the slaves under her direct power. In one fictional account published in 1839, the model mistress was described as one who ran her home with "perfect system" and where "each servant was allotted his or her respective duties, and to each was assigned the time when those duties were to be performed" (Glymph 2008, 79). Although the realities of life in plantation homes were quite different, paternalism assumed that the natural authority of the mistress, not her coercive power, would ensure domestic order.

Enslaved people, like those shown here on the J. J. Smith Plantation in Beaufort, South Carolina, in 1862, formed strong communities that protected their members against the dehumanization inherent in the slave system. These communities shared resources and preserved crucial aspects of African American culture. (Library of Congress)

Based upon mountains of evidence collected over the past thirty years, historians have decisively rejected the notion that slaveholders actually operated their plantations along paternalistic lines. With their livelihood and social status linked irrevocably to the capitalist market in cotton and other staple crops, planter families regularly and often egregiously violated the terms of their own proslavery rhetoric in order to extract every last shred of profit from the labor of the people they owned. Faced with a choice between their own economic self-interest or their ability to look and act like benevolent masters, white slaveholders nearly always chose the former over the latter, a fact that enslaved people knew only too well. Former slave Henry Bibb accused his former owner Albert Sibley of the grossest form of hypocrisy for selling his mother and youngest sister after making repeated promises to grant them freedom after two years of service. "You have an awful account to render to the great Judge of the Universe," he warned Sibley. He pronounced the "slave holding religion" of the South, with its paternalistic assumptions about reciprocal obligations between master and slave, to be "of the devil" (Blassingame 1977, 55).

But even as their actions betrayed their own ideological justification for enslaving black people, slaveholding men and women continued to insist to others, and often to themselves, that their system was the right one and that they were the embodiment of a benevolent ruling class. In so doing, they created an opening for enslaved people to hold them to their own standards, to insist that slaveholders act like the benevolent and decent Christians they claimed to be. As the pioneering historian Eugene Genovese once wrote, the slaves found "an opportunity to translate paternalism into a doctrine different from that understood by their masters" and to "forge it into a weapon of resistance" and a "powerful defense against the dehumanization implicit in slavery" (Genovese 1972, 7). While such resistance did not always work, slaves recognized that while the distribution of power on plantations was vastly imbalanced in favor of masters and mistresses, the planters' desire to see themselves as paternalistic provided a limited but still important source of power over them.

One example of the way in which this dynamic might function was in the care of elderly slaves who could no longer contribute to the economic profitability of the plantation. While there are numerous examples of masters who demonstrated cruelty, neglect, and malice toward those whose age made them unfit for work, enslaved people nevertheless leaned heavily on paternalistic rhetoric to pry concessions out of their owners. Jake, an elderly slave no longer able to labor in fields, used the notion of reciprocity to confront his master and insisted that "I've labored for you for forty years now . . . and I done earned my keep. You can sell me, lash me, or kill me. I ain't caring which but you can't make me work no more." Although Jake's mode of speech might easily have been seen as insubordination and elicited a violent response, the master instead agreed to his terms, saying, "All right Jake, I'm retiring you" (Genovese 1972, 521). Jake could no longer contribute to the productive labor of the plantation and could not be sold for profit in the slave trade, and thus the planter's decision to "retire" Jake involved little or no economic loss and allowed him to preserve his own self-image as a "good master." In using the language of reciprocal obligations to make his appeal, however, Jake demonstrated a shrewd understanding of the possibilities, though limited, that paternalism could be turned to his own advantage.

Enslaved people often used similar techniques to prevent masters from selling them or members of their families. The threat of sale was undoubtedly the most powerful weapon that slaveholders wielded in their quest to control the labor and obedience of the people they owned, and slaves fought back against it in many ways, including appeals to paternal obligations. Maryland slave William Green remembered that when his mother heard that William was to be sold to a slave trader and sent into the Deep South, she "went with a bursting heart to my young master and begged him not to take her poor child away from her no more to return" (Johnson 1999, 36). Reminding him that she had "nursed him when a child," he agreed to allow her to find a local buyer. Enslaved people who strategically employed the language of paternalism to fight off the possibility of sale insisted that only disobedience or rebelliousness could ever justify it. The family of one enslaved woman was incensed when they discovered that her owner had sold her to a slave trader in order to pay off a gambling debt. "The people told him 'twas a shame to let me go to the trader—that I was too good a girl for that, having taken care of him in sickness—that I ought to have a chance to find someone to buy me." Apparently, the argument worked as the owner "became ashamed of what he had done and bought me back" (Drew 2008, 312).

It is crucial to understand that while enslaved people sometimes used paternalism to their advantage, they rejected its most basic assumptions. Indeed, the chief obstacle to the slaveholders' ability to translate their paternalistic ideals of plantation government into effective practice was the simple fact that enslaved people refused to play their own assigned roles as loyal and grateful servants. Whether in the fields or in the plantation houses of the antebellum South, slaves refused to work at the pace that masters, mistresses, or overseers demanded. In contrast to the mythical stories of cheerful, happy slaves that filled the pages of the proslavery rhetoric emanating from the South before and after the Civil War, enslaved African Americans were often sullen, insolent, angry, or even violent in their responses to the brutal exploitation that was endemic to the system of slavery. Told when, how, and how long to work, slaves routinely slacked off, feigned illness, produced poor or half-finished work, and in many other ways flouted the demands of the planters and their families. Deeply racist slaveholding whites insisted that such actions were the outgrowth of the innate inferiority of black people. But, in fact, they were acts of resistance by which slaves challenged the political hierarchy of the plantation regime and demanded concessions from those who owned them.

THE POLITICS OF FIELDWORK

The dynamics of plantation politics most fundamentally revolved around the production of cash crops, and planters recognized that successful "government" of enslaved people was critical to that end. One slaveholder stated very clearly that "the profits of the planter" depended upon his ability to establish "rule and system" in the management of farms and plantations, including set times for slaves to rise in the morning, when they were to appear in the fields, what tasks they were to perform during the working day, when they could eat, and when the workday was to end. During the antebellum period, in fact, Southern periodicals contained an endless stream of advice literature that persistently warned planters of the economic ruin that would result from the absence of firm, consistent "government" of their workers (Breeden 1980, 41).

At the same time, however, such literature tacitly acknowledged that the universal application of rules was not always possible and that the best plantation government rested upon limited forms of consent from the enslaved people themselves. Ruling by threats of violence alone, or what one planter described as "the simple and low principle of fear," would never produce the effective laborers that resulted from "peace and harmony" on the plantation or the "contentment and consequent happiness of the slaves." Though clearly not all slaveholders followed such principles, many could not help but recognize, even if grudgingly, that the people they owned were human and therefore subject to the same physical and emotional forces that made all human beings more or less effective at their daily tasks. Admitting the ruthless self-interest that lay at the heart of this thinking, one planter stated simply that because of the enormous economic value of slaves, "it behooves those who own them to make them last as long as possible." The interplay between the economic self-interest of the planter and the humanity of the slaves is where plantation politics took place, and it began at dawn each day (Breeden 1980, 40).

According to the advice literature on slave government, slaves were to rise before first light and to be in the fields as the sun rose, with severe punishment meted out to those who failed to appear. But within this set of rules, planters or overseers were often confronted with enslaved people who were ill or injured and whose labor in the fields might permanently damage their long-term health and value as laborers. A similar calculation occurred in evaluating the condition of female slaves in the later stages of pregnancy, who, if overworked, might miscarry and thus deprive their owners not only of valuable labor but also of the economic value of the children they carried. While overwork, poor clothing, and inadequate food and living conditions meant that enslaved people experienced legitimate illnesses quite often, feigning sickness or "playing possum" should also be seen as a form of resistance to the dominant plantation order, and planters were intensely frustrated by their inability to tell the difference between playacting and legitimate ailments. Thomas Chaplin of South Carolina complained bitterly about his slave woman Peggy, who always seemed to be ill "when I am most pushed for work" and whose illnesses seemed to last much longer than he expected. While it is impossible to know for sure whether Peggy's illness was real or feigned, her insistence on her inability to work meant that she was able to spend more time away from the fields just after giving birth to a baby girl. Slaves took a significant risk in deceiving their owners, and evidence suggests that many planters refused to excuse injured or sick slaves from work, but "playing possum" allowed some enslaved people to "rest their bodies, to relieve some of the extra stresses of pregnancy," and to "affect the pace of work" (Fett 2000, 185–186).

In demanding attention to their maladies, whether real or pretended, slaves forced their owners to provide various forms of medical care as well as the construction of rudimentary plantation hospitals called "sickhouses." More common on large plantations than small ones, these dwellings allowed planters to quarantine slaves whom they suspected of having contagious diseases. Placed at a safe distance from the plantation house but close enough to the fields to enable regular inspections by the overseer, sickhouses sometimes became spaces where the power struggles inherent to plantation life became overt and even violent. "Great care must be taken to prevent persons from lying up when there is nothing or little the matter with them," wrote one planter. In the absence of a physician, however, it was very difficult to assess the condition of slaves, and most planters seem to have relied on something like instinct to decide which slaves were "shamming" and thus should be "turned out" of the sickhouse and forced into the fields (Breeden 1980, 192). To discourage any such "shamming," some overseers resorted to what can only be described as barbarous behavior. Former slave Charles Ball remembered a slave woman named Lydia who had become deeply depressed after the death of her child and failed to appear in the field when the horn was blown one morning. The overseer, convinced that she was "pretending to be sick," refused to allow her to go to the sickhouse and instead forced her to drink a grotesque mixture of iron sulfate that made her vomit incessantly (Ball 1837, 266). Lydia's attempts to escape the field and to grieve her child were unsuccessful, but they must be understood as another form of resistance to the incessant demands of the plantation government.

One of the striking features of this form of resistance is the fact that the slaveholders refused to recognize that it was resistance at all. Rather than entertain the disturbing conclusion that slaves, in fact, hated the plantation regime and were using every means at their disposal to subvert its control over their lives, planters insisted that slaves simply lacked a work ethic comparable to that of whites. They developed an extensive vocabulary, including words like "malingering" or "playing possum" to describe what they contended was an innate racial tendency toward laziness. Unfortunately, it has taken historians until quite recently to see through the language of the slaveholders to perceive the subtle, yet significant ways in which enslaved people used their own health as a bargaining chip in their ongoing negotiation with masters over power and labor. However they explained it, slaveholders could neither ignore the health of their workforce nor overlook the possibility that slaves were using illness as a way to avoid the labor that plantations required for their long-term profitability. Each morning when the call to work was sounded, slaves and their owners faced one another over this critical issue.

For those who were unable to avoid that morning call, the fields constituted the next space in which the politics of plantation life were enacted. On cotton plantations, slaves were generally required to work from sunup to sundown, though at harvest times they might be forced to continue their labor into the night. On rice or sugar plantations, the work hours might be shorter or longer depending upon the seasonal demands of the crops or the specific arrangements made between masters and slaves. By the antebellum period, however, most planters had adopted many of the same notions of efficiency and time discipline that governed factory life in the North, and they demanded high levels of productivity from their slaves. This meant that fieldwork was done in most cases under direct white supervision and under a system of productivity quotas that were designed to ensure the profitability of the plantation. Thus, the successful "government" of slaves meant that work was done in accordance with plantation rules and that the authority of the master and overseer could be measured objectively by the volume of crops produced by enslaved workers. "In the labors of the day," wrote one efficiency-minded planter from Georgia, "there must be uniformity and system" and "all must move off like clockwork" (Breeden 1980, 66).

In reality, the increasing productivity demands of planters placed dehumanizing burdens on the bodies and minds of enslaved people and elicited another subtle but vastly important politics of daily resistance. During the critical cotton harvest season, the cardinal rule of field government was the quota system in which slaves were expected to pick a designated weight that was established on the picker's best day. Punishments would be meted out to workers who failed to meet their assigned quota, and exceeding it would result in a higher quota being set by the master. "A slave never approaches the gin-house with his basket of cotton but with fear," wrote former slave Solomon Northup (Northup 1853, 167). Yet even within this seemingly ironclad system of control, enslaved people resisted in clever and at times even humorous ways. For example, when enslaved Mississippian Israel Campbell struggled to meet his assigned a 100-pound quota, he began slipping watermelons into his sack to make up the shortfall. After the sacks had been weighed and stored for the night, Campbell would make an excuse to return to the cotton house, take the melons from the bag and eat them. The plan worked so well that Campbell taught the other slaves on the plantation how to beat the quota system. "Before the season was over," he recalled, "every one of the delinquents knew how to save their backs, and they found it much easier to pick melons and pumpkins than to have their backs cut to pieces" (Campbell 1861, 38).

In addition to their crafty evasions of the quota system, enslaved people took advantage of the fact that masters and overseers could not observe all of their workers at the same time. Northern journalist Frederick Law Olmsted, who traveled throughout the cotton South during the early eighteenth century, noticed that slaves were keenly aware when the overseer was looking the other way. "As often as he visited one end of the operations, the hands at the other end would discontinue their labor," the Northerner wrote. He also noted that when the cotton plants were in full bloom, their height effectively hid the bodies of the workers so that their pace of work could not be constantly monitored. A related strategy stemmed from the fact that enslaved people had more direct experience with the labor of cotton production than either masters or overseers and sometimes used their knowledge to disrupt the process. One planter, who "did not take the time to see how the work [of ploughing] was done," found himself completely bamboozled by disgruntled field hands who followed his orders but did so in a way that nearly destroyed the crop. "All the hands slighted their work," observed a neighboring planter, "and where they did plow, they would let the plow run over the grass and not plow it up" (Johnson 2017, 167). Determined to establish a pace and style of work that suited them rather than conform to externally imposed notions of efficiency, enslaved people contested the rules of plantation government even as they toiled in the fields.

Yet perhaps the most dramatic expression of the ways in which slaves renegotiated the field labor demands of their masters can be seen in the emergence of the "task system" of labor that prevailed on the rice plantations of the South Carolina and Georgia lowcountry. In this region, where the black population significantly outnumbered that of whites, enslaved people worked out a system in which a day's task, rather than dawn to dusk labor disciplined by a quota, was the standard by which a slave's work would be judged. The precise circumstances out of which this system emerged during the eighteenth century are complex, but by the nineteenth century, enslaved people in the lowcountry insisted upon their right to define a reasonable task and to work on their own time once the assigned task had been completed. One overseer unfamiliar with these rules faced unexpected resistance from a slave named Philip Coleman, who had very clear ideas about what constituted a "stint" or day's work. "One day he directed me to cover what to me seemed more than a day's work, and I told him I would go as far as I could." While the angry overseer was ready to inflict punishment for such an insubordinate response, the planter intervened to uphold the traditions of the task system. "[He] told me to do the best I could, and let the rest of the stint go for the day" (Blassingame 1977, 561). When masters or overseers overstepped the bounds of what the slave community regarded as an acceptable day's task, there were many ways in which displeasure could be expressed. The ever-observant Northern journalist Frederick Law Olmsted provided his readers with a concrete list of what might happen: "gates left open and bars left down . . . rails removed from fences . . . mules lamed and implements broken" and even flat boats untied from their moorings and allowed to "go adrift on the river" (Schwalm 1997, 40).

THE POLITICS OF THE BIG HOUSE

While the dynamics of oppression and resistance in the cotton fields of the antebellum South constituted one of the most dramatic elements of plantation politics, a more intimate political struggle occurred within the plantation household itself. Southern plantation mistresses were expected to manage homes that were beautiful, refined expressions of their families' elite status. The quality of the food served to family members and guests, the cleanliness of the clothing worn by husbands and children, and the careful maintenance of the furnishings available for entertainment and leisure all fell within the responsibility of the mistress. And yet as members of the plantation class, elite Southern women were not expected to perform the physical labor required to meet these demanding standards. Instead, their ability to meet expectations depended almost entirely on their ability to manage and control the labor of enslaved men, women, and children. Like their husbands, whose economic success depended upon their capacity to establish effective government over field slaves, plantation mistresses attempted to create "efficient" households in which the work of cooking, washing, cleaning, sewing, mending, and serving would be done regularly and according to the rules of "household management" (Glymph 2008, 76). But as in the fields, slaves refused to internalize the rules of efficiency imposed upon them by whites and, whenever possible, resisted them.

Perhaps no better introduction to the politics of domination and resistance in the plantation household can be found in the writings of former slave Louis Hughes who was born in Charlottesville, Virginia, and, at the age of twelve, sold for $380 to a Mississippi cotton planter named Edward McGee. When he arrived on the plantation, Hughes was immediately presented to the mistress as a "Christmas gift" and put to work as a "house servant and errand boy" in the "great house" under her direct supervision. Hughes remembered the mistress as "naturally irritable" and willing to inflict beatings upon any household servants who failed to meet her exacting standards or who displeased her in any way. "Servants always got an extra whipping when she had any personal trouble, as though they could help it," he remembered. "She seldom let a day pass without beating some poor woman unmercifully" (Hughes 1897, 13, 72–73). As the wife of an ambitious, upwardly mobile planter, Sarah McGee's irritability and her almost obsessive surveillance of the servants may have resulted from her struggle to raise four children while maintaining the outward trappings of a refined domestic life. Hughes noted that when the family moved to a larger and even more ornate house in Memphis, Tennessee, her "severity" became even more unbearable.

Whether in Mississippi or Tennessee, Sarah McGee sought to establish a clear system by which she could "govern" the household slaves. Each morning would begin with a rigorous inspection of the various worksites around the "great house," including the interior rooms of the home itself as well as its adjacent barn, smokehouse, and henhouse. Accompanied by a young slave girl whose task was to carry a basket containing the keys to every room in the house, the mistress made her "rounds" and confronted her servants with anything that failed to please her eye. "She rarely returned to the house from these rounds without having whipped two or three servants," Hughes recalled. But in language that demonstrates a rejection of both her standards and her authority, he also insisted "that the number and severity of these whippings depended more upon the humor of the madam than upon the conduct of the slaves." Young Louis was especially vulnerable to her cruelty because of his age, his separation from family back in Virginia, and the fact that he was responsible for the appearance of the parlor, a room where guests to the home were entertained by the family. Convinced that Louis was slacking off, Mrs. McGee regularly slapped him, pinched him, boxed his ears, and whipped his naked back even when he had worked hard to please her. Although Hughes confessed that he was initially afraid of his mistress and wept when she abused him, her cruel and arbitrary behavior eventually summoned up feeling of rebelliousness. "After the first burst of tears," he recalled, "the feeling came over me that I was a man, and it was an outrage to treat me so—to keep me under the lash day after day" (Hughes 1897, 72–74).

The feelings of anger, resentment, and rebelliousness that Sarah McGee's brutality created in Louis Hughes can be seen in the behavior of other household slaves whose age and experience allowed them to resist in subtle but important ways. As historian Thavolia Glymph has demonstrated, domestic servants, like field slaves, subverted the household regime by refusing to work according to the rules, even if it meant punishment. One plantation mistress, Tryphena Fox, complained bitterly that the enslaved women in her home simply would not do their assigned tasks in the time and manner that she directed. Two slaves in particular, Mary and Susan, seem to have driven Fox almost to despair because of what she called their "laziness and impudence" (Glymph 2008, 68). Mary concealed her son, an escaped slave, in her room and apparently kept her own a secret stash of whiskey as well. She also engaged in acts of petty pilfering from the plantation kitchen, taking cream and butter that were reserved for the use of the white family. Susan was, if anything, more exasperating to her mistress because of her insistence that the slightest injury to her hand meant that she should be excused from sewing, cleaning, or other necessary tasks for weeks at a time. When Fox attempted to discipline her, Susan screamed at her and ran away, which meant that the care of the white family's three children would fall to their mother, a burden that Fox was ill equipped to carry for long. Though Susan's escape might have been used as an excuse to sell her, Fox was so dependent on her labor that she was allowed to return to the house and take up her assigned tasks.

The intense frustration of so many plantation mistresses with "good-for-nothing" black servants suggests that resistance to household discipline was widespread and, at least in one way, extremely successful. When they washed clothes poorly, cooked barely edible food for guests, left parlors dusty or stairways dirty, domestic slave women made it impossible for plantation mistresses to create what Victorian Southerners regarded as essential standards for civilized homelife and thus threatened their self-image as successful domestic managers. At times, their dissatisfaction with the work of servants forced mistresses to do at least some of the work themselves, which violated class-based standards of elite female conduct, effectively conceded their lack of authority in the home, and even undermined their own refinement. After years of struggling with Mary, Susan, and other female servants, Tryphena Fox confessed that she was worn down physically and emotionally and had almost become a "scare crow" in outward appearance. Another frustrated plantation mistress, Keziah Brevard, whose slave Sylvia "hates a white face" and from whom she could not "get a civil word," even wished that she had been born in a world without slavery (Glymph 2008, 75, 103). While women like Fox and Brevard attributed the actions or inaction of their domestic servants to irrational hatred or laziness, they are far better understood as acts of resistance to a domestic regime that sought to erase the humanity and individuality of enslaved people and remake them according to the desires of their owners.

DISRUPTING THE PLANTATION HIERARCHY

As noted earlier, antebellum plantations were governed in hierarchical terms, with masters, mistresses, and overseers exercising discreet forms of authority over the daily lives of enslaved people. The master, because his personal ownership of the landed and slave property, sat at the top of the pyramid of power and was the final authority on all important matters related to the smooth running of the plantation complex. Yet like plantation mistresses who were expected to create refined homes without performing the labor themselves, masters, especially those on large plantations, preferred to delegate the sometimes dirty and violent work of day-to-day government of slaves to white overseers. Often related to the planters by blood, overseers certainly wielded enormous power over the daily lives of slaves, and their close supervision and frequent punishment of the field laborers meant that they were the most visible manifestations of white supremacy on some plantations. Enslaved people, however, understood that the power of the overseer was not absolute and was therefore subject to both subtle and overt forms of resistance. If appealed to in the correct way, in other words, masters might reverse the decisions of overseers or reprimand them for cruelty or neglect. Enslaved women, moreover, also recognized that plantation mistresses might, in certain instances, act on their behalf against overseers or even against the authority of the master himself. Finding and exploiting weaknesses in the plantation hierarchy, therefore, is another key element in the politics of plantation life and demonstrates the always-contested dynamics of power within Southern slavery.

Playing masters against overseers was a key political strategy for enslaved people and provides another example of the ways in which slaves sometimes used the ideology of paternalism in their own cause. Although slaveholders warned each other that enslaved people would be sure to take advantage of "any little jarring between master and overseer," they were often unable to prevent such circumstances from occurring. When overseers were left in charge of plantations on behalf of absentee planters, for example, slaves who believed that they were being treated cruelly or unfairly found ways to communicate their grievances to the master. John Grimball, a South Carolina planter who spent most of the year in Charleston, routinely received critical reports from his slaves about the conduct of the overseer. His slave Bachus, for example, reported that the overseer's brother had been allowed to feed his own horse from the plantation stores, a fact that the master found "displeasing." A second slave Richard complained that the overseer had demoted him as the plantation's black "driver" and replaced him with another, less-capable slave. The master immediately fired off a letter reminding the overseer that the power of "making and displacing drivers is one which no one has a liberty to exercise without my permission" and that such liberty "has not been given to you." In case the overseer planned to punish Richard for complaining in this way, Grimball warned that the slave "is not to be punished for this offense" until he had conducted a full investigation of the circumstances (Genovese 1972, 17, 18–19). Former slave Frederick Douglass reported that while slaves like Richard risked being punished by both masters and overseers for subverting the plantation chain of command, the most common result of their actions was often a relaxation of the overseer's disciplinary rigor.

Because overseers were often used by planters who did not reside on their estates year round, enslaved people who wanted to appeal directly to their masters had to take the radical and very risky step of fleeing from the plantation. One elderly ex-slave named John Jackson, for example, remembered a remarkable instance in which a risky flight from the brutality of an overseer resulted in a favorable outcome. Living on the plantation of an absentee planter in eastern Virginia, Jackson "slipped away" after receiving a vicious beating from an overseer whom he described as "mean and cruel clean through." While on the road he encountered an elegant white gentleman mounted on a white horse who asked whose slave he was and how he was treated. After hearing Jackson's scathing description of the poor food, scant clothing, and unspeakably harsh treatment he had received on the plantation, the "fine-looking" gentleman handed him $2 and instructed him to return home. Once back on the estate, Jackson discovered that the gentleman was none other than the absentee planter who, instead of punishing his escaped slave, confronted the overseer about his poor treatment of the workers. "The slave owner's wrath was kindled," Jackson recalled, and he thoroughly lambasted the overseer for mismanagement of the slaves before firing him. "There was great rejoicing in the slave cabins that evening," Jackson reported (Blassingame 1977, 552–553). Although this story was told more than half a century after the end of slavery and likely mixes memory and myth, it is nevertheless a powerfully symbolic narrative pointing to the ways in which enslaved people understood and exploited the very real differences of class and power that existed between wealthy planters and their white employees.

A related political dynamic existed when slaves appealed to plantation mistresses against the actions of both overseers and masters. Perhaps the most dramatic example of this form of interaction can be seen in the journals of Fanny Kemble, a famous British actress who married wealthy planter Pierce Butler and who came to reside on his extensive estates near Darien, Georgia. As soon as she arrived, the female slaves shrewdly cultivated both her goodwill and her sympathy for their wretched condition. When she was introduced to the new mistress, for example, the plantation's black midwife gushed over her physical beauty and somewhat theatrically asked Pierce Butler where he had obtained this "lilly, alabaster baby" of a wife. Another female slave, whom Kemble recalled had embraced her with "irresistible zeal" on the day of her arrival, soon asked to speak with her privately outside the plantation house. "She was the mother of a very large family," Kemble recalled, "and complained to me that, what with child-bearing and hard field labor, her back was almost broken in two" (Kemble 1863, 30–31). In a dramatic gesture that shocked and horrified the new mistress, the woman tore off her clothes to reveal an emaciated body suffering from a panoply of ailments that Kemble promised she would "attend to" as best she could. These enslaved women appealed both to her vanity and to her identity as a woman and mother, hoping that she would exert influence over her husband and his hired overseer.

If that was their intent, it was a remarkably successful strategy as Kemble soon found herself in a pitched battle with the male plantation hierarchy over their treatment of the slaves. The most immediate point of conflict was the female slaves' bitter complaint that the demands placed upon them as field laborers prevented them from caring adequately for their sick children. The overseer denied this charge, but what infuriated Kemble the most was the fact that the overseer mercilessly flogged the woman who had made it. The result was a confrontation with her husband in which she told him in no uncertain terms "that if the people were to be chastised for anything they said to me, I must leave the place" (Kemble 1863, 57). The slaves on Butler's plantation increasingly regarded their new mistress as an ally against what they regarded as a cruel and unreasonable overseer. She told them that her husband was the final authority in such matters, but they entreated her that if "'missis' begged 'massa' for them, he would lighten their task." Ultimately, her decision to intervene repeatedly on behalf of the slaves resulted in Butler's unequivocal reassertion of the male plantation hierarchy. Accusing his wife of reinforcing the slaves' natural irresponsibility and laziness, Pierce Butler forbade her from bringing him any more complaints. "Why do you believe such trash?" he asked her with both frustration and anger, "don't you know the niggers are all d—d liars?" (Kemble 1863, 170, 215).

Fanny Kemble's limited power as a planter's wife meant that she was unable to make a decisive change in the plantation regime, but the slaves' coordinated attempts to cultivate her as an advocate indicate their understanding of the ways in which white women might, under certain circumstances, become temporary allies. While Kemble's British origins and extended residence in the North made her far more critical of slavery than most Southern-born white women, other plantation mistresses opposed excessive cruelty or ignorant neglect simply because of its detrimental effect of the value of slave property. In other words, "financial necessity" rather than "domestic caregiving" led some slaveholding women to challenge the male plantation hierarchy (Fett 2000, 115–116). Either way, enslaved people understood that white mistresses occupied a distinctive place in the plantation hierarchy and that their special responsibilities for the health of the slaves meant that they might challenge or at least mitigate the actions of masters or overseers. Like all forms of government, the plantation regime was a human institution, and as such, it was subject to internal fissures, conflicts over power and responsibility, and questions of moral legitimacy. Although they started from a position of weakness and enormous vulnerability, enslaved people exploited those fissures, conflicts, and doubts as often as they could.

In addition to the negotiations between the slaves and key members of the plantation hierarchy, slave hiring created opportunities for enslaved people to challenge or influence the decision-making powers of their owner. When slaves were hired out, families were often separated. Historian Jonathan Martin has demonstrated that enslaved people developed a variety of strategies to maintain contact with their spouse or children. In some cases, they asked their master to include permission to visit their loved ones as part of the hiring contract. In other cases, enslaved people threatened to run away, to harm themselves, or to refuse the assigned work. Some owners calculated that it was in their interest to heed the hiring preferences of their slaves and to intervene in conflicts between a slave and the white hirer. If slave owners ignored the wishes of their slaves, the consequences were sometimes disastrous. When Fanny, an enslaved woman, was hired out to a Richmond resident, Emanuel Seaman, he refused to let other slaves visit her. Fanny objected to Seaman's policy and told him that she wanted to leave. She also complained about her treatment to her owner. When neither responded positively, Fanny

Frances Anne "Fanny" Kemble (1809–1893) was a famous British actress who married wealthy Georgia slaveholder Pierce Butler. While residing on her husband's plantation, she recorded her observations of enslaved people and her efforts to intercede on their behalf. (Library of Congress)

set fire to the coal house of a Masonic lodge next to the room where she slept. For the crime of arson, she was "tried & convicted & sentenced to be hanged" (Zaborney 2012, 43).

Slave flight was another tool slaves used in their negotiations with masters. When an enslaved person ran away from an abusive situation, he or she often hoped to convince a slave owner to intervene, even if it was only to protect his or her economic interest. Frederick Douglass, who had been sent by his master to live with a notorious slave breaker named Edward Covey, attempted just this gambit after receiving a brutal beating from Covey that left him "covered in blood." Convinced that his master Thomas Auld would intervene if he understood the full extent of Covey's brutality, Douglass determined that he would "go to my master, enter a complaint, and ask for protection." The calculated risk Douglass took in this instance was based on the fact that Auld, not Covey, was his owner and that Auld would perceive his slave's bloody and battered condition as a threat to the potential value of his human property. In this instance, however, he was mistaken, as Auld refused to protect him from Covey's abuse and, after giving him rudimentary medical treatment and allowing him to stay the night, sent him back. This was a critical turning point in Douglass's life however, as Auld's refusal to act paternalistically at a critical point shattered any remaining illusions about using the proslavery ideology as a protective buffer against violence. The next time Douglass was assaulted and beaten by Covey, he thought not of fleeing to Thomas Auld but rather of physical self-defense, and he successfully fought off his attacker. The ensuing "battle" with Covey, he recalled, "was the turning-point in my career as a slave" as it "rekindled the few expiring embers of freedom and revived within me a sense of my own manhood" (Douglass 1845, 67–68). In Douglass's case as in that of Fanny, the failure of owners to listen to the complaints of slaves hired out or temporarily controlled by others meant the possibility of dramatic forms of resistance.

ENSLAVED PEOPLE AND AMERICAN POLITICS

The bulk of this chapter has focused on the informal politics of plantation life, but it will conclude with an examination of the subtle ways in which more formal political ideas and activities intersected with the lives of enslaved people. To understand this intersection, it is crucial to recall that American slavery reached its fullest development at a time when the political system of the United States was undergoing a transition to electoral democracy. Emerging mass-based political parties such as the Democrats and Republicans, as well as social movements like abolitionism, were finding innovative ways of reaching the white electorate that included open-air speeches and debates, the distribution of newspapers and cartoons, and the organization of parades and mass rallies. Although enslaved people could be prevented from participating in both formal and informal activities related to partisan politics, the political life of the nation could not be hidden from them. Slaveholders themselves were deeply interested in the political life of the period and talked about it over the dinner table with family and guests within the full hearing of their servants who listened carefully. In a variety of ways then, enslaved people absorbed information about American political life and formed their own opinions about it, especially as the political system experienced increasing conflict over slavery. During the Civil War itself, moreover, slaves demonstrated a remarkably sophisticated grasp of the political dynamics that were transforming the nation and seized the opportunity to act decisively against their masters.

Former slaves who wrote about their experiences in the South left substantial evidence that the political life of the larger nation was not only of interest to them but also the subject of discussion in the slave quarters. Perhaps the subject of their greatest attention was the rise of the abolitionist movement that profoundly affected the political life of the nation beginning in the 1830s. "Every little while, I could hear something about the abolitionists," wrote former slave Frederick Douglass in 1841, and he "always drew near when that word was spoken, expecting to hear something of importance to myself and fellow-slaves" (Douglass 1845, 42). John Sella Martin, who like Douglass had gained the rudiments of literacy during his childhood as a slave in Alabama, became fascinated by abolitionism after reading an article in a Southern newspaper condemning the abolitionist "tendencies" of Kentucky senator Henry Clay's speeches and writings. He recalled that while he did not fully understand the article, it was clear that slaveholders regarded abolitionism as evil, and that fact increased his interest in the topic. More important, Martin conveyed his discoveries to his fellow slaves, reading passages of the article out loud to them. "What I read or pretended to read," he recalled many years later, "gave the most intense satisfaction, and awakened the wildest hopes about freedom among my hearers" (Blassingame 1977, 711). These examples suggest that the more loudly Southern slaveholders condemned abolitionists in speech and writing, the more interested their slaves became in the movement.

As these examples from Frederick Douglass and John Sella Martin indicate, enslaved people who had obtained literacy skills or lived in urban areas of the South were best positioned to gain knowledge of the formal political world. For Douglass, who lived in Baltimore as a young boy, printed material was easily available, and his ability to read meant access to ideas that were subversive in the context of a slave society. Obtaining a copy of the *Columbian Orator*, a cheap rhetoric textbook containing essays on politics and reform, Douglass encountered the key themes of the classical republican tradition, including concepts of citizenship, limited government, and the corrupting nature of absolute power. He was powerfully affected by an essay of the Irish playwright Richard Sheridan, who passionately condemned the oppression of Irish Catholics by the British State. "What I got from Sheridan was a bold denunciation of slavery, and a powerful vindication of human rights," he remembered of his encounter with the *Columbian Orator*. When Douglass was sent back to rural Maryland to take up his life as a field slave, these political ideas went with him, and they played a powerful role in his continuing resistance to slavery. Although he had to act with extreme care, he communicated what he had learned to his fellow slaves to "imbue their minds with thoughts of freedom" (Douglass 1845, 40, 83–84).

For enslaved people who could not read books or newspapers, knowledge of abolitionism and other political subjects was, nevertheless, accessible through the burgeoning visual culture that accompanied democratic politics in antebellum America. In the mid-1830s, abolitionists sent hundreds of thousands of antislavery prints into the South, many of which contained visual images depicting the cruelties of slavery. Drawing inspiration from British abolitionists who had used horrifying images of the Atlantic slave trade to bring about a parliamentary ban, antislavery activists in the United States recognized that evocative imagery could be a powerful means of awakening the consciences of their fellow white Americans. As historian Stephanie Camp has argued, however, enslaved African Americans also obtained access to these images through clandestine communication networks. Relying on black sailors, carriage drivers, personal servants, and other "mobile bondpeople," slaves came to understand that there was a political world beyond the plantation where important allies in the struggle for freedom might be found. During the 1840s, for example, a

Mississippi slave woman named California was found to possess numerous abolitionist images in her cabin, a fact that her owner used to explain her resistant attitude toward his authority. "She has an idea she is free . . . goes & comes & does what she pleases," he wrote with obvious irritation (Camp 2004, 108, 97, 89).

As the Civil War approached, enslaved people recognized that the formal political life of the nation was increasingly divided over slavery, a fact that already preoccupied their owners. Just after the 1860 election, for example, Louis Hughes recalled that his master Edward McGee and his wife Sarah were intently reading the newspapers for information about Lincoln, the Republican Party, and the possible secession of the South. He overheard McGee express his disgust at the fact that an "old rail splitter" had been elected president and his absolute certainty that Lincoln would "never take his seat" as chief executive. Hughes said nothing to indicate his interest in the subject, but it is clear that he was carefully gathering all of the information he could about the political crisis as the country slid into Civil War. "When Lincoln was inaugurated," he recalled "Boss, old Master Jack and a great company of men met at our house to discuss the matter, and they were wild with excitement." Although Lincoln did not issue the Emancipation Proclamation for another two years, it was clear to Hughes and the other slaves on the McGee plantation that the success of the Union cause was far more likely to bring about their freedom than that of the Confederacy. "I tried to catch everything I could about the war," he remembered. "It was common when the message of a Union victory came to see the slaves whispering to each other: 'We will be free'" (Hughes 1897, 111, 114).

The same clandestine communication networks that had spread news of abolitionism throughout the plantations of the South also informed them of the Emancipation Proclamation when it was issued in 1863. The result was what some slaveholders referred to as a "great stampede" in which African Americans fled their plantations for Union army lines and, if they were adult men, volunteered to take up arms against their former masters (Camp 2004, 119). Indeed, the Civil War brought the informal politics of plantation resistance and the formal politics of the United States together for the first time in the nation's history. Refusing to work in the fields, houses, and yards of their former masters any longer, enslaved people took advantage of new and startling weaknesses the war had created in the system of plantation government. As the Union cause took on a formal antislavery character, moreover, enslaved people reached out beyond the plantations to forge alliances with those sympathetic Northern whites they had learned of in the abolitionist literature they had risked so much to obtain. Emancipation, in other words, was a deeply political act in which slaves expanded their subtle and sometimes unsuccessful strategies of plantation resistance into a full-scale assault on the power and legitimacy of the slaveholding regime itself.

DOCUMENT: LOUIS HUGHES, *THIRTY YEARS A SLAVE: FROM BONDAGE TO FREEDOM* (1896)

Louis Hughes was born in 1832 as a slave in Virginia, but as a young child he was sold away from his family and purchased by Edmund McGee, an ambitious Mississippi cotton planter. Near the end of the Civil War, Hughes escaped and managed to contact Union forces near Memphis, Tennessee. With the help of Union troops, he secured the freedom of his family and the other slaves trapped on the McGee plantation. Louis Hughes's description of the early years of the Civil War shows how deeply aware many slaves were of the political and military events going on around them.

I remember well when Abraham Lincoln was elected. Boss and the madam had been reading the papers, when he broke out with the exclamation: "The very idea of electing an old rail splitter to the presidency of the United States! Well he'll never take his seat." When Lincoln was inaugurated, Boss, old Master Jack and a great company of men met at our house to discuss the matter, and they were wild with excitement. Was not this excitement an admission that their confidence in their ability to whip the Yankees, five or six to one, was not so strong as they pretended?

The war had been talked of for some time, but at last it came. When the rebels fired upon Fort Sumpter [sic], then great excitement arose. The next day when I drove Boss to town, he went into the store of one Williams, a merchant, and when he came out, he stepped to the carriage, and said: "What do you think? Old Abraham Lincoln has called for four hundred thousand men to come to Washington immediately. Well, let them come; we will make a breakfast of them. I can whip a half dozen Yankees with my pocket knife." This was the chief topic everywhere. Soon after this Boss bought himself a six shooter. I had to mold the bullets for him, and every afternoon he would go out to practice. By his direction, I fixed a large piece of white paper on the back fence, and in the center of it put a large black dot. At this mark he would fire away, expecting to hit it; but he did not succeed well. He would sometimes miss the fence entirely, the ball going out into the woods beyond. Each time he would shoot I would have to run down to the fence to see how near he came to the mark. When he came very near to it—within an inch or so, he would say laughingly: "Ah! I would have got him that time." (Meaning a Yankee soldier.) There was something very ludicrous in this pistol practice of a man who boasted that he could whip half a dozen Yankees with a jackknife. Every day for a month this business, so tiresome to me, went on. Boss was very brave until it came time for him to go to war, when his courage oozed out, and he sent a substitute; he remaining at home as a "home guard." One day when I came back with the papers from the city, the house was soon ringing with cries of victory. Boss said: "Why, that was a great battle at Bull Run. If our men had only known, at first, what they afterwards found out, they would have wiped all the Yankees out, and succeeded in taking Washington."

Right after the bombardment of Fort Sumpter [sic], they brought to Memphis the Union flag that floated over the fort. There was a great jubilee in celebration of this. Portions of the flag, no larger than a half dollar in paper money, were given out to the wealthy people, and these evidences of their treason were long preserved as precious treasures. Boss had one of these pieces which he kept a long time; but, as the rebel cause waned these reminders of its beginning were less and less seen, and if any of them are now in existence, it is not likely that their possessors will take any pride in exposing them to view.

As the war continued we would, now and then, hear of some slave of our neighborhood running away to the Yankees. It was common when the message of a Union victory came to see the slaves whispering to each other: "We will be free." I tried to catch everything I could about the war, I was so eager for the success of the Union cause. These things went on until Boss came hurrying in one morning, right after breakfast, calling to me: "Lou, Lou, come; we have a great victory! I want to go up and carry the boys something to eat. I want you and Matilda to get something ready as quickly as you can." A barrel of flour was rolled into the kitchen, and my wife and I "pitched in" to work. Biscuit, bread, hoe-cake, ham, tongue—all kinds of meat and bread were rapidly cooked; and, though the task was a heavy one for my wife and me, we worked steadily; and, about five o'clock in the afternoon the things were ready. One of the large baskets used to hold cotton was packed full these provisions. Our limbs ached from the strain of the work, for we had little help. One reason for the anxiety of the Boss for the preparation of this provision for the soldiers was that he knew so many in one of the companies, which was known as the "Como Avengers," and he had a son, a nephew and a brother of his wife connected with it; the latter a major on Gen. Martin's staff. On the following morning I got up early, and hurried with my work to get through, as I had to go to the post office. Madam hurried me off, as she expected a letter from her husband, who had promised to write, at the earliest moment, of their friends and relatives. I rushed into the city, at full speed, got some letters and a morning paper, and, returning as rapidly as possible, gave them to her. She grasped them eagerly, and commenced reading the paper. In a short time I heard her calling me to come to her. I went in, and she said, in great excitement: "Louis, we want to have you drive us into town, to see the Yankee prisoners, who are coming through, at noon, from Shiloh." I went and told Madison to hitch up, as soon as he could. In the meantime I got myself ready, and it was not long before we were off for the city. The madam was accompanied by a friend of hers, a Mrs. Oliver. We were at the station in plenty of time. About twelve o'clock the train from Shiloh drew into the station; but the prisoners that were reported to be on board were missing—it proved to be a false report. While they were looking for the prisoners, Mrs. Oliver saw Jack, a servant of Edward McGee, brother of madam. "Oh! Look," said Mrs. Oliver, "there is Edward's Jack. Lou, run and call him." In a minute I was off the carriage, leaving the reins in madam's hands. Jack came up to the carriage, and the women began to question him: "Where is your Master, Ed," asked both of them. "He is in the car, Missis—he is shot in the ankle," said Jack. In a minute the women were crying. "I was going to get a hack," said Jack, "to—" "No, No!" said both of them. "Go, Lou, and help Jack to bring him to our carriage. You can drive him more steadily than the hackman." Jack and I went to the car, and helped him out, and after some effort, got him into our carriage. Then I went and got a livery hack to take the women and his baggage home. When we reached home, we found there old Mrs. Jack McGee, mother of the madam, Mrs. Charles Dandridge, Mrs. Farrington, sisters of madam, and Fanny, a colored woman, Edward's housekeeper and mistress—a wife in all but name. All of these had come to hear the news of the great battle, for all had near relatives in it.

Source: Louis Hughes. *Thirty Years a Slave: From Bondage to Freedom: The Institution of Slavery as Seen on the Plantation and in the Home of the Planter*. Milwaukee, WI: Southside Printing Co., 1896, 111–116.

FURTHER READING

Ball, Charles. 1837. *Slavery in the United States: A Narrative of the Life and Adventures of Charles Ball*. New York: John S. Taylor.

Blassingame, John, ed. 1977. *Slave Testimony: Two Centuries of Letters, Speeches, Interviews, and Autobiographies*. Baton Rouge: Louisiana State University Press.

Breeden, James O., ed. 1980. *Advice among Masters: The Ideal in Slave Management in the Old South*. Westport, CT: Greenwood.

Camp, Stephanie. 2004. *Closer to Freedom: Enslaved Women and Everyday Resistance in the Plantation South*. Chapel Hill: University of North Carolina Press.

Campbell, Israel. 1861. *An Autobiography. Bond and Free: Or, Yearnings for Freedom, from My Green Brier House. Being the Story of My Life in Bondage, and My Life in Freedom*. Philadelphia: printed by the author.

Douglass, Frederick. 1845. *Narrative of the Life of Frederick Douglass, an American Slave. Written by Himself*. Boston, MA: Antislavery Office.

Drew, Benjamin, ed. 2008. *The Refugee: Narratives of Fugitive Slaves in Canada*. Toronto, Canada: Dundurn Press.

Fett, Sharla M. 2000. *Working Cures: Healing, Health, and Power on Southern Slave Plantations*. Chapel Hill: University of North Carolina Press.

Genovese, Eugene D. 1972. *Roll Jordan Roll: The World the Slaves Made*. New York: Pantheon Books.

Glymph, Thavolia. 2008. *Out of the House of Bondage: The Transformation of the Plantation Household*. New York: Cambridge University Press.

Hammond, James Henry. 1858. "Debate over Kansas, LeCompton Constitution." Congressional Globe 35th Congress, 1st Session. March 4. http://memory.loc.gov/ammem/amlaw/lwcglink.html

Hughes, Louis. 1897. *Thirty Years a Slave: From Bondage to Freedom: The Institution of Slavery as Seen on the Plantation and in the Home of the Planter*. Milwaukee, WI: South Side Printing Company.

Johnson, Walter. 1999. *Soul by Soul: Life inside the Antebellum Slave Market*. Cambridge, MA: Harvard University Press.

Johnson, Walter. 2017. *River of Dark Dreams: Slavery and Empire in the Cotton Kingdom*. Cambridge, MA: Harvard University Press.

Kemble, Frances Anne. 1863. *Journal of a Residence on a Georgian Plantation in 1838–1839*. New York: Harper & Brothers.

Martin, Jonathan. 2004. *Divided Mastery: Slave Hiring in the American South*. Cambridge, MA: Harvard University Press.

Moore, John Hammond. 1993. *A Plantation Mistress on the Eve of the Civil War: The Diary of Keziah Goodwyn Hopkins Brevard, 1860–1861*. Columbia: University of South Carolina Press.

Northup, Solomon. 1853. *Twelve Years a Slave: Narrative of Solomon Northup, a Citizen of New-York, Kidnapped in Washington City in 1841, and Rescued in 1853*. Auburn, NY: Derby and Miller.

Schwalm, Leslie A. 1997. *A Hard Fight for We: Women's Transition from Slavery to Freedom in South Carolina*. Champaign: University of Illinois Press.

Stringfellow, Thornton. 1856. *Scriptural and Statistical Views in Favor of Slavery*. Richmond, VA: J. W. Randolph.

Zaborney, John J. 2012. *Slaves for Hire: Renting Enslaved Laborers in Antebellum Virginia*. Baton Rouge: Louisiana State University Press.

6
INTELLECTUAL LIFE

Perhaps the most powerful expression of the meaning of intellectual life for enslaved African Americans can be found in the 1845 *Narrative of the Life of Frederick Douglass: An American Slave*. That work, which was to play an enormous role in the antislavery movement before the Civil War, told white readers that enforced ignorance, perhaps even more than violence itself, was the most powerful tool in the hands of slaveholders. In one dramatic episode, Douglass recalled the day when his master, Hugh Auld, discovered his Northern-born wife teaching young Frederick to read and spell. Incandescent with rage he commanded her to stop and proclaimed that knowledge would make any slave "unmanageable and of no value to his master." Learning of any kind, he insisted "would make him unfit to be a slave." For Douglass, Hugh Auld's panicked outburst had exactly the opposite result from the one intended because it revealed to him that the deepest sources of slaveholders' power rested in their ability to control the mental world of those they owned. "I now understood . . . the white man's power to enslave the black man," Douglass wrote. Although he no longer had the aid of his mistress in learning to read and write, his desire to obtain those skills and to acquire knowledge through them became insatiable. "From that moment," he later insisted, "I understood the pathway from slavery to freedom" (Douglass 1845, 33).

As in the discussion of their political life, understanding the intellectual life of enslaved people in the American South requires new concepts and definitions that are appropriate to the experiences of oppressed people. At a time when the intellectual life of white Americans was shaped by rising literacy rates, the creation of public schools in parts of the United States, and the proliferation of institutions of higher learning, enslaved African Americans were denied, often by the law itself, any of these advantages. Yet despite this, enslaved people did not, as their masters so often insisted, lack curiosity about the world they lived in, and they recognized that various forms of knowledge were necessary in order to survive and to ultimately resist the system of slavery. The narratives of former slaves like Frederick Douglass, moreover, demonstrate the ability of some enslaved people to make significant contributions to the intellectual life of the United States, in this case its rich antislavery culture. Douglass, in particular, fits the definition of an "organic intellectual," a concept pioneered by the twentieth-century Italian social critic Antonio Gramsci. For Gramsci, an organic intellectual is someone who rises out of an oppressed social condition to level a penetrating attack on the oppressive system or ideology. Reflecting the "specific working conditions and cultural milieu with which

Frederick Douglass (1818–1895), who became the foremost African American leader of the nineteenth century, was born a slave on Maryland's Eastern Shore. His *Narrative of the Life of Frederick Douglass, An American Slave* was published in 1845 and included a scathing critique of slavery. It also documented the role of slave literacy in fomenting resistance to the system. (Library of Congress)

they are involved," such figures express the feelings and aspirations of their entire social group (Chrisman 2013, 68). As we have seen, enslaved people rejected the racist ideology of paternalism that slaveholders used to defend the system, and they used all the ideas at their disposal, both religious and secular, to resist its hold on their own mental worlds. While only a successful escape from slavery allowed some to express that rejection in its most developed form, their writings should be seen as an extension of the ongoing intellectual resistance on plantations throughout the South.

SLAVERY AND LITERACY IN THE ANTEBELLUM SOUTH

Soon after the establishment of slavery during the colonial period, Southern slaveholders became aware that reading, writing, and other forms of formal learning among slaves constituted a serious threat to the system. This position sometimes put them at odds with Anglican missionaries or evangelical preachers who hoped to encourage Bible reading as part of their attempts to convert enslaved people to Christianity. Nonetheless, planters in both South Carolina and George feared that printed or written documents might be used to foment insurrection, and thus they prohibited whites from teaching literacy to slaves well before the American Revolution. The desire for knowledge among the slaves themselves, however, was extremely strong, and authorities in South Carolina remained concerned that slaves were holding "underground" meetings to obtain various forms of "mental instruction." The result was another law, passed in 1800, that made such meetings among both free and enslaved African Americans a criminal offense and punishable by up to twenty lashes. This law, as historian Heather Williams has noted, encouraged authorities to seek out secret gatherings of slaves that occurred before dawn or after sunset, to "break down doors" and "disperse" those who were engaging in prohibited activity (Williams 2007, 13).

Although these statutes suggest a long-standing desire on the part of slaveholders to prevent slaves from obtaining literacy, a more systematic legal assault on slave learning occurred during the 1830s in response to the twin threats of abolitionist sentiment in the North and Nat Turner's 1831 rebellion in Southampton County, Virginia. In contrast to the moderate, gradual tone of antislavery sentiment in the early republic, the abolitionism of the 1830s insisted on the sinfulness of slavery and demanded its immediate abolition.

The enormous volume of printed material circulated widely by abolitionists during the 1830s, moreover, was highly confrontational in tone, condemning the Southern slave system as utterly corrupt and ungodly. Some of this material, especially the incendiary *Appeal to the Colored Citizens of the World* written by black abolitionist David Walker, was carried into the South by African American sailors and secretly disseminated among free and enslaved black people. The resulting fear among whites produced a new and more punitive set of statutes throughout the South prohibiting black literacy, including a law in North Carolina that overtly acknowledged the link between all forms of learning and slave resistance. "The teaching of slaves to read and write has a tendency to excite dissatisfaction in their minds and to produce insurrection and rebellion, to the manifest injury of the citizens of this state" (Williams 2007, 15). Frederick Douglass's master used slightly different language to express his disapproval of slave literacy, but his sentiments echoed those of the vast majority of slaveholders.

Nat Turner's violent rebellion simply reinforced the growing fear that slaves were getting ahold of dangerous ideas through access to the written word. Turner was a literate black preacher, and his infamous *Confessions* demonstrated that he had forged a powerful critique of slavery through his distinctive readings of biblical texts. A wave of laws followed, indicating not only how much whites feared black literacy but also how they believed such skills were being spread. Alabama's laws, for example, criminalized the teaching of slaves, prohibited the unauthorized interaction between free blacks and slaves, and outlawed all black preaching unless at least five slaveholders were present to ensure that it was confined to acceptable topics. Indicating their belief that at least some significant part of the slave population had become literate, moreover, many Southern states simply banned the circulation of any and all abolitionist material. Both Virginia and Mississippi, for example, prohibited any printed material calling into question the legitimacy of slavery with whites facing a $1,000 fine and three-month term in state prison for breaking Mississippi's ban. Although the slaveholders in these states clearly hoped to inoculate their own white populations against the possible "contamination" of antislavery sentiment, their laws were especially concerned with the effect of such sentiments on the slaves themselves (Camp 2004, 104). As a justice of the Georgia Supreme Court put it, "Everything must be interdicted which is calculated to render the slave discontented" (Genovese 1972, 562).

Despite the intensifying suspicion of black literacy in the antebellum South, enslaved people continued to acquire it during the years before the Civil War. Although it is impossible to know precisely how many slaves were able to read, it is likely around 5 percent of the total population, with a higher percentage of literate slaves living in urban parts of the South. Yet since plantations were dispersed throughout the rural South, it was difficult for state or local authorities to monitor the extent to which anti-literacy laws were being followed by slaveholding families, and historians have identified a variety of contexts in which learning occurred. Some planter families, for example, especially those who lacked the services of white overseers, occasionally needed the help of literate slaves in matters of business and thus encouraged limited forms of education in reading and basic mathematics. Ned Walker who grew up a slave on a large plantation in upcountry, South Carolina, vividly recalled his young master's dismissive response when he was told that teaching his slaves to read and write was a violation of the law. "To hell wid de law, I got to have somebody dat can read and write 'mong de servants" (Rawick 1973, 3: 178). Walter Long, another former slave from South Carolina, recalled that his master had been a well-educated "businessman" and that the mistress taught many of the slaves "how to read, write and figure, 'nough to help us in small business" (Rawick 1973, 3: 119). It is clear that slaves who were trusted or useful members of the household or plantation system sometimes received instruction, regardless of the larger prohibitions on black literacy.

Along with the practical need for masters to teach perhaps one or two slaves how to read, other members of the white family also offered instruction under certain circumstances. Plantation mistresses, sometimes motivated by a sense of religious obligation or familial leadership, responded favorably to their slaves' efforts to read. Caroline Farrow's mistress, for example, insisted that all of her household slaves attend her church and appears to have responded to their own desire to read the scriptures for themselves. "She would often teach us to read and write at home when we would try to learn," Farrow recalled (Rawick 1973, 2: 39–40). Another former slave remembered that his mistress had fought with her husband over her insistence on teaching the slaves to read the Bible but reported with satisfaction that his objections did not deter her. "I learned how to spell considerable," he insisted, "and afterwards I got so I could read a little" (Blassingame 1977, 417). These actions were rare, however, and indicated a willingness among certain slaveholding families to defy not only the law but also the widespread view that educating slaves was dangerous. Former Texas slave Jerry Moore told a Federal Writers' Project interviewer that his mistress Fanny Van Zandt and her daughters "shared with their darkies and larned 'em all how to read." The Van Zandt's neighbors, however, were extremely unhappy with this practice and referred to the slaves on their farm as "Van Zandt's free niggers" and "wouldn't have none" of them on their property (Rawick 1973, 5: 121).

The response of the Van Zandt's neighbors was far more indicative of Southern white attitudes toward black literacy, which forced most enslaved people to learn in secret. Mandy Jones, a former slave from Mississippi interviewed during the 1930s, provided a fascinating description of what she called "pit schools," secret places where illegal learning took place. "Dey would dig pits, an' kiver the spot wid bushes and vines . . . and de slaves would slip out de Quarters at night, an go to dese pits" where another member of the slave community "dat had some learnin would have a school." While Jones did not specify the times when instruction took place, it is likely that most of it happened after dark or on Sunday when, at least on many plantations, no fieldwork was required. Jones did testify, however, to the importance of these "pit schools" to the larger history of African education in the South during the era of slavery and emancipation. She recalled that an enslaved man named Gunn, whose master had taught him to read, started a "pit school" in her neighborhood and that his son Henry had learned to read there. When the Civil War ended, Henry used the knowledge he had acquired in his father's "pit" to start a formal school for "de cullud chilluns" where Jones received instruction. "He was my onlies' teacher," she remembered, "we learned firs' de ABC . . . yo knows how it goes" (Berlin, Favreau, and Miller 1998, 206).

Mandy Jones also alerted her interviewers to another clever strategy that enslaved people employed to obtain literacy. "De way de cullud folks would learn to read was from de white chillun," she recollected. When white children left school with their books in hand, she reported, they liked nothing better than to "slip off somewhere" and teach their black playmates the lessons they had just learned from their own teachers (Berlin, Favreau, and Miller 1998, 206). This method took various forms such as that of Thomas H. Jones, an enslaved man born in North Carolina, whose intense desire for books and relentless drive for literacy led him to pay a young white boy named Hiram to instruct him. Meeting Hiram secretly each day in a stable near the print shop where he worked, Jones paid six cents for basic education in the alphabet and simple phonetics. Although the arrangement was soon ended by Hiram's father, Jones had learned enough to allow him to improve his skills without a teacher, and he secretly pored over his little spelling book, carefully hiding it among the shop's barrels each night. Surprised one afternoon by his master, Jones only had time to toss his book away before facing a furious interrogation by a suspicious owner who was certain he was stealing. When he refused to answer satisfactorily, the master whipped him so mercilessly that he could not remove his blood-soaked shirt without "tearing off some of the skin with it." But in language that testified to the enormous value he placed on books and reading, Jones later wrote that he "got well of my mangled back, and my book was as still left. This was my best, my constant friend" (Jones 1858, 17). Jones's hard-won literacy allowed him to play an important role in the abolitionism and civil rights activism in the North following his escape from slavery in 1849.

Like Frederick Douglass, Thomas Jones saw reading and writing as a path to personal empowerment, but there was a more practical reason why many enslaved people hoped to acquire the ability to write. As historian Heather Williams has shown, writing skills allowed slaves to forge documents that could lead directly to freedom itself, a fact that was certainly not lost on slaveholders. Enslaved Tennessean James Fisher, for example, was furious with his owner for separating him from his mother and began copying down words on paper even before he had any idea what they meant, just in case the chance arose for him to write out his own pass. "I copied every scrap of writing I could find," he wrote, "and thus learned to write a tolerable hand" (Williams 2007, 22). Like Jones, Fisher paid a white man to tutor him but was discovered with writing implements before he could complete his pass. Other enslaved people were more successful, however, and there are numerous examples of slaves who used their literacy skills in escaping from slavery entirely. Many of the advertisements offering rewards for the return of escaped slaves reported that the fugitive in question had forged either a pass or papers identifying him or her as a free person. It is grotesque but not surprising that owners periodically threatened to cut of the hands or fingers of slaves whom they suspected of learning to write.

This 1863 photograph of Isaac and Rosa, emancipated slave children from the free schools of Louisiana, illustrates the intense desire for literacy among all enslaved African Americans. Long denied access to education, freed people sought all forms of learning, even in the midst of the Civil War. (Library of Congress)

Along with covert strategies for obtaining education, there were a few direct attempts to challenge the enforced illiteracy that characterized the Southern slave system. Perhaps the most dramatic was the case of Margaret Crittenden Douglass, a Southern white woman who set up a school in Norfolk, Virginia, in direct violation of the state's anti-literacy law. Although Douglass herself had owned slaves and, by her own profession, was not an abolitionist, she and her teenage daughter Rosa felt compelled by "feelings of humanity" to offer instruction to the "free colored children" of Norfolk, Virginia. Seemingly unaware that Virginia's anti-literacy laws prohibited the teaching of free as well as enslaved blacks, their school eventually enrolled as many as twenty-five students who made rapid progress in basic literacy and mathematical skills. Douglass later argued that her belief in the legality of teaching free black children was based on the fact that many of the city's churches operated Sunday schools where both free *and* enslaved children received instruction each week by prominent members of the white community. In May 1853, however, the Norfolk City constable raided the school, arrested Douglass, took down the names of the children and their parents, and then herded all of them to city court for examination by the mayor.

After being served with a grand jury indictment two months later, Douglass appeared for trial in city court where she was convicted of violating several explicit provisions of Virginia's anti-literacy law. In her own final speech to the jury, however, Douglass defended her actions as fully justified by moral and religious convictions, and they were moved enough by it to impose the nominal sentence of a $1 fine. Unfortunately, Judge Richard Baker, who presided in the case, regarded Douglass's activities as far more dangerous and overruled the jury in favor of a month-long prison sentence. His final opinion in the case clearly indicates the widespread belief among slaveholders that instructing free blacks in Virginia amounted to teaching the slaves themselves and would result in the overthrow of the whole system of slavery. Laws like the one Margaret Douglass had violated, he proclaimed, were necessary for the "self-preservation and protection" of the slave states, lest slaves learn to read incendiary abolitionist literature that was designed to "stir up insubordination among our slaves." In the early 1850s, moreover, Virginia slaveholders like Judge Baker were becoming increasingly anxious about slave escapes and rebellion, which made it especially important to suppress activities like those of Margaret Douglass. "Teaching the negroes to read and write is made penal by the laws of this state," he told Douglass, because otherwise they might easily be induced to "cut our throats" (Douglass 1854, 47–48).

Like Hugh Auld, who angrily forbade his wife to teach Frederick Douglass to read, men like Judge Baker clearly recognized that their ability to control enslaved people's bodies required the suppression of critical sources of information. But the ability to do so was, in some ways, a losing battle as enslaved people found numerous ways to obtain the very ideas slaveholders were eager to deny them. Indeed, the very fact that so many Southern states passed, and at least sometimes enforced, such stringent laws indicates their very real concern that literacy skills were spreading into the slave population. It is also worth noting that in the case of Margaret Douglass, the state of Virginia levied a harsh criminal penalty on an otherwise respectable white woman whose actions, rooted as they were in religious and moral commitment, elicited the sympathies of at least some segment of Norfolk's white community. In a society that otherwise placed an extremely high value on literacy, the necessity of sending a woman like Margaret Douglass to prison for teaching children to read the Bible raised implicit questions about the legitimacy of the slave system itself. In their intense desire for learning and their willingness to take risks in acquiring it, therefore, enslaved African Americans forced the white South to reveal the glaring contradictions at the heart of their society.

THE MEANINGS OF LITERACY

While slaveholders feared that literate slaves might read abolitionist literature or forge passes, the deepest threat posed by reading was its capacity to provide enslaved people with understandings of themselves that differed dramatically from the crass, stereotyped identities imposed upon them by their owners. While it is certainly true that slave families, communities, and religious convictions also provided critical sources of identity and meaning, access to books and learning opened even deeper and sharper understandings of the world and provided a foundation for resisting the power of proslavery ideas. Paternalism, the proslavery racist ideology of the slaveholding class, insisted that enslaved people were fundamentally inferior to whites and incapable of living independently of them. As such, the identity of slaves was to be rooted in their dependent relationship to masters whose claim to their labor was understood as a legitimate return for the "civilization" conferred upon them by supposedly benevolent Southern whites. The notion that slaves occupied their "proper" place in Southern society was reinforced constantly through the differences in food, clothing, living conditions, and personal freedoms. In this environment, access to countervailing views could be revelatory and offer new possibilities of mental freedom.

For many enslaved people, the process of becoming literate amounted to something akin to a religious conversion experience in which a new sense of self was born. To Frederick Douglass, it was as if "the silver trump of freedom had roused my soul to eternal wakefulness." After encountering highly developed antislavery ideas for the first time in his life, he recalled, "freedom now appeared, to disappear no more forever. It was heard in every sound and seen in everything" (Douglass 1845, 41). Thomas Jones, who endured a brutal beating rather than allow his master to take a book from him, said that even before he knew how to read the letters on the page, he sensed intuitively that simple possession of a book had the potential to change his life forever. "I hid my book in my bosom, and hurried on to my work, conscious that a new era in my life was opening upon me through the possession of this book," he later wrote. "It seemed to me now, that, if I could learn to read and write, this learning might . . . point out to me the way to freedom" (Jones 1858, 13). Ironically, it was the masters' insistence on preventing slaves from becoming literate that, at least in part, generated such intense desire to gain access to printed materials. The fundamental relationship between literacy and power was not lost on enslaved people whose oppression was partly rooted in written documents like bills of sale, wills, passes, and laws.

The radical shift in perception that Douglass and Jones expected when they acquired literacy was far from fanciful, and there are numerous examples of enslaved people whose lives were altered by the words they found in books. Since many slaves learned to read in order to have access to the Bible, it was often there that they found antidotes to the proslavery notion that human bondage was somehow natural or morally legitimate. Taught to read in secret by his master's son, enslaved North Carolinian James Curry found the Bible full of ideas that undercut his master's authority. "I learned that it was contrary to the revealed will of God, that one man should hold another as a slave," he wrote after escaping from the South. While he had heard other slaves say that "we ought not to be held as slaves" and "that our fore-fathers and mothers were stolen from Africa, where they were free men and free women," his Bible reading provided him with what he regarded as an authoritative basis for condemning slavery. The masters' defense of slavery as the natural position for an inferior or degraded race of people unraveled for Curry as he read Acts 17:12, stating that "God hath made of one blood all nations of men to dwell on all the face of the earth" (Williams 2007, 23). As in the narratives of other literate escaped slaves, it is clear that Curry's eventual decision to risk the dangers of flight stemmed in large part from their encounter with antislavery ideas in printed form.

Enslaved men who could read the Bible not only found subversive ideas there but also gained status within the slave community and opportunities to spread the message they had encountered. One former slave, for example, reported that the slave community regarded literate men as ideal candidates for preaching and called upon them to read from the Bible "at times and places unknown to the master" (Cade 1935, 330). Since slaves suspected that white preachers quoted selectively from the scriptures in order to defend and uphold slavery, literate slave preachers were critical in providing an alternative reading of the holy texts. Slave communities recognized this and made sacrifices for those who could open up such reading to the group. One ex-slave named Byrd Day reported that when his community discovered he was literate, they pooled their money, purchased a Bible for him, and agreed to work on his provision grounds so that he would have time to study the scriptures and preach to them on Sunday. The literate black preacher, as one scholar has argued, was "their key to unlocking the Bible's power" to break the intellectual and moral foundations of slaveholder paternalism (Cornelius 1983, 182). And in addition to reading from the text and speaking from its authority, moreover, black preachers functioned as teachers themselves, using the biblical texts as reading primers so that their flock might find meaning and comfort on their own.

The most explosive connection among literacy, Bible reading, preaching, and slave rebellion can be seen in Nat Turner whose rebellion in 1831 prompted Southern states to clamp down on all forms of slave literacy. Turner appears to have possessed enormous intellectual gifts that allowed him to obtain literacy skills with "perfect ease" at an age so young that he had "no recollection whatever of learning the alphabet" (Greenberg 1996, 45). He claimed that his ability to spell out the names of any object around him was a source of "wonder in all the neighborhood, particularly among the blacks" and put him in a special category among his fellow slaves. Printed materials of any kind were intensely interesting to him, and he used his proximity to white children to obtain access to their school books. But it was through the reading of biblical prophecy, however, that Turner found inspiration for the war he would wage against the slaveholders of southeastern Virginia. The book of Revelation, with its images of holy violence, the destruction of the sinful, and the advent of a new Jerusalem, confirmed and focused Turner's revolutionary inclinations and provided him with the authority to lead his fellow rebels into battle.

Prior to his rebellion, however, Nat Turner used books to satisfy his insatiable curiosity about the workings of nature and about the practical arts of making paper and gunpowder, both important items in the conflict between enslaved people and those who claimed ownership over them. "In books," he later said, "I would find many things that the fertility of my own imagination had depicted to me before" (Greenberg 1996, 45). It is clear that Turner's captors were fascinated by his intellectual gifts, and his published *Confessions*, compiled by Virginia lawyer Thomas Gray, contained an extending rendering of his views on the meaning of scripture and Christian theology. Yet while Turner's captors went out of their way to depict him as an exotic, almost bizarre exception to the common run of enslaved people, his intense and relentless desire to obtain knowledge through books or other printed materials can be seen in the lives of many others, including Frederick Douglass and Thomas Jones. The role of literacy in Turner's rebellion was simply the most dramatic example of the way in which self-education enabled oppressed African Americans to see the world differently and to act decisively on what they had learned.

The Bible, however, was not the only place where literate slaves could find subversive ideas. Frederick Douglass's famous narrative provides the most comprehensive and self-conscious description of the ways in which secular reading could transform enslaved people's view of the world. Using various "stratagems" to make himself fully literate, the twelve-year-old Douglass came across a book entitled *The Columbian Orator*, a rhetoric textbook assembled by a New England editor that contained examples of great dialogues and speeches. Two texts in the anthology spoke directly to Douglass, a fictional antislavery "dialogue between a master and his slave" written by two English writers and a speech by the Irish playwright and parliamentarian Richard Sheridan who argued for the emancipation of oppressed Catholics in the British Empire. In the first selection, an unnamed slave about to be punished by his master for running away makes a sophisticated and ultimately successful argument for his natural right to freedom. To Douglass, the fact that the slave in the dialogue was "made to say some very smart as well as impressive things" seemed a radical departure from the assumed inferiority of enslaved people. In Sheridan's speech, moreover, he encountered "a bold denunciation of slavery and a vindication of human rights," which made a mockery of the slaveholders' racist paternalism (Douglass 1845, 39).

What Frederick Douglass encountered in the *Columbian Orator* were elements of the Anglo-American Enlightenment and its abiding belief that the human capacity for reason, freed from the shackles of oppression, superstition, and ignorance, was the key to all forms of progress. While not all Enlightenment intellectuals endorsed the abolition of slavery, they tended to regard the institution as cruel, irrational, and founded upon brute force rather than reason. For Douglass, exposure to these ideas was life changing because they allowed him to give a much sharper and intellectually precise shape to his own deepest longings for freedom. "The reading of these documents enabled me to utter my thoughts," he wrote, "and to meet the arguments brought forward to sustain slavery." Suddenly he was aware that the world contained sophisticated ideas antithetical to slavery and that there were important, highly educated people willing to express their opposition to the system in ways that would have been dangerous in the South. Whatever hold the paternalist ideology had exerted over his mind prior to his encounter with the *Columbian Orator*, Douglass now developed a scathing critique of slavery that drove him toward escape. "The more I read, the more I was led to abhor and detest my enslavers," he wrote. "I could regard them in no other light than a band of successful robbers who had . . . gone to Africa and stolen us from our homes and in a strange land reduced us to slavery" (Douglass 1845, 40).

SLAVE NARRATIVES: EX-SLAVES AS ORGANIC INTELLECTUALS

Because of the enormous obstacles placed in the way of enslaved people's ability to develop or express their intellectual lives, their most sophisticated contributions to American culture were made by those who escaped from slavery. In the years before the Civil War, ex-slave narratives formed an impressive assault on the proslavery ideology of the white South, giving enslaved people a distinct and authentic voice by which to counter the moral, religious, and economic defenses of the institution. While literate slaves within the South remained a vital source of resistance, escaped slaves who wrote about the horrors of the system were able to speak more freely and to reach a much wider audience. The popularity of their writings suggests that Northern readers were interested in the inner workings of the slave system and were at least willing to consider what slaves themselves had to say about it. Northern-born white abolitionists, who were often charged with exaggerating the brutality of a system of which they had little direct knowledge, saw the slave narratives as a convincing rebuttal to such accusations. Wherever possible, they encouraged escaped slaves to speak and write about their experiences, often publishing excerpts in abolitionist newspapers or pamphlets.

Yet while slave narratives represented an element of the antislavery movement in the North, it is crucial to recognize that the themes of these works emerged out of the daily experiences of enslaved people in the South. Escaped slaves like Frederick Douglass and Harriet Jacobs, argues scholar Robert Chrisman, can be understood as "organic intellectuals," a term developed in the early twentieth century by Italian social critic Antonio Gramsci. According to

Gramsci, social oppression is often maintained by the power of a dominant ideology, and we have seen the role that paternalism played in justifying the enslavement of African Americans in the antebellum South. To resist such domination, however, Gramsci suggests that oppressed groups frequently developed a counter ideology, an alternative system of thought that challenges the basic assumptions of their oppressors and opens an intellectual path toward resistance. Slave religion and access to antislavery ideas played this role in the daily lives of enslaved African Americans, providing an important mental barrier against the dehumanization and resignation that the brutal system of slavery might well have produced.

In this context, an organic intellectual, a member of the oppressed group with special access to skills and information, has an important role to play in giving systematic shape and development to the ideas of his or her group. Reared amid the same oppressive circumstances as other members of their class, organic intellectuals nevertheless find avenues for the collection and dissemination of ideas and information that challenges the power and cultural authority of the "ruling class" (Chrisman 2013, 67). When enslaved people escaped to the North during the antebellum period, they played just this role by producing highly effective narratives undermining the slaveholders' paternalistic image of their system. These narratives were written in the North, but ex-slaves wrote with a powerful sense of their connection to and responsibility for those they had left behind in the South. Frederick Douglass concluded his 1845 narrative with the earnest hope that his "little book may do something toward throwing light on the American slave system and hastening the glad day of deliverance to the millions of my brethren in bonds" (Douglass 1845, 125).

In giving precise intellectual shape to enslaved people's rejection of paternalism, the writings of escaped slaves developed a series of powerful themes that ran through many of their works. Among the most common was the notion that, despite the repeated claims of slaveholders, slavery was an utterly unnatural institution that distorted the moral development of both masters and slaves. In a variety of ways, they showed that slavery corrupted whites and led them to ignore basic standards of decency. Harriet Jacobs, for example, who had been a domestic slave in North Carolina before escaping to the North, wrote that as a twelve-year-old girl she had become the object of her middle-aged master's sexual desire and that he pursued her relentlessly while his own wife looked on in disgust and rage. Although Jacobs was taught "pure principles" by her grandmother, she told her readers that the constant exposure to her owner's unbridled lust had corrupted her childhood innocence. "He peopled my young mind with unclean images," she remembered. "The degradation, the wrongs, the vices, that grow out of slavery, are more than I can describe." While Jacobs provided her readers with a detailed description of her own highly unusual response to the persecution she endured as a young woman, she was always careful to connect her story to the larger experience of enslaved women. "If God has bestowed beauty upon her, it will prove her greatest curse," she wrote. "That which commands admiration in the white woman only hastens the degradation of the female slave" (Jacobs 1861, 44, 46). Responding directly to slaveholders' claim that the system was both natural and beneficial to the moral development of enslaved people, Jacobs demonstrated that slaveholding blunted the natural human responses to beauty and to childhood innocence.

Frederick Douglass makes a similar argument in his own narrative, focusing on the ways in which slaveholding required white people to ignore their own natural human impulses. As a child he was sent to live with owners in Baltimore and found that his new mistress, Sophia Auld, was "a woman of the kindest heart and finest feelings" and initially acted in maternal ways toward him. Douglass carefully explained to his readers that she had never owned a slave before her marriage and that as a result she was "unlike any other white woman I had ever seen." Over the next seven years, however, the narrative documents the destructive effects of slaveholding on Sophia Auld's character and its capacity to twist positive traits into negative ones. The cause, he argued, was the "irresponsible power" that slavery placed in the hands of whites which acted as a "fatal poison" upon the moral values of even the best-intentioned owner. Sophia's tender heart, he explained, "became a stone," and her calm demeanor was replaced by a "tiger-like fierceness" always on the lookout for signs her authority was not being respected. What had been the face of an angel soon became that of a "demon." Her intelligence and respect for education, which had initially led her to instruct Douglass in basic literacy, became a weapon by which to assert her authority over others. Because she was "an apt woman," she learned quite quickly that "education and slavery were incompatible with each other" (Douglass 1845, 32, 37). Like Harriet Jacobs, Douglass took pains to communicate what enslaved people throughout the South knew from their own direct experience, that slavery could turn white people into monsters.

For enslaved people, however, the most painful example of the ways in which slaveholders violated their vaunted paternalism was their callous decision to separate black families on the auction block. Though nearly all ex-slave narratives emphasize this common experience of loss and grief, one of the most powerful examples can be found in Solomon Northup's *Twelve Years a Slave*, written in 1853 by a free black man from the North who had been kidnapped and sold into slavery in Louisiana. Transported to New Orleans for sale, Northup met an enslaved woman named Eliza who hoped to be sold along with her two small children, Randall and Emily. It became clear, however, that the children would be sold separately, and Northup detailed not only the terrible agonies their mother suffered but also the brutality and indifference of the slave trader as the little girl begged them not to take her away. When Eliza tried to prevent the trader from taking Emily, "he struck her such a heartless blow, that she staggered backward, and was like to fall." Northup wrote, "Oh! how piteously then did she beseech and beg and pray that they might not be separated." He went on to say that Eliza was destroyed both mentally and physically by the loss of her children, beaten and abused because of her inability to work, and ultimately left to die alone and uncared for in her grief. He was aware that middle-class white readers of his narrative revered the family, especially the bonds between mother and child, and thus Northup's recounting of Eliza's tragic fate was an especially powerful rebuttal to proslavery thought. "This is no fiction, no exaggeration," he told his readers. "If I have failed in anything, it has been in presenting to the reader too prominently the bright side of the picture" (Northup 1853, 321).

Another key element of the proslavery ideology, which ex-slaves contested successfully, was its insistence that the system was the very basis of order in the South. Slaveholders routinely argued that in contrast to the growing labor conflict that accompanied the emergence of industrialization in the North, slavery had produced a stable social order that rested upon the authority of masters. The slave narratives, however, consistently painted a very different picture, one that depicted slaveholders or overseers as utter lawless tyrants who committed murder and other heinous acts without any legal accountability. Frederick Douglass described an overseer named Gore whose "savage barbarism" was symbolic of the endemic role of violence in the maintenance of slavery. After a slave named Demby ran to a nearby creek to relieve the pain from a flogging he had received from Gore, the brutal overseer raised his musket and took aim. "In an instant poor Demby was no more," Douglas wrote. "His mangled body sank out of sight, and blood and brains marked the water where he had stood." Almost as horrific as the murder itself was the fact that Gore was never held accountable for his homicidal actions after the master concluded that it was necessary as an example to other slaves. Rather than the orderly, law-bound society slaveholders so often celebrated, Douglass reminded his readers that the slaveholding South was a place where the "guilty perpetrator of one of the bloodiest and most foul murders goes unwhipped of justice, and uncensured by the community in which he lives" (Douglass 1845, 23–24).

Harriet Jacobs's narrative, moreover, made it clear that the slaveholders' descriptions of their society as a stable natural hierarchy masked a deep-seated fear of the slaves that sometimes resulted in indiscriminate brutality. In the weeks following Nat Turner's rebellion, for example, whites in Virginia and several neighboring states became hysterical and reacted with almost unimaginable brutality against innocent blacks. "Those who never witnessed such scenes can hardly believe what I know was inflicted at this time on innocent men, women, and children," she recalled. They were pulled from their dwellings and "whipped till the blood stood in puddles at their feet." Yet even in periods of relative calm, Jacobs reported that violence was constant and at times resulted in the most horrific atrocities. She knew a young slave named James who took to the woods to escape the whip of his sadistic master only to be captured, "cut with the whip from head to toe," washed in brine, and then locked into a cotton gin where he could barely move. After four days, his dead body was recovered from the wooden box, and it was discovered that his flesh had been eaten by "rats and vermin" perhaps while he was still alive. Jacobs took pains to tell her readers that the master who was responsible for this unspeakable murder was "highly educated" and "boasted the name and standing of a Christian" (Jacobs 1861, 98, 77).

Many of the slave narratives connected the lawless violence of white masters and overseers with their unrestrained sexual exploitation of black women. Solomon Northup, for example, explained that his master's infatuation with his female slave Patsey led to the most violent beating he witnessed in his twelve years as a slave in the South. Convinced that Patsey had just returned from a sexual liaison with a neighboring planter, Master Edwin Epps was consumed with jealous rage and ordered Northup to whip her. Stripped naked and tied to stakes in the ground, Patsey was whipped first by Northup and then, when he became too exhausted to continue, by Epps until he had literally flayed her skin. Frederick Douglass as a young child witnessed a similar scene in which his fourteen-year-old aunt Hester was confronted by her jealous master, who, like Edwin Epps, was furious that she had taken up with a young slave on a neighboring plantation. While the child Frederick Douglass cowered in a closet, the master cursed Hester profanely, ripped down the top of her dress, tied her to a doorframe, and whipped her until blood pooled at her feet. The narratives made it clear that incidents of this kind were quite common in the South and that slaveholders' claims about the moral benefits of slavery were nothing more than a thin mask concealing lawless outrages against basic human decency.

These examples were part of the larger argument made by these organic intellectuals that slaveholding was itself a sin, a violation of the Christian moral code. In doing so, they helped to advance the central ideas of the Northern antislavery movement, which called for the immediate abolition of the institution on the basis of its inherent sinfulness. Indeed, one clear indication of the intellectual achievement of the ex-slaves' narratives can be found in the overwhelming support they received from Northern reformers who regarded them as an authentic and highly original witness against slavery's intrinsic depravity. In his preface to Douglass's 1845 narrative, for example, abolitionist editor William Lloyd Garrison argued that Douglass's work proved beyond a doubt that the slaveholders' defenses of slavery were self-serving lies. Douglass, he argued, had shown that slavery was a system that "reduces those who by creation were crowned with glory and honor to a level with four-footed beasts, and exalts the dealer in human flesh above all that is called God!" (Douglass 1845, ix–x). Abolitionist minister and religious reformer Theodore Parker agreed but went even further in saying that slave narratives constituted the only example of a truly American literary genre, one that could not have been produced anywhere else in the world. "We have one series of literary productions that could be written by none but Americans," he told the graduating class at Colby College in 1849. "I mean the lives of Fugitive Slaves." Although Parker conceded that the narratives were not written by "men of superior culture," he seemed to sense that they were products of organic intellectuals, men and women who spoke from and for the collective experience of enslaved African Americans (Parker 1907, 37).

FOLK MEDICINE: HEALING KNOWLEDGE IN THE SLAVE COMMUNITY

So far in this chapter we have considered the intellectual life of enslaved people in traditional terms, focusing on issues of education, literacy, and the production of formal literary works in the form of ex-slave narratives. In this concluding section, we will examine a different, but equally significant form of intellectual life in the slave community's transmission and practice of healing knowledge or what might be called folk medicine. Drawing upon African healing practices that were passed from one generation to another, enslaved people used herbs, amulets, and charms along with social practices that were intended to restore those stricken with illness to full membership in the slave community. Slave healers who employed these methods, moreover, operated with profoundly different assumptions about illness and health from those of their masters. Rather than assessing health in relation to a person's ability to work, the overriding concern of white Southern planters, they understood it as the physical and emotional capacity to resist the dehumanizing effects of slavery itself. Since they did not make a distinction between matter and spirit, moreover, slave healers believed that the power to heal could be exercised by those who understood how to locate and deploy the restorative properties inherent in the natural world. Operating with these assumptions, slaves often placed greater confidence in the power of their own healers than in professionally trained white doctors acting on their owners' behalf.

Herb lore, or the power of sacred plants to provide healing, was a central element of the African healing tradition, and antebellum slaves combined it with Native American and European practices to develop a rich array of "herbal recipes" to treat various ailments. Due to the nature of their work, moreover, African American slaves developed an intimate and highly detailed knowledge of the natural landscape, especially its flora, which provided them with a "veritable pharmacy" of plant recipes. Pepper and dogwood tea, for example, were often used to treat fevers, while snakeroot was widely believed to relieve the symptoms associated with abdominal pain. Various kinds of tree bark were used to treat headaches or to rouse an afflicted person from a stupor or extended period of unconsciousness. Not everyone in the slave community was equally schooled in the ability to locate healing herbs, however, as this required a level of expertise and observational talent that only some members could master. One former slave from Maryland said that there were some elderly healers who could almost literally "read the woods just like a book" and were immediately able to locate the plant or bark that was needed to treat the specific ailment afflicting their patients (Fett 2000, 72). Whether or not the remedies prescribed by these healers produced biomedical results in our modern sense, their ability to "read the woods" should be understood as an element in the intellectual lives of enslaved people.

In addition to their ability to locate the correct healing plants, slave healers possessed a detailed knowledge of the complex preparations necessary to make them effective on patients. According to the traditions of slave folk medicine, sacred healing plants would be potent remedies only if they were harvested at precise moments in their growth cycle and then prepared in the correct way. The multiple uses of pokeberries, as medical historian Sharla Fett demonstrates, are a perfect example of the precise knowledge required in the preparation of healing cures. Depending upon when they were picked, what part of the plant was used, and what mixture was developed, pokeberries could treat rheumatism and boils or provide an energy boost in the early spring. Treatment for rheumatism required mixing the crushed berries with alcohol, while poultices for boils were made from the tops of the pokeberry leaves, and the energy drink could be made effective only with young leaves that appeared in the spring. Beyond the complexity of these preparations, moreover, healers had to be careful to avoid the potentially dangerous parts of this plant. "Healing with pokeweed required a practiced hand," Fett notes, "for the roots could be poisonous and the tops also became toxic as the plant matured" (Fett 2000, 74). The fact that white Southerners sometimes approached elderly slave healers for advice on how to locate and prepare their herbal remedies suggests that they too recognized their specialized knowledge. Unwilling or unable to seek the advice of white doctors, planter families were forced to seek the assistance of those who could "read the woods."

Yet if white families and their slaves shared a belief in herbal remedies, they operated from different assumptions about why such treatments were effective. Influenced by the scientific materialist principles that had emerged in Europe beginning in the seventeenth century, planter families saw plants as useful only for their positive effects upon the body. Sickness was understood as a physical phenomenon and treated accordingly. For enslaved people, however, illness was produced as much by malign spiritual and social forces as by physical causes, and thus, healing practices required attention to these causes. As a key aspect of their African spiritual heritage, for example, enslaved African Americans believed that physical suffering was often the direct result of conflict between members of the slave community or violations of community norms. Disrespect for parents, failure to honor ancestors, sexual transgressions, and stealing from other slaves might easily result in physical pain or affliction and thus required intervention from healers who could read the signs of supernatural causes. Conversely, a person might become ill because the person had been cursed by a "conjurer" who had the ability to deploy the power of roots or plants in bringing about a rival's illness or death. In this case, a cure could only be found in the deployment of an antidote prepared by an equally effective conjure doctor who understood the nature of the illness and wielded the "great power" of "hair and nail clippings, a piece of clothing or personal object belonging to the victim, [or] dirt from a person's footprint" (Raboteau 1978, 82). Enslaved people believed that in such cases white doctors were essentially useless because they understood illness only in a material sense and thus lacked any ability to respond in an effective way.

In general terms, the intellectual life of antebellum slaves provided them with another powerful tool to resist the dehumanizing effects of their enslavement. Although Southern whites insisted that slaves neither possessed nor wanted an intellectual life, this was just another facet of their propaganda campaign to defend their brutal system against its critics. Ironically, the attempts by slaveholders to criminalize literacy, to suppress access to information, and to punish all efforts by slaves to obtain education may itself be the most powerful evidence that the intellectual aspirations of enslaved people not only were strong but also presented a serious challenge to the system of slavery. Despite the extraordinary obstacles they faced, some African Americans did obtain literacy and found ways to document the daily lives of slaves and to produce a damning critique of the system's inhuman character. For those who remained in bondage, African traditions of healing combined with new ideas and practices developed in the context of the American South helped to ease the burdens of illness and affliction and offered a path toward wholeness in the midst of their daily trials.

DOCUMENT: THOMAS JONES, *THE EXPERIENCE OF THOMAS H. JONES, WHO WAS A SLAVE FOR FORTY-THREE YEARS* (1862)

Before his escape in 1849, Thomas Jones lived as a slave in Wilmington, North Carolina, where he worked as a domestic servant and as an assistant in his master's store. Hearing rumors that his wife and several children were about to be sold away from him, he helped them flee from slavery and then escaped himself by stowing away on a ship bound for New York City. In the mid-1850s, he wrote a narrative of his life under slavery in order to raise funds to purchase his son Edward who was still living as a slave in the South. In this excerpt from his narrative, Jones illustrates the intense determination of enslaved people to obtain literacy skills.

I had discovered that I could not get a spelling-book if I told what I wanted to do with it, and so I told a lie, in order to get it. I answered, that I wanted it for a white boy, naming one that lived at my master's, and that he had given me the money to get it with, and had asked me to call at the store and buy it. The book was then handed out to me, the money taken in return, and I left, feeling very rich with my long-desired treasure. I got out of the store, and, looking around to see that no one observed me, I hid my book in my bosom, and hurried on to my work, conscious that a new era in my life was opening upon me through the possession of this book. . . .

But I could not go on alone. I must get someone to aid me in starting or give up the effort to learn. This I could not bear to do. I longed to be able to read, and so I cast about me to see what I could do next. I thought of a kind boy at the bake-house, near my own age. I thought he would help me, and so I went to him, showed my book, and asked him to teach me the letters. He told their names and went over the whole alphabet with me three times. By this assistance I learned a few more of the letters, so that I could remember them afterwards when I sat down alone and tried to call them over. I could now pick out and name five or six of the letters in any part of the book. I felt then that I was getting along, and the consciousness that I was making progress, though slow and painful, was joy and hope to my sorrowing heart, such as I never felt before. I could not with safety go to the bake-house, as there I was exposed to detection by the sudden entrance of customers or idlers. I wanted to get a teacher who would give me a little aid each day, and now I set about securing this object. As kind Providence would have it, I easily succeeded, and on this wise: A little boy,

Hiram Bricket, ten years old, or about that age, came along by the store one day, on his way home from school, while my master was gone home to dinner, and James was in the front part of the store. I beckoned to Hiram to come round to the back door; and with him I made a bargain to meet me each day at noon, when I was allowed a little while to get my dinner, and to give me instruction in reading. I was to give him six cents a week. I met him the next day at his father's stable, the place agreed upon for our daily meeting; and, going into one of the stalls, the noble little Hiram gave me a thorough lesson in the alphabet. I learned it nearly all at that time, with what study I could give it by stealth during the day and night. And then again I felt lifted up and happy.

I was permitted to enjoy these advantages, however, but a short time. A black boy, belonging to Hiram's father, one day discovered our meeting and what we were doing. He told his master of it, and Hiram was at once forbidden this employment. I had then got along so that I was reading and spelling in words of two syllables. My noble little teacher was very patient and faithful with me, and my days were passing away in very great happiness under the consciousness that I was learning to read. I felt at night, as I went to my rest, that I was really beginning to be a man, preparing myself for a condition in life better and higher, and happier than could belong to the ignorant slave. And in this blessed feeling I found, waking and sleeping, a most precious happiness.

After I was deprived of my kind little teacher, I plodded on the best way I could myself, and in this way I got into words of five syllables. I got some little time to study by daylight in the morning, before any of my master's family had risen. I got a moment's opportunity at noon, and sometimes at night. During the day I was in the back store a good deal, and whenever I thought I could have five minutes to myself, I would take my book and try to learn a little in reading and spelling. If I heard James, or master Jones, or any customer coming in, I would drop my book among the barrels, and pretend to be very busy shoveling the salt or doing some other work. Several times I came very near being detected. My master suspected something, because I was so still in the back room, and a number of times he came very slyly to see what I was about. But at such times I was always so fortunate as to hear his tread or see his shadow on the wall in time to hide away my book.

When I had got along to words of five syllables, I went to see a colored friend, Ned Cowan, whom I knew I could trust. I told him I was trying to learn to read and asked him to help me a little.

He said he did not dare to give me any instruction, but he heard me read a few words, and then told me I should learn if I would only persevere as nobly as I had done thus far. I told him how I had got along, and what difficulties I had met with. He encouraged me and spoke very kindly of my efforts to improve my condition by getting learning. He told me I had got along far enough to get another book, in which I could learn to write the letters, as well as to read. He told me where and how to procure this book. I followed his directions, and obtained another spelling-book at Worcester's store, in Wilmington. Jacob showed me a little about writing. He set me a copy, first of straight marks. I now got me a box which I could hide under my bed, some ink, pens, and a bit of candle. So, when I went to bed, I pulled my box out from under my cot, turned it up on end, and began my first attempt at writing. I worked away till my candle was burned out, and then laid down to sleep.

Source: Thomas Jones. *The Experience of Thomas H. Jones, Who Was a Slave for Forty-Three Years*. Boston: Bazin & Chandler, 1862, 15–19.

FURTHER READING

Berlin, Ira, Marc Favreau, and Steven F. Miller, eds. 1998. *Remembering Slavery: African Americans Talk about Their Personal Experiences of Slavery and Emancipation*. New York: The New Press.

Blassingame, John, ed. 1977. *Slave Testimony: Two Centuries of Letters, Speeches, Interviews, and Autobiographies*. Baton Rouge: Louisiana State University Press.

Cade, John B. 1935. "Out of the Mouths of Ex-Slaves." *The Journal of Negro History* 20, no. 3 (July): 294–337.

Camp, Stephanie. 2004. *Closer to Freedom: Enslaved Women and Everyday Resistance in the Plantation South*. Chapel Hill: University of North Carolina Press.

Chrisman, Robert. 2013. "Black Studies, the Talented Tenth and the Organic Intellectual." *The Black Scholar* 43, no. 3 (Fall): 64–70.

Cornelius, Janet. 1983. "'We Slipped and Learned to Read': Slave Accounts of the Literacy Process, 1830–1865." *Phylon* 44, no. 3 (September): 171–186.

Douglass, Frederick. 1845. *Narrative of the Life of Frederick Douglass, an American Slave. Written by Himself*. Boston, MA: Antislavery Office.

Douglass, Margaret. 1854. *Educational Laws of Virginia: The Personal Narrative of Mrs. Margaret Douglass*. Boston, MA: John P. Jewett & Co.

Fett, Sharla M. 2000. *Working Cures: Healing, Health, and Power on Southern Slave Plantations*. Chapel Hill: University of North Carolina Press.

Genovese, Eugene D. 1972. *Roll Jordan Roll: The World the Slaves Made.* New York: Pantheon Books.

Greenberg, Kenneth, ed. 1996. *The Confessions of Nat Turner and Related Documents.* New York: Bedford/St. Martins.

Jacobs, Harriet. 1861. *Incidents in the Life of a Slave Girl. Written by Herself.* Boston: printed by the author.

Jones, Thomas H. 1858. *Experience and Personal Narrative of Uncle Tom Jones.* Boston: H. B. Skinner.

Northup, Solomon. 1853. *Twelve Years a Slave: Narrative of Solomon Northup, a Citizen of New-York, Kidnapped in Washington City in 1841, and Rescued in 1853.* Auburn, NY: Derby and Miller.

Parker, Theodore. 1907. *The American Scholar.* Boston, MA: American Unitarian Association.

Raboteau, Albert. 1978. *Slave Religion: The "Invisible Institution" in the Antebellum South.* New York: Oxford University Press.

Rawick, George P., ed. 1973. *The American Slave: A Composite Autobiography, vol. 2: South Carolina Narratives,* Part 2. Westport, CT: Greenwood Press.

Rawick, George P., ed. 1973. *The American Slave: A Composite Autobiography, vol. 3: South Carolina Narratives,* Parts 3 and 4. Westport, CT: Greenwood Press.

Rawick, George P., ed. 1973. *The American Slave: A Composite Autobiography, vol. 5: Texas Narratives,* Part 3. Westport, CT: Greenwood Press.

Williams, Heather. 2007. *Self-Taught: African American Education in Slavery and Freedom.* Chapel Hill: University of North Carolina Press.

7

RECREATIONAL LIFE

In November 1850, a detachment of the Richmond, Virginia, police entered the city's Washington Hotel and began arresting nearly one hundred African Americans, both free and enslaved, whose only crime was to attend a "grandiose" subscription ball being held in the basement (Takagi 1999, 102). Dressed in their finest dancing clothes, the ball-goers were just about to enter the dance floor when the police arrived, and instead of enjoying a rare evening of happy conviviality, they now faced criminal charges for participating in what the city authorities were calling an illegal assembly. The fact that the slaves at the ball carried passes from their owners specifically granting them permission to attend did not spare them from being paraded through the streets to the courthouse the next morning. Yet, as they were marched toward their uncertain fate that morning, they were no doubt surprised and heartened by the thousands of their fellow African American residents who came out to communicate their solidarity with the persecuted partygoers. Though Richmond's white population regarded this show of support as "idle curiosity" and perhaps itself an "unlawful assembly," it instead represented the determination of African Americans to assert their place in Southern society and to resist white attempts to control or prohibit their recreational activities. In the end, most of those who appeared before the court were released without charge.

As the example of the subscription ball arrests shows, white Southerners looked upon the recreational activities of enslaved people with mixed feelings. Focused intently on their ability to control and exploit black labor, slaveholders were generally reluctant to leave much time or opportunity for leisure or recreation. When slaves gathered in groups as large as the one in Richmond, they feared the possibility that subversive ideas would be exchanged or even rebellion plotted. At the same time, however, slaveholders also understood that some concession to the humanity of enslaved people was essential to ensure that they labored effectively. That meant that pauses in the otherwise-incessant demands for work were necessary for the physical and mental health of the people whose productive capacities were crucial to the functionality and profitability of the plantation. In general, then, planters permitted enslaved people to engage in recreation, including various forms of music, dance, holiday making, and different kinds of "frolics" as well as storytelling. But at the same time, they attempted to control or co-opt the recreational customs of slaves, hoping to use them in ways that furthered their own power and their ability to obtain the slaves' productive labor.

Fortunately, the recreational activities of slaves, like other aspects of their culture, proved impossible for slaveholders to fully control or direct. Because the recreational traditions of enslaved people were rooted in West African ways, slaveholders often missed the meaning or significance of their activities and failed to recognize the subtle forms of resistance they contained. Though slaveholders encouraged slaves to sing as they worked in order to speed up and maintain the pace of labor, for example, they paid little attention to what was being sung or the role of singing and dancing in forging bonds of solidarity within the slave community. The stories or folktales that slaves told one another and their children, moreover, were powerful weapons against the dehumanization of slavery and provided an important tool for the preservation of a distinctive African American culture and consciousness. The recreational lives of slaves, in other words, are yet another way to study the fundamental dynamics of power within the society of the antebellum South.

MUSIC

Music was an integral part of the lives of enslaved people who played and sang in a distinctive style that surprised, fascinated, and at times even frightened whites. The famous architect Benjamin Latrobe, who traveled through the Deep South in the early years of the nineteenth century, was unable to relate to the musical culture of enslaved people. Because his ear was trained to hear the music of the Western classical tradition, he used words like "savage," "uncouth," and "noise" to describe the singing and drumming he heard in New Orleans's Congo Square (Latrobe 1905, 180, 181). Other whites, such as the journalist and poet William Cullen Bryant, were more sympathetic to the musical expressions of the slaves, but they still found the sounds and styles "extravagant," "singularly wild," and difficult to process (Bryant 1884, 32). What neither Latrobe nor Bryant could fully understand was that the West African heritage of enslaved people had provided them with a rich array of rhythmic, tonal, and harmonic options for expressing themselves in musical form and laid the basis for the later emergence of blues, ragtime, and modern jazz.

Equally important, and equally confusing to white observers, was that the music of enslaved people was a participatory and improvisational activity rather than a performance and that in many cases it was inseparable from dance or other forms of physical motion. Although slave songs, whether explicitly religious or not, were often built around a simple line of melody, they left open spaces in which individuals could add their own melodic variations and created opportunities for singers or players to interact musically with those who were dancing or moving to the music. As a powerful expression of community solidarity and human uniqueness, the music of the slaves constituted a powerful rejection of the slave system itself.

Enslaved people used a variety of musical instruments that were brought from Africa during the Middle Passage and then modified over the centuries under New World slavery. Perhaps the most famous was the banjo, an instrument with a long neck with several strings stretched over a hollow bowl sometimes made of wood but even more commonly from a gourd. During the era of the slave trade, European traders and missionaries commented periodically on the rich array of stringed instruments played by Africans and sometimes described their construction in ways that suggest that they were prototypes of the banjo. Though they were known by different names, the term "banjo" emerged as a generic term for the four- or five-string version that enslaved people played in colonial and nineteenth-century America. Sometimes the fifth string of these instruments was shorter than the others and used as a "drone" or unfretted string as in the modern version of the banjo. In Africa, moreover, those who played stringed instruments similar to the banjo often combined their instrumental performances with storytelling. The *xalam*, which originated among the Wolof peoples of Senegal and Gambia, was played by special performers called *griots*, who were key figures at rituals of naming or in wedding ceremonies.

In nineteenth-century America, the banjo became an inseparable part of Southern plantation culture, and its spread from coastal plantations through the Cotton Kingdom of the Deep South followed the expansion of slavery itself. Eventually, white Southerners adopted the instrument themselves, and it became the primary "folk instrument" in the development of white roots music (Katz-Hyman and Rice 2011, 43). Yet if banjos eventually became key instruments in the development of American folk music more generally, historians Philip Gura and James Bollman have traced the history of the instrument through the seventeenth and eighteenth centuries and find abundant evidence that banjos were constructed and played exclusively by slaves during these years. Advertisements offering rewards for escaped slaves often mentioned that their fugitive being sought was skilled on the banjo, and one free black man living in New York was even known by his neighbors as "Billy Banjo." During the 1840s, when white musicians became interested in the banjo as part of the racist blackface minstrel shows, they "got their instruments and lessons primarily in the plantation South" (Gura and Bollman 1999, 24).

Another crucial instrument in the musical culture of enslaved people was the drum, another critical legacy of West African religion and culture. Observers of antebellum slaves seemed to see and hear drums almost everywhere in the plantation South, and the varieties of instruments appeared almost endless. There were drums made of old kettles, hollow gourds, and tree trunks covered with goatskins, as well as "cylindrical drums," "single-staved drums," and "cricket bat drums." Historians Shane and Graham White note that all these drums produced different sounds, either because of the material that made up the drum's membrane or the method by which that membrane was struck by the player. In the case of the "open-staved" drum, a slave drummer could raise or lower the pitch by squeezing or releasing the sides of the instrument with his or her legs to increase the tension on the membrane. The "cricket bat" drum that Benjamin Latrobe observed in Congo Square was made by creating an aperture in the side of a piece of wood that was about the length and width of a bat that was struck by a stick or some other implement. Both drums closely resemble instruments that were developed in West Africa prior to the slave trade and thus represent an important aspect of cultural survival under slavery. The different volumes, pitches, and timbres they were able to produce, moreover, allowed drummers to interact with or respond to one another as well as with those who were singing to or dancing along to the music: "drummers engaging with drummers, drummers with dancers, dancers with singers, and so on" (White and White 2005, 44–45). Because of the rhythmic and sonic complexity of the musical heritage they had preserved, enslaved musicians were able to produce a highly participatory and improvisational result.

The sounds of drumming made whites nervous, and Southern slaveholders feared that the sounds made by drums might be coded messages presaging some form of slave rebellion. In South Carolina, for example, whites believed that the Stono Rebellion of 1739, in which a group of enslaved people had killed whites and fled toward Spanish Florida, had been organized by the sound of beating drums. The notion that drums somehow "talked" and encouraged rebellion led some Southern states to pass outright bans on drumming, especially on Sundays when plantation discipline was relaxed due to Sabbath observance. Just after the rebellion, for example, South Carolina prohibited the "keeping of drums, horns, or other loud instruments" that might allow slaves to "call together or give sign or notice to one another of their wicked designs" (Thompson 2014, 102). But enforcing such bans was next to impossible as drums could be created out of any number of implements and they were small enough to conceal even when their sounds could be heard from afar. One enslaved man named Wash Wilson recalled that a sheep's rib or a cow's horn or a piece of scrap iron could serve as drum as could the hollow of a tree. He also remembered one fellow slave who sat behind a barrel which he struck with his fingers or hands and "iffen he git to feelin de music in he bones, he'd beat on dat barrel with he head" (White and White 2005, 47). Whatever state law might say about the legality of drumming, there was no way to ban sheep ribs, cow horns, barrels, and heads.

Fiddles were also present in the slave quarters on Southern plantations during the antebellum period and, like the drum and the banjo, there were West African bowed instruments such as the one-stringed *goge* that prepared African American slaves to play fiddles. But enslaved people such as Andy Brice of South Carolina appear to have learned the specific techniques of fiddle playing from whites. "One day I see Mars Thomas a twistin' de ears on a fiddle and rosinin' de bow," he told a Federal Writers' Project interviewer in the 1930s. "Sumpin bust loose in me and sing all through my head and tingle in my fingers. I make up my mind right den and there to save and buy me a fiddle" (Katz-Hyman and Rice 2011, 219). In addition to the banjo, the drum, and the fiddle, enslaved people created and played a variety of other instruments, including the pan flute or quill. The quill was made from cane or reed tubes of varying sizes and lengths to produce different pitches and then tied together into a row or rack. Blowing over the open end of the quill produced a sound not unlike the flute, and the instrument could be played in conjunction with a banjo or fiddle at corn shuckings or frolics. Accomplished players who developed the capacity to play notes in quick succession were respected by fellow slaves for their virtuosity. "Boy I sho' could blow you out a dar wid a rack a quills," remembered former slave George Fleming. "Gals wouldn't look at nobody else when I start blowin'" (Eisnach and Covey 2009, 184).

Enslaved people were resourceful in making or purchasing musical instruments, but the most common instrument they possessed was, of course, the human voice. Though clearly an aspect of the recreational life of slaves, singing appears to have been inseparable from life itself under slavery in the antebellum South. Slaves sang while they were working in the fields, cooking food, worshipping, dancing, or caring for children, and, as one contemporary observer put it, "always and everywhere they are singing" (White and White 2005, 40). White observers were often especially struck by the relationship between singing and the most intense forms of work, even in contexts where it seemed inappropriate or incongruous. Fredrika Bremer, a Swedish woman who toured the South in the early 1850s, was fascinated by the vigorous singing of half-naked slaves whose job was to feed the fiery furnaces on the steamboat she took down the Mississippi River. Describing the scene as "fantastic" and "strange," she could not help but admire their ability to turn a dangerous and brutally demanding task into a kind of performance (Bremer 1853, 174). Yet the integration of singing into all aspects of daily life was yet another West African tradition that enslaved people brought with them and preserved into the antebellum period.

Among the most distinctive elements of slave singing was its improvisational character. When enslaved people sang, they did so in a highly creative and interactive way that began with familiar melodies and lyrics but quickly branched out into new forms of expression. As historians Shane and Graham White have so aptly described it, a song was "never a stable text and an unvarying tune" but rather "a frame to be filled as the moment dictated" (White and White 2005, 59). Indeed, lines or stanzas from one well-known song could be used either fully or partially in an entirely different one if the singer or group of singers chose to do so. Often, a lead singer would sing in ways that would invite a response from the others who might in turn respond in ways that influenced the direction of the song. The ability of a lead singer to improvise effectively with both the tune and lyrics, moreover, was regarded as a mark of virtuosity among the slaves and elevated them to positions of local fame. Former slave Francis Fedric recalled one evening in which a slave named Reuben led a large group in song during a long corn shucking session that lasted into the wee hours of the morning. Reuben's energy and his brilliant extemporaneous lyrics, some of which openly criticized the master, led his group to victory in the competition to shuck the most corn. Reuben was sold not long after his triumph of song and work, but his musical leadership had spoken to his fellow slaves as "another tongue, one that the first one often could not" (Baptist 2014, 160).

Whether their instruments were voices, banjos, quills, or fiddles, enslaved people made music in many different contexts, including some that bore the marks of oppression. In their attempts to defend the institution of slavery against its critics, for example, slaveholders routinely argued that the musical culture of enslaved people indicated their contentment within the system, and there are numerous accounts of slaveholders forcing slaves to perform musically to prove this point. On some plantations, owners required slaves to build stages upon which musical and other kinds of performances could take place under the watchful and paternalistic eye of slaveholders and their guests. Competitions were even arranged between dancers and musicians from neighboring plantations, while white families acted as spectators and judges, awarding prizes of various kinds to the winning performers. Although the slaveholders regarded these activities as forms of leisure for their slaves, these were, in fact, command performances and, in several ways, they reinforced the notion of black subordination and inferiority. First, it was whites, not blacks, who chose the winners of these competitions and thus imposed their own cultural norms on performers from a dramatically different musical tradition. Second, the observation of these events, in which black musicians were required to

Solomon Northup, a free black man from New York, was kidnapped and sold into slavery in 1841. Once freed, he published a poignant narrative of his ordeal entitled *Twelve Years a Slave*. It included detailed descriptions of the suffering of slaves as they lived, worked, and endured painful separations from loved ones. (Northup, Solomon. *Twelve Years a Slave: Narrative of Solomon Northup . . .* , 1853)

perform cheerfully for white observers, allowed slaveholders to see themselves as benevolent guardians of happy, child-like slaves whose "innate" musicality indicated their intellectual inferiority. Having spent her childhood watching such events, one white Virginia woman asserted confidently that her parents' slaves were all "merry hearted, and among them I never saw a discontented face." She was certain that the only recreation they needed was "dancing to the music of the banjo" (Thompson 2014, 84).

In other instances, black musicians were compelled to perform simply to gratify the whims of masters. Solomon Northup, who had become a highly skilled fiddle player prior to his kidnapping and enslavement, recalled the ways in which his master Edwin Epps coerced him and other slaves on his plantation into performing. After a long day in the fields, Northup was sometimes summoned to the plantation house and, while the master stood by with a whip in his hand, told to play dance tunes on the fiddle while the other slaves danced. These performances would sometimes go on through the night until nearly dawn, and Northup recalled that if he paused even briefly to rest his bow hand or to give the dancers a moment of respite, he would be "spurred by an occasional sharp touch of the lash" and told to play on. At the end of a long night of such "performances" which men like Edwin Epps used as evidence of their slaves' happiness, Northup reported that while they had been "made to dance and laugh" they would rather have "cast ourselves upon the earth and weep" (Northup 1853, 181–182). The extent to which slaveholders genuinely believed that coerced recreation was truly evidence of their slaves' acceptance of bondage is difficult to assess, but at least one former slaveholder saw the truth of the matter quite clearly. "I have never seen a happy slave," wrote abolitionist Angelina Grimké after leaving her slaveholding family for the North. "I have seen him dance in his chains, it is true, but he was not happy" (Thompson 2014, 98).

Another way in which slaveholders co-opted the recreational activities of enslaved musicians was by sending them out for hire. This was especially true among fiddle players like Solomon Northup whose ability on the instrument made him a popular performer among the white families in rural Louisiana. He noted that as he traveled by mule to one "jollification" or another he was constantly asked to play little tunes for passersby and gained a reputation for skills that allowed his master to collect extra money from his playing. Because he was playing for a white audience, however, the music Northup and other enslaved musicians played at these events was a mix of dance tunes familiar in African American culture as well as "minuets and cotillions" that were expected at dances held in plantation homes (Southern 1997, 177). In fame and popularity, however, no slave fiddler surpassed Simeon Gilliat who was once owned by the royal governor of Virginia and who became a stock figure at parties and balls in the Richmond area until his death in 1820. Although Gilliat was clearly a highly accomplished musician, he appears to have been sought after, in part, because his regal appearance and courtly dress attracted the mirth of white audiences.

Yet even as white Southerners sought to use African American music for their own purposes, enslaved people made music for themselves in ways that differed sharply from coerced performances demanded by owners. The first problem, however, was finding the time, and since the demands of plantation labor dominated the workweek, Sundays provided the greatest opportunity for slaves to make music of their own. As we saw in the chapter on religious life, the most common context for musical production was the Sunday religious gathering in which spiritual singing, in conjunction with the ring shout spiritual dance, played a central role. The nature of this "shout" singing, however, was quite distinct from the musical culture of white churches in that it was interactive, improvisational, and inseparable from physical movement. Former slave Vinnie Brunson reported that when the shout began, the best singers would start the song, and as the singing accelerated in tempo and increased in volume, they would join hands in a circle while other members of the congregation joined in with rhythmic clapping and making "a big noise." The tempo of the singing, Brunson recalled, was faster or slower depending upon the occasion, so that a song like "Swing Low Sweet Chariot" might be sung quickly as a shout or a "praise song" and more slowly and sadly at a funeral (Berlin, Favreau, and Miller 1998, 184).

In addition to religious gatherings, recreational music was played at dances that often occurred on Saturday evenings in the woods or some other area far from the plantation house. Unlike the plantation stages where they were compelled to perform for white observers, dances or frolics were places where enslaved people could express themselves musically in a more authentic and autonomous way. Banjos, fiddles, drums, quills, and singing were central elements of the frolics, and slaves who were unable to perform plantation work sometimes found a special role at these events as musicians. Fannie Berry remembered that on the Virginia plantation where she lived there was a banjo player named Dennis who was always present to play jigs, reels, and other music for the dancers. "Dennis had a twisted arm, an' he couldn't do much work," she reported, "but he sho could pick dat banjer" (Berlin, Favreau, and Miller 1998, 177). Former Arkansas slave James Bolton remembered many different kinds of dances but said that his favorite was when they would "git in a ring an' when the music started we would begin wukkin' our footses, while we sung, You steal mah True Love, an' Ah Steal You'en" (Berlin, Favreau, and Miller 1998, 172). Music was also featured when slaves gathered for marathon corn shucking events when as many as 500 barrels of corn were husked by a large group of slaves. Sometimes the corn would often be divided into two large piles and two groups of enslaved people would sing short responsive verses as they competed to shuck the fastest. As one historian has put it, music made it possible for slaves to feel "truly alive, as people who mattered for their unique abilities and contributions, as a people in a common situation who could celebrate their individuality together" (Baptist 2014, 160).

DANCING

As we have seen, the musical expression of African American slaves was often inseparable from their culture of dance; indeed, much of the music they created was specifically designed to accompany or encourage dancing or other forms of physical motion.

Europeans and white Americans often dismissed the dance traditions of West African peoples as chaotic or condemned them as sexualized performances, but in doing so they failed to appreciate the varied contexts and meanings of dance in the African and African American experience. Like music, dance served a "functional" as well as recreational purpose in the daily lives of enslaved people, used to mark rites of passage, to celebrate milestones in the agricultural year, and to express spiritual devotion, or as an element of courtship rituals. As in white culture, moreover, rules governed the nature and character of dancing, and while sexuality played a role in the West African culture of dance, dancers were required to observe certain expectations of "modesty" and "decorum" in their physical movements (Thompson 2014, 28). Under slavery in the United States, African Americans continued to regard dance as an integral part of their lives and sought out spaces where they might express themselves freely in this way.

When former slaves wrote and spoke about dancing, they most often discussed its role in their youthful rituals of courtship. In 1937, Fannie Berry recalled dances with more than a hundred slaves in attendance where everyone did their best to dress well, "eben ef dey ain't got nothin but a piece of ribbon to tie in dey hair." Since "field shoes" were uncomfortable and made too much noise, she said, most of the dancers took them off before stepping out onto the floor. She also insisted that these dances were governed by strict rules of modesty so that men and women were not "squeezed up close to one another" or wrapping their arms together like "young folks do today." When Berry was asked to say what sorts of dances were most popular, she remembered one called "cuttin' de pigeons wings" in which the dancers flapped their arms and legs while holding their necks stiff "like a bird do." Another was "gwine [going] to de east and gwine to de west" in which couples could kiss one another while keeping their bodies slightly apart for modesty's sake. Fiddlers at these dances were masters of ceremonies, often deciding on the dance by calling out a number that signified the number of steps the couples were to "cut." There were also dances that required individual skill and competitions such as dancing with a glass of water on the head or dancing quickly around a circle without touching the end. The latter dance often went on until all the dancers except one were disqualified and the winner was awarded a cake. "No, I never did win no cake," Berry recalled, "but I was purty good at it jus' de same I reckon" (Berlin, Favreau, and Miller 1998, 179–180).

Both clothing and dancing skills were very important to young slaves who attended these dances, and the efforts of the dancers sometimes created tragic-comical scenes. Jacob Green, who grew up a slave in Maryland, wrote that as a sixteen-year-old he was "very fond of dancing" and was determined to attract the attention of the young women at a "shindy" that was being held a few miles from his home. Dressed in his finest clothes and carrying a jingling mixture of pennies and brass buttons in his pocket to create the impression of vast wealth, he proceeded to the dance only to tear his trousers on a nail, splitting them "up to the seat." Pinning his shirt and pants as thoroughly as he could, he entered the dance, requested the fiddle player to play a fast jig, and began dancing with a young woman "round the room" with the change jangling in his pocket. As all eyes focused on his fine appearance and skillful dancing, Green discovered with horror that the pins in his "breeches" had come loose and his long shirt tail was flapping through the hole in the seat. His young lady partner, instead of helping him to conceal his embarrassment, grabbed ahold of the loose shirt tail and held it up for everyone to see, an act that resulted in uproarious laughter from the entire assembly. Even more humiliating for Green was that "the gals had turned my pockets out" and discovered that brass buttons rather than silver dollars were the primary currency he carried (Green 1864, 12–13).

Dancing often involved prolonged and extreme physical exertion that turned courtship into a test of endurance. Solomon Northup recalled a dance in which a fellow slave named Sam was determined to win the affection of "Miss Lively," whose ability to dance at top speed for long periods of time was legendary in the area. To the chagrin of his rivals, Sam began dancing a fast "figure" with Lively and, according to Northup, his "legs flew like drumsticks down the outside and up the middle, by the side of his bewitching partner." Eventually, however, Sam found that he could not keep up with Lively and was overcome with exhaustion, whereupon other young men sought to take this place. As Lively continued "whirling like a top" without pause, she proved her physical superiority to all her partners, "outwinding" them and leaving them feeling like an "empty bag." Northup also recalled that sometimes the dancers outlasted even the fiddle players, determined to win the applause of the group for being last on the dance floor. When the fiddle music stopped, he reported, the dancers were accompanied by "a music peculiar to themselves," which he called "patting." Patting involved a coordinated series of rhythmic claps on the knees, hands, and shoulders while "keeping time with the foot" and singing (Northup 1853, 124). Patting and dancing were two sides of the same coin for enslaved people as those who patted most enthusiastically often felt moved to get up and join those on the floor.

Because dances involved relatively large public assemblies of enslaved people, some planters prohibited them, while others regulated attendance or supervised them as well. Mollie Booker who was born free in Virginia recalled with bitterness that planters would not allow members of her family to attend dances with slaves for fear that interactions with free blacks might be dangerous (Perdue, Barden, and Phillips 1976, 54). Former slave Bailey Cunningham told an interviewer that he remembered that the "big dances" held off the plantations in the evening could be attended only by those who had a written pass and that the "master would have eight or ten men on horses watching and anyone caught without a pass was taken up and punished." Still, the ability of whites to control or regulate dancing seems to have been, like attempts to ban drumming or other forms of music, limited at best. An anonymous former slave from Virginia reported that when slaves were required to work on the Saturday of a big dance, their excitement for the upcoming event spilled out of the slave quarters and into the fields. While their leader sang rhythmic verses with a call and response pattern of "feet de de diddle diddle" and "gwine to de ball," slaves in the potato field began "kickin' de clod in step" and "steppin' high and choppin' right in tune." The irritated overseer attempted to lash the slaves nearest him with a cowhide to stop the impromptu dancing, but he was powerless to enforce his will (Perdue, Barden, and Phillips 1976, 82, 106).

HOLIDAYS AND FESTIVITIES

The music and dancing that formed such an important part of slave culture were expressed most often during the various holidays, especially Christmas, when many planters allowed their slaves time to rest and celebrate. Some former slaves, Frederick Douglass foremost among them, believed that slaveholders used holiday festivities as a means of controlling enslaved people. "The holidays are part and parcel of the gross fraud, wrong and inhumanity of slavery," he wrote in his 1845 autobiography. "They do not give the slaves this time because they would not like to have their work during its continuance, but because they know it would be unsafe to deprive them of it." In many cases, Douglass noted, planters provided the slaves with prodigious quantities of alcohol, which, after months of the most grueling labor, was consumed in copious quantities. Ordered into the fields after two weeks of such "dissipation," he argued, many "slaves were, upon the whole, rather glad to go, from what our master had deceived us into a belief was freedom, back to the arms of slavery" (Douglass 1845, 75). As we have seen in our discussion of music and dance, slaveholders were often cunning in their ability to use the recreational practices of enslaved people to reinforce their subordination.

And yet not all slaves fell into the trap that Douglass believed slaveholders had set for them at holiday celebrations, and Christmas stood out in the minds of many former slaves as a moment of communal solidarity and personal joy. Elderly ex-slave Harriet Jones remembered Christmas as a rare time to enjoy "good things to eat," and, while her owner did supply a keg of cider or wine to enhance their "Christmas spirit," he also allowed the slaves to use the yard of the plantation house for their Christmas dinner, which included chicken and wild turkey. This unusually sumptuous meal was, however, partly a command performance that the slaveholding family clearly used to reinforce their self-image as paternalists, and Jones carefully noted in her interview that "after de white folks eats, dey watches de servants have dey dinner." Yet once the Christmas feast was over, the celebration moved to the slave quarters where nearly everything was moved out of the cabins to make way for the dancing. As in other kinds of frolics, the fiddle player was the leader and choreographer, calling out dances and encouraging couples to partner up and lead the others. At the end of the night, Jones remembered, the fiddler would always play the "Virginny Reel" as a signal that the festivities were coming to an end, and most years the master would give the slaves the next day off to recuperate from a long night of partying (Berlin, Favreau, and Miller 1998, 175–176).

Like Southern whites, enslaved people associated Christmas with gift giving, and some slaveholders provided small presents for their slaves, including hats or pipe tobacco for men and little items of clothing for women. Yet as former slave Jacob Stroyer recalled, a ritual of subservience was required before slaveholders would bestow these gifts as men were required to remove their hats and bow ceremonially and women made an obligatory "low curtsey" (Stroyer 1879, 34). In some cases before they handed over the gifts, masters required that enslaved people perform for them by dancing, telling an amusing story, or singing a pleasing song. Another pastime that slave children associated with Christmas was "catching" presents from white people, which consisted of hiding along a path, jumping out on unsuspecting pedestrians, and demanding a gift in exchange for their release from "capture." This was something of a risky business, however, as even a holiday-inspired reversal of everyday power relations could produce negative or even violent reactions in slaveholders. One escaped slave, Peter Bruner, recalled that as a ten-year-old he decided to take that risk with his unpredictable master and decided to "catch his Christmas gift" as the man was returning from town. Rather than give the young boy a gift, however, the startled and enraged slaveholder picked him up, threw him into a vat of tanning water, and held him down until "I was almost dead." Though he scrambled out several times, his master would grab ahold and "kick" him back in again until he finally managed to slip out the other side of the vat (Bruner 1918, 22).

For other enslaved people, the respite from the demands of the master or overseer gave them the opportunity to do some work for themselves, at times earning money for the various items they produced. Kentucky-born ex-slave William Wells Brown recalled that while enslaved women worked to mend clothing for members of their families, young men and boys took the week between Christmas and New Year to make brooms, mats, and axe handles, which they sold for cash. And despite his general disdain for the way in which Christmas was celebrated on plantations in the South, Frederick Douglass admitted that many slaves avoided excessive alcohol consumption and used their time to improve their material circumstances. "The sober, thinking, industrious ones would employ themselves in manufacturing corn-brooms, mats, horse-collars, and baskets," he wrote. "Another class spent their time in hunting opossums, coons, rabbits, and other game" (Douglass 1845, 180). For those in the slave community who had embraced evangelical Christianity, revival denominations such as Methodists and Baptists regularly scheduled tent or camp meeting revivals during the week between Christmas and New Year when slaves were likely to have the time and the permission from their masters to attend.

But Christian celebrations of the Christmas holiday did not monopolize the season. In some areas of the South, for example, the celebration of Junkanoo, an Afro-Caribbean masquerade procession, occurred at the same time. Former slave Harriet Jacobs, whose region of eastern North Carolina had an especially strong Junkanoo tradition, went as far as to say that without it "Christmas would be shorn of its greatest attraction." The festival had its origins in West Africa and, though it was performed there at different times of the year, enslaved people in the Americas used their brief Christmas respite from labor to preserve and pass on the tradition. The Junkanoo procession involved large groups of slaves dressed in a variety of ornate, brightly colored costumes, some garbed as animals, with "cows' tails . . . fastened to their backs" and heads "decorated with horns." Beginning their parade around noon on Christmas day, marchers proceeded through the local community to the rhythm of a "gumbo box," a drum covered with sheep skin or goat skin and struck with jawbone (Jacobs 1861, 179–180). The parade stopped at the homes of anyone likely to bestow a gift, either a small amount of money or "a glass of rum," and those who refused to contribute were likely to be serenaded with songs chiding them sarcastically for their stinginess.

Although not holidays in the formal sense, enslaved people regarded "quiltings" and "corn shuckings" with only somewhat less anticipation than Christmas itself. These were moments of community celebration when communal solidarity, individual skills, special foodways, and various forms of cultural reproduction came together in brief, but often joyous, ways. Enslaved women possessed prodigious skills as quilters, a tradition that extended from their West African roots where the production of elaborate textiles was a key aspect of the culture. While fabrics for quilt making were far less available under slavery, former slaves made repeated references to quilting when they were interviewed during the 1930s. On special occasions, older women gathered in one of the slave cabins and worked together to complete quilts that they had been working on little by little for as long as a month, sometimes finishing as many as twelve in one evening. It is unclear whether the quilts produced at these events were intended for the use of the slaves themselves or for their owners, but in any case, the production process was associated with various forms of recreation.

Former slaves who were interviewed in the 1930s remembered quiltings as festive occasions in which there was extra food, dancing, and unsupervised playtime. "Colored people would have quiltings to one of dey own house, up in de quarter, heap of de nights," recalled Sallie Paul of South Carolina, "en dey would frolic en play en dance dere till late up in de night." Rather than shuckings, which were arranged by masters, quiltings were organized by enslaved people themselves, a fact that gave them added significance. Sallie Paul had a strong sense of quiltings as community events that mixed labor and recreation in ways that defied easy description. Members of the community "would enjoy themselves better den de peoples do dese days, dey would be glad to get together," she insisted (Rawick 1973, 3: 244). Because she was a small child at the time, Sallie Paul probably did not understand the process of quilt making itself and therefore did not comment on the skill of the quilters or on the nature of the final product. There were, however, a variety of styles made by enslaved women, with "patchwork" quilts, patches of cloth in various sizes and colors sewn together in various patterns, being the most prevalent.

Corn shucking had a similar festive atmosphere, and sometimes the two activities occurred at the same time, with men husking the corn and women doing the quilting. When slave owners had a large quantity of corn to shuck, they often decided to invite slaves from neighboring plantations to shuck all the corn in one night and then have a party. There were drinking games and various forms of competition involved in these events. One ex-slave from North Carolina recalled that anyone who shucked a red ear of corn would receive an extra pull from the whiskey bottle. In many cases, corn shuckings were competitive, with two captains dividing up all the workers and then racing to see which one finished first. The captain's job was to "encourage his team by making up humorous verses that the team would then repeat or answer even as they in ceaseless motion pulled off shucks, [and] tossed the naked ears into the 'clean' pile" (Baptist 2014, 159). Prince Johnson remembered that after winning a shucking in Mississippi, "we put our Captain on our shoulders and rode him up and down while every body cheered and clapped their hands like the world was coming to an end" (Berlin, Favreau, and Miller 1998, 171). On some plantations, moreover, prizes were awarded, including money or extra allocations of clothes, to the person or people who shucked the most corn, a production incentive that some efficiency-minded planters no doubt encouraged. But once all the corn had been shucked, the fun would begin. The slave owner provided alcohol and food, and enslaved people danced into the night. According to Eliza Washington of Arkansas, corn shuckings were times when members of the community "talked and sang and had a good time" (Rawick 1974, 11: 53). James Bolton loved going to corn shuckings because once they finished their work, they "could have the whole night fer frolic" (Berlin, Favreau, and Miller 1998, 173). Careful observers recognized that these were primarily group events in which slaves reinforced their bonds of community by singing, working, and laughing together in a harmonious whole.

CHILDREN'S GAMES

Games of various kinds, which required no special occasion, also played a role in the daily lives of enslaved people. Slave children who were too young to work in the fields played games that encouraged their physical and moral development, even under the repressive conditions in which they lived. Jumping rope or playing tag were not uncommon among slave children, and climbing trees in the woods or swimming in the lakes or rivers around the plantations occurred as well. Sundays were particularly important days for enslaved children as they were often released from the job of watching their younger siblings while their parents worked in the fields. Exploring the land around the margins of the plantation, they would often gather wild plants or berries and return to the cabin with "dresses full of hickory, walnuts, and berries" (Wiggins 1980, 23). Because the slave patrollers did not require slave children to carry passes, moreover, they often traveled to neighboring plantations on Sundays to visit with and play with other children who were sometimes blood relations. The only requirement that owners and parents imposed was the necessity of returning by nightfall. It also appears that there was very little sex segregation in the recreational activities of slave children as boys and girls played side by side. One former slave recalled that his little sister followed him wherever he went and refused to sit out any of the physical challenges in his various forms of play. "If I jumped in the river tuh swim, she did hit too; if I clum a tree or went th'ough a briar patch, she don hit right behin' me" (White 1999, 93).

Whether on the plantation or not, slave children played a wide variety of games. Among the most widespread were "ring games," which were similar to the dances and shouts their parents performed in Christian worship. Using a stick or rock, children would scratch a ring in the dirt as wide as 30' and congregate inside it to dance, sing, clap, and make up words to various tunes. Other former slaves recalled a game they called "hide the switch," in which children would search for a hidden switch, with the successful hunter (lightly) flogging the others. Some slave children obtained marbles and played a variety of games with them, and one historian has argued that winning at marbles gave slave children a sense of ownership and power that they were denied in nearly every other aspect of life. Slave children who could not obtain marbles to play with developed creative solutions that turned the most ordinary objects into items of play. The game known as "smut," for example, used grains of corn in ways that were very similar to playing cards. "We played it just like you would with cards only we would have grains of corn and call them hearts and spades," recalled one former slave from Tennessee. The denominations of the various "cards" were determined by "the spots on the corn" (Wiggins 1980, 24).

More traditional athletic events were also common on plantations in the South, including early forms of what became the game of baseball. But more often they participated in competitions involving physical prowess: running, jumping, throwing, swimming, and lifting extremely heavy objects. Perhaps the most telling aspect of slave children's recreational lives, however, is the games they did not play. Historian David Wiggins has noted that references to boxing or other forms of violent competition appear only infrequently in the accounts of ex-slaves or in the writings of those who escaped from bondage in the South. "Physical abuse of one child by another was considered unjustifiable and a veritable threat to the general well-being of the group," he argued. Wiggins concluded that while slave children undoubtedly fought with one another, "they understood that their mutual advantage required them to care for each other and to refrain as much as possible from foolish 'skirmishes'" (Wiggins 1980, 28). Another significant choice slave children made in their recreational lives was to refrain from any games that required the exclusion or elimination of participants who performed less successfully. It is likely that this reflected the same ethos of communal solidarity that also discouraged more violent forms of play. Whether parents intervened directly to prohibit or modify violent play or rules of elimination, the recreational patterns of enslaved children indicate the process in which they internalized the basic rules of the slave community.

STORYTELLING

Children's games were part of the educational and socialization process in the slave community, but storytelling was among the most important ways in which the worldview and values of enslaved people were articulated and passed on. Storytelling was done in the same venues and contexts as music, dancing, and holiday making, and thus it can be seen as a form of recreation. Skilled storytellers interacted with their audiences who laughed, cried, and gasped at critical points in the entertaining narratives they heard. It is important to recognize, however, that the profound meanings embedded in stories made their telling and reception akin to religious life. As one scholar has put it, stories provided a "condensed representation of cultural ideas and social necessities" as well as "a frame for experience" (Joyner 1984, 190). The characters who appeared in these tales, particularly Brer Rabbit, Brer Squirrel, Brer Wolf, and the other animal tricksters, possessed moral qualities, some good and some decidedly not good, and thus their interactions with one another and with the larger world conveyed messages that informed the lives of the people who heard the stories. The stories provided a rich imaginative world in which an oppressed people sought to confront and navigate the harsh realities of the society they lived in while providing the tools for envisaging a new and more just order.

Storytelling had deep roots in West African culture, and it served a variety of psychological and emotional functions that were also essential for surviving slavery in the Americas. Originating in the struggles of daily existence, West African folktales allowed people to relieve and channel their anger, frustration, or mirth away from the individuals or groups who had caused it toward the generic characters who appeared in the stories. In this sense, storytelling functioned well as a mechanism for mitigating conflict, reaffirming group identity, and permitting audiences to laugh at people or systems they were otherwise prohibited from mocking. A key element of West African folktales was the pervasive role of animal tricksters, "relatively powerless creatures who attained their ends through the application of native wit and guile rather than power and authority" (Levine 2007, 103). The specific trickster in question differed from one West African region to another but might be a hare, a tortoise, a spider, or a rabbit. Yet regardless of the species, the mythical animal tricksters in these stories possessed fully human characteristics and lived in a world that was easily recognizable by the audiences who heard them. Brer Rabbit, who became the dominant trickster figure in slave folktales in the United States, bears a close resemblance to similar figures among the peoples of Ghana, Angola, Nigeria, and Sierra Leone.

The trickster stories often revolved around attempts by stronger and more powerful figures, Brer Wolf for example, to capture supposedly weaker and more vulnerable creatures like Brer Rabbit. In one comical and revealing tale, Brer Wolf tries to catch Brer Rabbit by cornering him in the hollow of a tree, setting it on fire, and preparing to seize the smaller animal as he tries to escape the flames. The rabbit has other means at his disposal, however, and finds a small opening in the back of the tree, which he uses to get away from the confused and frustrated wolf. To ensure the wolf's total humiliation, moreover, the rabbit slyly shows himself to the wolf and expresses sarcastic gratitude for the fire since it has melted the honey trapped in the tree and afforded him a tasty snack. But as historian Lawrence Levine has argued, stories like this one were not simply quaint tales of hairbreadth escapes and unexpected treats but rather of "vicarious triumph" in which the powerful and greedy are punished for their malevolent designs (Levine 2007, 107). When Brer Wolf finds that the rabbit has tricked him and consumed all the honey, he wedges himself into another tree hoping to find a similar reward. This time, however, there is no escape hole, and he is burned alive by the rabbit who stands by and, despite the pleas of the wolf, is unwilling to come to his aid. The reversal of power in this story and the overt desire for revenge against what was once both strong and unmerciful demonstrate the emotional intensity that these tales revealed in the tellers and in those they addressed.

In many ways, the trickster stories that were told and retold by enslaved people reflected the specific material circumstances of their lives and the distinctive approaches they took to address chronic hunger, violence, and sensory deprivation. The world of the stories, like the world of the slaves, was a constant struggle for survival in which simple moral principles, many of them derived from Christianity, were inapplicable or out of place. Like Brer Rabbit, enslaved people sometimes needed to lie to or steal from their masters to obtain enough food or to avoid brutal beatings, and the tales reflected this reality. In one story, for example, Brer Rabbit and Brer Wolf purchased a cow together but had no knife to butcher it, and the rabbit suggested that he would watch the cow while the wolf set off in search of the necessary object. While the more powerful animal was away, the rabbit killed the cow, hid the meat, and stuck the horns and tail into the mud to make it look as if the cow had sunk deep into the ground. When the witless wolf returned, the clever rabbit cried out that the cow was stuck in the mud, sinking fast and needed to be pulled out by the strength of a powerful wolf. Pulling the horns with all his might until they suddenly popped out the ground, the wolf was thrown far into the distance only to repeat the same humiliating act with the tail. When the wolf appeared unable to figure out what had happened, the cunning rabbit told him that the cow had simply gone down into the mud "as fast as he pull" (Roberts 1989, 36). As they listened to tales like this, enslaved African Americans could retain the core of their moral compass while also recognizing that the ruthless power of the slaveholders could be resisted only by wit, quick thinking, and razer-sharp instincts for survival.

While animal trickster stories offered an allegorical discussion of the slaves' daily struggles for survival, there were other storytelling traditions that were set fully and overtly in the human world. The characters of John or Jack appeared in several stories and represented a subversive slave folk hero who, like Brer Rabbit, used all forms of trickery and humorous ruses to dupe his master or to avoid punishment. In one comical tale, John's master was hunting and ordered his slave to sit behind the deer blind with a gun and to be sure that he shot any deer that happened to pass by. When a huge buck with a fully developed set of antlers suddenly came into view, John became frightened, fell flat on his face, and completely forgot his master's instructions to shoot. Just as John's master returned, however, the deer suddenly bolted and in its terrified flight it fell down a steep hill and broke its neck. When the angry master asked, "Why didn't you shoot that deer," the quick-thinking John responded calmly that "it's like dishyer: the way dat deer was goin' down dat hill, I know he was goin' to break his own neck" (Anderson 1961, 420–421). In other stories, John acted in more directly subversive ways, calling his master "evil," praying that God would take him to hell, or even cursing him (Blassingame 1977, 129). Yet as in the tales of Brer Rabbit and Brer Wolf, in which the rabbit consistently wins out but remains a vulnerable object of prey, John's victories over his master are always temporary and, for all his wit and cunning, he remains a slave.

Other stories seemed to combine the fantastical with the earthly in ways that clearly fused pure entertainment with messages of survival or temporary empowerment. One remarkable tale focused on a family of slave conjurers, a father, mother, and son, who possessed the ability to transform themselves and the bodies of others. Nursing a strong "spite" for the overseer on the plantation where they lived, the father and son took on ghostly form, slipped through the man's keyhole, and proceeded to transform the overseer and his own son into a bull and yearling. In order to punish and humiliate them, the conjurers mount the bull and yearling and ride them into the wheat field of an equally objectionable neighboring planter, trampling and ruining the crop. Knowing that the overseer would be held responsible for the behavior of his animals, the slave conjurers' victory over him was nearly total. What made it even sweeter, however, was that upon waking, the overseer and his son "feel very tired and know 'dat de witches been ridin' em, but they never find out what witches it was" (Blassingame 1972, 128). This story is especially revealing in that it combines multiple elements of slave culture, including the tradition of conjure, the moral critique of white authority, and the ability of enslaved people to use conflicts between whites to their own advantage.

The telling of stories like this one often occurred at holiday time or in conjunction with corn shucking or frolics. Former slave Charles Ball remembered an evening of dancing, singing, and banjo playing that also included stories from "those who were too old to take any part in our active pleasures." The tales he heard that night "were sufficiently fraught with demons, miracles, and murders, to fix the attention of many hearers" (Ball 1837, 201). The ritual of the story was, however, a strong and distinct element in recreational events, and the tellers announced its commencement with specific introductory lines like "once upon a time," "this is a story about," or other phrases that signaled its importance and demarcated the act of storytelling from other activities going on at the same time (Joyner 1984, 190). As storytellers performed their tales, they expected their audiences to become active participants in the process, expressing brief verbal agreement or disagreement with what the characters might be doing or saying. In this dialogue between storyteller and audience, one historian argues, came "subtle changes" in the meaning of stories that were repeated quite often in different social or recreational contexts (Joyner, 1984, 190).

The recreational lives of enslaved people were part and parcel of the larger slave culture that emerged in the antebellum South. Since slavery was a system that conceptualized black people as property rather than as fully realized human beings, the determination of slaves to laugh, play, celebrate, and make music was fundamentally an act of resistance to that system. It also signified their ongoing hope that a different world in which their humanity would be recognized and supported might someday become a reality. As we have seen, moreover, recreational activities also represented another conduit through which the African roots of the slave population could be performed and passed on. Their musical traditions, dance culture, and folktales are especially strong examples of the cultural continuities that bound the slave population of North America to their African ancestors.

Yet perhaps the most inspiring aspect of the slaves' recreational lives was their role in forming communal bonds and reinforcing solidarity among a brutally oppressed people. Frolics, dances, quiltings, and corn shuckings allowed enslaved men, women, and children to see one another in ways that were fundamentally different from the identities their owners attempted to force upon them. Watching their mothers make complex and beautiful quilts; watching their mothers and fathers play, sing, and dance; and listening to their elders tell stories that uniquely reflected communal experience, slave children were socialized into a community that protected and celebrated its own. Recreation bolstered the bonds that gave enslaved people a chance to survive the physical and emotional degradation of slavery and to celebrate a culture of "mutual cooperation, joyful camaraderie, humor, respect for elders, and an undisguised zest for life" (Blassingame 1972, 148).

DOCUMENT: WILLIAM WELLS BROWN, *MY SOUTHERN HOME* (1880)

When he was twenty years old, William Wells Brown escaped from slavery in Kentucky and became one of the most prominent black abolitionists in the United States. Living in northern New York, Brown was committed to independent black political action and was a key organizer in the African American convention movement during the Civil War era. Brown traveled to Great Britain to spread the antislavery message and was the author of the popular antislavery novel Clotel. *In this excerpt from his final work, Brown provides evidence for the persistence of West African patterns of music and dance among enslaved people in antebellum America.*

Throughout the Southern States, there are still to be found remnants of the old time Africans, who were stolen from their native land and sold in the Savannah, Mobile, and New Orleans markets, in defiance of all law. The last-named city, however, and its vicinity, had a larger portion of these people than any other section. New Orleans was their centre, and where their meetings were not uninteresting.

Congo Square takes its name, as is well known, from the Congo negroes who used to perform their dance on its sward every Sunday.... It was a gala occasion, these Sundays in those years, and not less than two or three thousand people would congregate there to see the dusky dancers. A low fence enclosed the square, and on each street there was a little gate and turnstile. There were no trees then, and the ground was worn bare by the feet of the people. About three o'clock the negroes began to gather, each nation taking their places in different parts of the square. The Minahs would not dance near the Congos, nor the Mandringas near the Gangas. Presently the music would strike up, and the parties would prepare for the sport. Each set had its own orchestra. The instruments were a peculiar kind of banjo, made of a Louisiana gourd, several drums made of a gum stump dug out, with a sheepskin head, and beaten with the fingers, and two jaw-bones of a horse, which when shaken would rattle the loose teeth, keeping time with the drums. About eight negroes, four male and four female, would make a set, and generally they were but scantily clad.

It took some little time before the tapping of the drums would arouse the dull and sluggish dancers, but when the point of excitement came, nothing can faithfully portray the wild and frenzied motions they go through. Backward and forward, this way and that, now together and now apart every motion intended to convey the most sensual ideas. As the dance progressed, the drums were thrummed faster, the contortions became more grotesque, until sometimes, in frenzy, the women and men would fall fainting to the ground. All this was going on with a dense crowd looking on, and with a hot sun pouring its torrid rays on the infatuated actors of this curious ballet. After one set had become fatigued, they would drop out to be replaced by others, and then stroll off to the groups of some other tribe in a different portion of the square. Then it was that trouble would commence, and a regular set-to with short sticks followed, between the men, and broken heads ended the day's entertainment.

On the sidewalks, around the square, the old negresses, with their spruce-beer and peanuts, cocoa-nuts and pop-corn, did a thriving trade, and now and then, beneath petticoats, bottles of tafia, a kind of Louisiana rum, peeped out, of which the gendarmes were oblivious. When the sun went down, a stream of people poured out of the turn-stiles, and the gendarmes, walking through the square, would order the dispersion of the negroes, and by gun-fire, at nine o'clock, the place was well-nigh deserted. These dances were kept up until within the memory of men still living, and many who believe in them, and who would gladly revive them, may be found in every State in the Union.

Source: William Wells Brown. *My Southern Home: Or, the South and Its People*. Boston: A. G. Brown & Co., 1880, 121–124.

FURTHER READING

Anderson, John Q. 1961. "Old John and the Master." *Southern Folklore Quarterly* 25, no. 3 (September): 418–429.

Ball, Charles. 1837. *Slavery in the United States: A Narrative of the Life and Adventures of Charles Ball.* New York: John S. Taylor.

Baptist, Edward. 2014. *The Half Has Never Been Told: Slaver and the Making of American Capitalism.* New York: Basic Books.

Berlin, Ira, Marc Favreau, and Steven F. Miller, eds. 1998. *Remembering Slavery: African Americans Talk about Their Personal Experiences of Slavery and Emancipation.* New York: The New Press.

Blassingame, John. 1972. *The Slave Community: Plantation Life in the Old South.* New York: Oxford University Press.

Blassingame, John, ed. 1977. *Slave Testimony: Two Centuries of Letters, Speeches, Interviews, and Autobiographies.* Baton Rouge: Louisiana State University Press.

Bremer, Fredrika. 1853. *Homes of the New World: Impressions of America,* vol. II. New York: Harper & Brothers.

Bruner, Peter. 1918. *A Slave's Adventures toward Freedom. Not Fiction, but the True Story of a Struggle.* Oxford, OH: s.n.

Bryant, William Cullen. 1884. *The Prose Writings of William Cullen Bryant.* New York: D. Appleton and Co.

Douglass, Frederick. 1845. *Narrative of the Life of Frederick Douglass, an American Slave. Written by Himself.* Boston, MA: Antislavery Office.

Eisnach, Dwight, and Herbert Covey. 2009. *What the Slaves Ate: Recollections of African American Foods and Foodways from the Slave Narratives.* Santa Barbara, CA: Greenwood.

Green, Jacob D. 1864. *Narrative of the Life of J. D. Green, a Runaway Slave, from Kentucky, Containing an Account of His Three Escapes, in 1839, 1846, and 1848.* Huddersfield, England: Henry Fielding.

Gura, Philip F., and James F. Bollman. 1999. *America's Instrument: The Banjo in the Nineteenth Century.* Chapel Hill: University of North Carolina Press.

Jacobs, Harriet. 1861. *Incidents in the Life of a Slave Girl, Written by Herself.* Boston: printed by the author.

Joyner, Charles. 1984. *Down by the Riverside: A South Carolina Slave Community.* Champaign: University of Illinois Press.

Katz-Hyman, Martha B., and Kym S. Rice, eds. 2011. *World of a Slave: Encyclopedia of the Material Life of Slaves in the United States,* vol. I. Santa Barbara, CA: Greenwood.

Latrobe, Benjamin. 1905. *The Journal of Latrobe.* New York: D. Appleton and Co.

Levine, Lawrence. 2007. *Black Culture and Black Consciousness: Afro-American Folk Thought from Slavery to Freedom.* 30th Anniversary Edition. New York: Oxford University Press.

Northup, Solomon. 1853. *Twelve Years a Slave: Narrative of Solomon Northup, a Citizen of New-York, Kidnapped in Washington City in 1841, and Rescued in 1853*. Auburn, NY: Derby and Miller.

Perdue, Charles, Jr., Thomas E. Barden, and Robert K. Phillips, eds. 1976. *Weevils in the Wheat: Interviews with Virginia Ex-Slaves*. Charlottesville: University Press of Virginia.

Rawick, George P., ed. 1973. *The American Slave: A Composite Autobiography, vol. 3: South Carolina Narratives*, Part 3. Westport, CT: Greenwood Press.

Rawick, George P., ed. 1974. *The American Slave: A Composite Autobiography, vol. 11: Arkansas Narratives*, Part 7. Westport, CT: Greenwood Press.

Roberts, John. 1989. *From Trickster to Badman: The Black Folk Hero in Slavery and Freedom*. Philadelphia: University of Pennsylvania Press.

Southern, Eileen. 1997. *The Music of Black Americans: A History*, 3rd ed. New York: W. W. Norton.

Stroyer, Jacob. 1879. *Sketches of My Life in the South, Part I*. Salem, MA: Salem Press.

Takagi, Midori. 1999. *"Rearing Wolves to Our Own Destruction": Slavery in Richmond, Virginia, 1782–1865*. Charlottesville: University Press of Virginia.

Thompson, Katrina D. 2014. *Ring Shout, Wheel About: The Racial Politics of Music and Dance in North American Slavery*. Urbana: University of Illinois Press.

White, Deborah Gray. 1999. *Ar'n't I a Woman? Female Slaves in the Plantation South*, 2nd ed. New York: W. W. Norton.

White, Shane, and Graham White. 2005. *The Sounds of Slavery: Discovering African American History through Songs, Sermons, and Speech*. Boston, MA: Beacon Press.

Wiggins, David K. 1980. "The Play of Slave Children in the Plantation Communities of the Old South, 1820–1860." *Journal of Sport History* 7, no. 2 (Summer): 21–39.

BIBLIOGRAPHY

GENERAL WORKS

Published Primary Sources

Ball, Charles. *Slavery in the United States: A Narrative of the Life and Adventures of Charles Ball*. New York: John S. Taylor, 1837.

Berlin, Ira, Marc Favreau, and Steven F. Miller, eds. *Remembering Slavery: African Americans Talk about Their Personal Experiences of Slavery and Emancipation*. New York: The New Press, 1998.

Bibb, Henry. *Narrative of the Life and Adventures of Henry Bibb, an American Slave*. New York: Printed by the author, 1849.

Blassingame, John W., ed. *Slave Testimony: Two Centuries of Letters, Speeches, Interviews, and Autobiographies*. Baton Rouge: Louisiana State University Press, 1977.

Breeden, James O., ed. *Advice among Masters The Ideal in Slave Management in the Old South*. Westport, CT: Greenwood Press, 1980.

Brown, Henry. *Narrative of the Life of Henry Box Brown*. Manchester: Lee and Glynn, 1851.

Brown, John. *Slave Life in Georgia: A Narrative of the Life, Sufferings and Escape of John Brown*. London: W. M. Watts, 1855.

Brown, William Wells. *Narrative of William W. Brown, a Fugitive Slave*. London: Charles Gilpin, 1849.

Bruce, Henry. *The New Man: Twenty-Two Years a Slave, Twenty-Nine Years a Free Man*. York, PA: P. Anstadt & Sons, 1895.

Campbell, Israel. *An Autobiography, Bond and Free*. Philadelphia: printed by the author, 1861.

Chesnut, Mary Boykin. *Mary Chesnut's Civil War*, edited by C. Vann Woodward. New Haven, CT: Yale University Press, 1981.
Douglass, Frederick. *My Bondage, My Freedom*. New York: Miller, Orton & Mulligan, 1855.
Douglass, Frederick. *Narrative of the Life of Frederick Douglass: An American Slave, Written by Himself*. Boston, MA: Antislavery Office, 1845.
Grandy, Moses. *Narrative of the Life of Moses Grandy, Late a Slave in the United States of America*. London: Charles Gilpin, 1843.
Green, Jacob D. *Narrative of the Life of J.D. Green, a Runaway Slave, from Kentucky, Containing an Account of His Three Escapes, in 1839, 1846, and 1848*. Huddersfield, England: Henry Fielding, 1864.
Henson, Josiah. *The Life of Josiah Henson, Formerly a Slave*. Boston: A. D. Phelps, 1849.
Hughes, Louis. *Thirty Years a Slave: From Bondage to Freedom*. Milwaukee, WI: South Side Printing Co., 1897.
Jacobs, Harriet. *Incidents in the Life of a Slave Girl*. Boston: printed by the author, 1861.
Jones, Thomas H. *The Experience of Thomas H. Jones, Who Was a Slave for Forty-Three Years*. Boston: Bazin & Chandler, 1862.
Keckley, Elizabeth. *Behind the Scenes: Thirty Years a Slave, and Four Years in the White House*. New York: G. W. Carleton & Co., 1868.
Kemble, Frances Anne. *Journal of a Residence on a Georgian Plantation in 1838–1839*. New York: Harper & Brothers, 1863.
Loguen, Jermain. *The Rev. J.W. Loguen, as a Slave and as a Freeman*. Syracuse, NY: J.G.K. Truair & Co., 1859.
Northup, Solomon. *Twelve Years a Slave: Narrative of Solomon Northup, a Citizen of New-York, Kidnapped in Washington City in 1841, and Rescued in 1853*. Auburn, NY: Derby and Miller, 1853.
Olmsted, Frederick Law. *The Cotton Kingdom: A Traveler's Observations on Cotton and Slavery in the American Slave States, Volume 1*. New York: Mason Brothers, 1862.
Olmsted, Frederick Law. *A Journey in the Back Country in the Winter of 1853–1854*. New York: Mason Brothers, 1860.
Parker, Allen. *Recollections of Slavery Times*. Worcester, MA: Chas. W. Burbank & Co., 1895.
Pennington, James W. C. *The Fugitive Blacksmith*. London: Charles Gilpin, 1849.
Pennington, James W. C. *A Narrative of Events of the Life of J.H. Banks, an Escaped Slave, from the Cotton State, Alabama, in America*. Liverpool, England: M. Rourke, 1861.
Perdue, Charles L., Thomas E. Barden, and Robert K. Phillips, eds. *Weevils in the Wheat: Interviews with Virginia Ex-Slaves*. Charlottesville: University Press of Virginia, 1976.
Rawick, George P., ed. *The American Slave: A Composite Autobiography*. 17 volumes. Westport, CT: Greenwood Press, 1973–1974.

Smith, James Lindsay. *Autobiography of James L. Smith*. Norwich, CT: The Bulletin, 1881.
Steward, Austin. *Twenty-Two Years a Slave and Forty Years a Free Man*. Rochester, NY: William Alling, 1857.
Stroyer, Jacob. *Sketches of My Life in the South, Part I*. Salem: Salem Press, 1879.
Tanner, Lynette Ater. *Chained to the Land: Voices from Cotton & Cane Plantations*. Winston-Salem, NC: John F. Blair Publishers, 2014.
Watson, Henry. *Narrative of Henry Watson, a Fugitive Slave*. Boston, MA: Bela Marsh, 1848.

Secondary Sources

Baptist, Edward. *The Half Has Never Been Told: Slavery and the Making of American Capitalism*. New York: Basic Books, 2014.
Campbell, Edward D. C., ed. *Before Freedom Came: African American Life in the Antebellum South*. Charlottesville: University Press of Virginia, 1991.
Fields, Barbara Jeanne. *Slavery and Freedom on the Middle Ground: Maryland during the Nineteenth Century*. New Haven, CT: Yale University Press, 1985.
Hudson, Larry. *To Have and to Hold: Slave Work and Family Life in Antebellum South Carolina*. Athens: University of Georgia Press, 1997.
Johnson, Walter. *Soul by Soul: Life inside the Antebellum Slave Market*. Cambridge, MA: Harvard University Press, 1999.
Jones-Rogers, Stephanie E. *They Were Her Property: White Women as Slave Owners in the American South*. New Haven, CT: Yale University Press, 2019.
Joyner, Charles. *Down by the Riverside: A South Carolina Slave Community*. Urbana: University of Illinois Press, 1984.
Kolchin, Peter. *American Slavery, 1619–1877*. New York: Hill and Wang, 2003.
Rosenthal, Caitlin. *Accounting for Slavery: Masters and Management*. Cambridge, MA: Harvard University Press, 2018.
Takagi, Midori. *"Rearing Wolves to Our Own Destruction": Slavery in Richmond, Virginia, 1782–1865*. Charlottesville: University Press of Virginia, 1999.
White, Deborah Gray. *Ar'n't I a Woman? Female Slaves in the Plantation South*. New York: W. W. Norton, 1999.

ECONOMIC LIFE

Baptist, Edward. "'Cuffy,' 'Fancy Maids,' and 'One-Eyed Men': Rape, Commodification and the Domestic Slave Trade in the United States." *American Historical Review* 106, no. 5 (December 2001): 1619–1650.

Berlin, Ira, and Philip D. Morgan, eds. *Cultivation and Culture: Labor and the Shaping of Slave Life in the Americas*. Charlottesville: University Press of Virginia, 1993.

Cecelski, David S. *The Waterman's Song: Slavery and Freedom in Maritime North Carolina*. Chapel Hill: University of North Carolina Press, 2001.

Finley, Alexandra. "'Cash to Corinna': Domestic Labor and Sexual Economy in the 'Fancy Trade.'" *The Journal of American History* 104, no. 2 (September 2017): 410–430.

Follett, Richard. *The Sugar Masters: Planters and Slaves in Louisiana's Cane World, 1820–1860*. Baton Rouge: Louisiana State University Press, 2005.

Martin, Jonathan D. *Divided Mastery: Slave Hiring in the American South*. Cambridge, MA: Harvard University Press, 2004.

O'Donovan, Susan Eva. *Becoming Free in the Cotton South*. Cambridge, MA: Harvard University Press, 2007.

Schwalm, Leslie A. *A Hard Fight for We: Women's Transition from Slavery to Freedom in South Carolina*. Urbana: University of Illinois Press, 1997.

Stevenson, Brenda. "What's Love Got to Do with It? Concubinage and Enslaved Women and Girls in the Antebellum South." *Journal of African American History* 98, no. 1 (Winter 2013): 99–125.

Wood, Betty. *Women's Work, Men's Work: The Informal Slave Economies of Lowcountry Georgia*. Athens: University of Georgia Press, 1995.

DOMESTIC LIFE

Dusinberre, William. *Strategies for Survival: Recollections of Bondage in Antebellum Virginia*. Charlottesville: University of Virginia Press, 2009.

Follett, Richard. "'Lives of Living Death': The Reproductive Lives of Slave Women in the Cane World of Louisiana." *Slavery and Abolition* 26, no. 2 (August 2005): 289–304.

Glymph, Thavolia. *Out of the House of Bondage: The Transformation of the Plantation Household*. New York: Cambridge University Press, 2008.

Hudson, Larry. *To Have and to Hold: Slave Work and Family Life in Antebellum South Carolina*. Athens: University of Georgia Press, 1997.

Hunter, Tera. *Bound in Wedlock: Slave and Free Black Marriage in the Nineteenth Century*. Cambridge, MA: Harvard University Press, 2017.

King, Wilma. *Stolen Childhood: Slave Youth in Nineteenth-Century America*, 2nd ed. Bloomington: Indiana University Press, 2011.

Malone, Ann Paton. *Sweet Chariot: Slave Family and Household Structure in Nineteenth-Century Louisiana*. Chapel Hill: University of North Carolina Press, 1992.

Pargas, Damian Alan. *The Quarters and the Field: Slave Families in the Non-Cotton South*. Gainesville: University Press of Florida, 2010.

Schwartz, Marie Jenkins. *Born in Bondage: Growing Up Enslaved in the Antebellum South*. Cambridge, MA: Harvard University Press, 2000.

Stevenson, Brenda. *Life in Black and White: Family and Community in the Slave South*. New York: Oxford University Press, 1996.

MATERIAL LIFE

Campbell, Edward D. C., Jr., ed. *Before Freedom Came: African-American Life in the Antebellum South*. Charlottesville: University Press of Virginia, 1991.

Eisnach, Dwight, and Herbert Covey. *What the Slaves Ate: Recollections of African American Foods and Foodways from the Slave Narratives*. Santa Barbara, CA: Greenwood, 2009.

Kiple, Kenneth F., and Virginia King. *Another Dimension to the Black Diaspora*. New York: Cambridge University Press, 1981.

Vlach, John Michael. *Back of the Big House: The Architecture of Plantation Slavery*. Chapel Hill: University of North Carolina Press, 1993.

White, Shane, and Graham White. *Stylin': African American Expressive Culture from Its Beginnings to the Zoot Suit*. Ithaca, NY: Cornell University Press, 1998.

RELIGIOUS LIFE

Akinyela, Makungu. "Battling the Serpent: Nat Turner, Africanized Christianity, and a Black Ethos." *Journal of Black Studies* 33, no. 3 (January 2003): 255–280.

Egerton, Douglas R., and Robert L. Paquette, eds. *The Denmark Vesey Affair: A Documentary History*. Gainesville: University Press of Florida, 2017.

Elizabeth. *Elizabeth, a Colored Minister of the Gospel, Born in Slavery*. Philadelphia, PA: The Tract Association of Friends, 1889.

Frey, Sylvia, and Betty Wood. *Come Shouting to Zion: African American Protestantism in the American South and the British Caribbean to 1830*. Chapel Hill: University of North Carolina Press, 1998.

Gomez, Michael A. *Exchanging Our Country Marks: The Transformation of African Identities in the Colonial and Antebellum South*. Chapel Hill: University of North Carolina Press, 1997.

Greenberg, Kenneth, ed. *The Confessions of Nat Turner and Related Documents*. New York: Bedford/St. Martins, 1996.

Harding, Vincent. *There Is a River: The Black Struggle for Freedom in America*. New York: Harcourt Brace, 1981.

Johnson, Thomas L. *Twenty-Eight Years a Slave: Or the Story of My Life in Three Continents*. Bournemouth, England: W. Mate & Sons, 1909.

Levine, Lawrence. "Slave Songs and Slave Consciousness: An Exploration in Neglected Sources." In *African-American Religion: Interpretive*

Essays in History and Culture, edited by Timothy Earl Fulop and Albert J. Raboteau. New York: Routledge, 1997, 57–58.

Long, John Dixon. *Pictures of Slavery in Church and State; Including Personal Reminiscences, Biographical Sketches, Anecdotes, etc. etc. with an Appendix, Containing the Views of John Wesley and Richard Watson on Slavery.* Philadelphia, PA: printed by the author, 1857.

Raboteau, Albert. *Slave Religion: The "Invisible Institution" in the Antebellum South.* New York: Oxford University Press, 1978.

Randolph, Peter. *Sketches of Slave Life: Or Illustrations of the Peculiar Institution.* Boston: printed by the author, 1855.

Robinson, William H. *From Log Cabin to the Pulpit, or, Fifteen Years in Slavery.* Eau Claire, WI: Publishing Printer, 1913.

Sidbury, James. "Reading, Revelation and Rebellion: The Textual Communities of Gabriel, Denmark Vesey, and Nat Turner." In *Nat Turner: A Slave Rebellion in History and Memory*, edited by Kenneth R. Greenburg. New York: Oxford University Press, 2003, 119–133.

Thompson, Katrina D. *Ring Shout, Wheel About: The Racial Politics of Music and Dance in North American Slavery.* Urbana: University of Illinois Press, 2014.

Turner, Richard Brent. "What Shall We Call Him: Islam and African American Identity." *Journal of Religious Thought.* 51, no. 1 (Summer/Fall 1994): 25–52.

Young, Jason R. "Spirituality and Socialization in the Slave Community." In *A Companion to African American History*, edited by Alton Hornsby, Jr. Malden, MA: Blackwell, 2008, 176–198.

POLITICAL LIFE

Camp, Stephanie. *Closer to Freedom: Enslaved Women and Everyday Resistance in the Plantation South.* Chapel Hill: University of North Carolina Press, 2004.

Drew, Benjamin, ed. *The Refugee: Narratives of Fugitive Slaves in Canada.* Toronto, Canada: Dundurn Press, 2008.

Genovese, Eugene D. *Roll Jordan Roll: The World the Slaves Made.* New York: Pantheon Books, 1972.

Moore, John Hammond. *A Plantation Mistress on the Eve of the Civil War: The Diary of Keziah Goodwyn Hopkins Brevard, 1860–1861.* Columbia: University of South Carolina Press, 1993.

Stringfellow, Thornton. *Scriptural and Statistical Views in Favor of Slavery.* Richmond, VA: J. W. Randolph, 1856.

Zaborney, John J. *Slaves for Hire: Renting Enslaved Laborers in Antebellum Virginia.* Baton Rouge: Louisiana State University Press, 2012.

INTELLECTUAL LIFE

Cade, John B. "Out of the Mouths of Ex-Slaves." *The Journal of Negro History* 20, no. 3 (July 1935): 294–337.

Chrisman, Robert. "Black Studies, the Talented Tenth and the Organic Intellectual." *The Black Scholar* 43, no. 3 (Fall 2013): 64–70.
Cornelius, Janet. "'We Slipped and Learned to Read': Slave Accounts of the Literacy Process, 1830–1865." *Phylon* 44, no. 3 (1983): 171–186.
Douglass, Margaret. *Educational Laws of Virginia: The Personal Narrative of Mrs. Margaret Douglass*. Boston, MA: John P. Jewett & Co., 1854.
Fett, Sharla M. *Working Cures: Healing, Health, and Power on Southern Slave Plantations*. Chapel Hill: University of North Carolina Press, 2002.
Greenberg, Kenneth, ed. *The Confessions of Nat Turner and Related Documents*. New York: Bedford/St. Martins, 1996.
Williams, Heather. *Self-Taught: African American Education in Slavery and Freedom*. Chapel Hill: University of North Carolina Press, 2007.

RECREATIONAL LIFE

Anderson, John Q. "Old John and the Master." *Southern Folklore Quarterly* 25, no. 3 (September 1961): 418–429.
Gura, Philip F., and James F. Bollman. *America's Instrument: The Banjo in the Nineteenth Century*. Chapel Hill: University of North Carolina Press, 1999.
Levine, Lawrence. *Black Culture and Black Consciousness: Afro-American Folk Thought from Slavery to Freedom*. 30th Anniversary Edition. New York: Oxford University Press, 2007.
Roberts, John. *From Trickster to Badman: The Black Folk Hero in Slavery and Freedom*. Philadelphia: University of Pennsylvania Press, 1989.
Southern, Eileen. *The Music of Black Americans: A History*, 3rd ed. New York: W. W. Norton, 1997.
Thompson, Katrina D. *Ring Shout, Wheel About: The Racial Politics of Music and Dance in North American Slavery*. Urbana: University of Illinois Press, 2014.
White, Shane, and Graham White. *The Sounds of Slavery: Discovering African American History through Songs, Sermons, and Speech*. Boston, MA: Beacon Press, 2005.
Wiggins, David K. "The Play of Slave Children in the Plantation Communities of the Old South, 1820–1860." *Journal of Sport History* 7, no. 2 (Summer 1980): 21–39.

WEBSITES

"Born in Slavery: Slave Narratives from the Federal Writers' Project, 1936 to 1938," n.d., accessed July 29, 2019. https://www.loc.gov/collections/slave-narratives-from-the-federal-writers-project-1936-to-1938/about-this-collection/
"The Geography of Slavery in Virginia." 2005, accessed July 27, 2019. http://www2.vcdh.virginia.edu/gos/index.html
Library of Congress. n.d. "Chronicling America: Historic American Newspapers," accessed July 27, 2019. https://chroniclingamerica.loc.gov/

University of North Carolina. n.d. "Documenting the American South," accessed July 29, 2019. https://docsouth.unc.edu/

Whitney Plantation. n.d., accessed July 27, 2019. https://www.whitneyplantation.com/

FILMS AND DOCUMENTARIES

Africans in America. 1998.
Amistad. 1997.
Glory. 1989.
Slavery and the Making of America. 2005.
12 Years a Slave. 2013.

INDEX

Abolitionism, 145, 147, 155, 171
Auld, Sophia, 168

Bacchus, Josephine, 57
Ball, Charles, 32, 148; cotton cultivation, 12–14; family, 42, 47; fishing, 32–33, 70–71, 76; food, 70–71, 73, 75, 76, 80, 81, 93; funeral practices, 102; housing, 84, 92; material goods, 31, 69, 86, 92; punishment, 133; recreation, 20; religion, 104; rice cultivation, 19; slave sales, 42
Banjo, 52, 120, 181–82, 184, 185, 186, 188, 201, 203
Bibb, Henry: conjure and courtship, 100–101; cotton picking, 15; criticism of master, 129; family separation, 129; marriage, 52–53, 54, 56; slave owner violence, 53
Biddle, Mary Minus, 7

Brown, Henry: punishment, 21; Richmond, 63, 87; sale of family, 62–64, 87; tobacco factory, 21
Brown, John: childcare, 60; food, 72, 78; marriage, 24; picking cotton, 13, 15; punishment, 12, 15, 25; slave sale, 42
Brown, William Wells: banjo, 203; Congo Square, 202–3; critique of slavery, 78; family, 49; music and dancing, 202–3; naming, 48; sexual coercion, 25; slave cabins, 83; slave sales, 25, 44; steward, 23; work, 193
Bruce, Henry: fishing, 76; hired out, 23
Bryant, William Cullen, 181
Butler, Pierce, 56–57, 58, 88, 141–42

Campbell, Israel, 15, 134–35
Chesnut, Mary, 56

Childrearing: accidents, 60; breastfeeding, 60; food, 61; gang system and, 61; mothers' return to work, 59, 60, 141; owners' involvement in, 60, 61; supervision of children, 60; task system and, 61; work and, 59–60

Clothing: children's, 31, 88–89, 92; domestic slaves, 88; field hands, 87; men's, 88; purchased for self, 31, 89–90; spinning and weaving, 90; style, 89, 90–91; supplied by master, 31, 87–88; women's, 88, 89, 91–92

Conjure, 100, 174, 200–201; and courtship, 100–101; Douglass, Frederick and, 101; and resistance, 101, 103

Corn: bread, 71, 73–74, 75, 92; diet of, 68, 80–81; games with, 197; grinding of, 1, 7, 48; growing of, 5, 7, 10, 11, 17, 18, 19, 31, 34; independent production, 51; selling, 30, 31; shucking, 6, 52, 188, 194, 195, 201, 202; Turner, Nat and, 118; uses of, 52, 86, 92, 193, 203; weekly ration, 31, 71–72, 93

Cotton, 3, 5, 73; gender division of labor, 7; growing of, 7, 12, 31, 33–34, 50; pace of work, 14–15, 68, 135; Petit Gulf, 12; picking of, 12–13, 34–35, 58, 68, 113; production of, 11, 14, 16, 21, 41, 134; slave clothing, 88, 90; and slave trade, 40, 62; weighing, 15, 35, 134

Courtship, 53; conjure and, 100–101; corn shucking, 195; dancing, 51–52, 189–91; music, 188

Covey, Edward, 101, 144

Dancing, 188, 203; courtship and, 51–52, 189–91; regulation of, 191

Denmark Vesey's conspiracy, 103, 110

Domestic slave trade: family separation, 2, 25, 39, 41–45, 46, 62–64, 98, 111, 129, 130, 137; Franklin and Armfield, 40; impact of, 40–41, 42, 44–45, 46; reasons for sale, 40, 41; rice cultivation and, 41; slave resistance to, 43–45, 130; traders, 40, 44

Domestic work: children and, 28, 61, 137; food and clothing, 27; plantation mistress, 28–29, 127–28, 136–39

Douglass, Frederick, 3, 23, 41, 145, 154, 171, 192; Auld, Sophia, 168; childhood, 62; conjure, 101; Covey, Edward, 101, 144; food, 61, 68, 72, 74, 80; literacy, 146, 153, 162, 165–66, 168; *Narrative of the Life of Frederick Douglass*, 153, 166, 171; organic intellectual, 167; punishment of, 29, 101, 140, 144, 169–70, 171; slave sales, 45; theft of food, 79; work, 11, 22, 193

Douglass, Margaret Crittenden, 160–61

Durham, Tempie Herndon, 55

Elizabeth: conversion, 106; direct revelation, 107; literacy, 107

Emancipation Proclamation, 147

Epps, Edwin, 21, 33, 35, 71–72, 85, 171, 186

Fancy trade, 25–26, 45

Festivities: Christmas, 191–93; corn shucking, 194–95; dances, 51–52, 189–91; subscription ball, 179–80

Folktales: Brer Rabbit, 198–200; Brer Wolf, 198–200; function,

Index 217

197–98, 199, 200; performance, 201; trickster stories, 199–201; West African roots, 198, 200–201
Food: cane juice, 18; children and, 61, 74, 80; clandestine trade, 32–33; corn, 71, 72, 74, 93; fishing, 61, 70, 75, 76; gardens, 75; harvest, 72; health and, 71, 80–81; holidays, 72–73, 192; hunting, 61, 75, 76, 193; independent production, 69; pork, 71–72; preparation, 73–74, 86; preserving meat, 6; preventing theft of, 79; theft of, 32, 70, 77–79, 116
Fox, Tryphena, 138–39

Games, 196–97
Garlic, Delia, 29, 43, 89
George, Ceceil, 16–17, 84
Grandy, Moses: boat pilot, 22–23; canal digger, 22, 72, 86; family separation, 42, 44, 111; food, 72; housing, 86; punishment, 111; religion, 111
Green, Jacob, 32, 190
Green, William, 84, 86, 130
Greene, Arthur, 78
Gudger, Sarah, 1

Hammond, James Henry, 54, 126
Health: African practices, 174; feigning illness, 132, 133; herbal remedies, 172–73; nutrition and, 71, 80–81; work and, 57–59, 132, 133, 141
Henson, Josiah, 10
Hill, Jennie, 67
Hughes, Louis: Civil War, 147, 148–50; holidays, 73; punishment of, 28, 138; religion, 114, 116; sale, 2, 137; slave owner violence, 28, 137
Hunt, Gabe, 10

Independent production: benefits of, 29–31, 50–51; clandestine trade, 32–33, 90; market transactions, 32, 89–90; work performed, 29, 31, 75–76

Jacobs, Harriet: childhood, 62; family, 48, 49; food, 79; Junkanoo, 193–94; marriage, 54, 56; miscarriages, 57; motherhood, 60; organic intellectual, 166; power of slave owners, 79, 168, 170; religion, 109, 115–16, 168; sexual coercion, 24, 54, 167–68; slave hiring, 20; violence, 170
Jones, Mandy, 158
Jones, Thomas H.: family separation, 42; literacy, 158–59, 162–63, 165, 175–77; marriage, 56; punishment of, 159; slave cabin, 85
Jumping the broom, 55
Junkanoo, 193–94

Keckley, Elizabeth: motherhood, 25; sexual coercion, 25; slave sale, 42
Kemble, Frances Anne (Fanny), 143; childbirth and fieldwork, 58, 59, 141; childcare, 60; interracial relationships, 56–57; slave clothing, 88, 90–91; slave diet, 80; slave management, 142; slave marriage, 56

Latrobe, Benjamin, 181, 182
Lincoln, Abraham, 147, 148
Literacy: abolitionism and, 145; anti-literacy laws, 155, 156, 174; *Columbian Orator*, 165; Curry, James, 163; Douglass, Frederick, 146, 153, 162, 165–66, 168; Douglass, Margaret, 160–61; Jones, Thomas, 158–59, 162–63,

165, 175–77; Martin, John Sella, 145; pit schools, 158; planter support for, 157–58; religion and, 106–7, 163–64; Turner, Nat and, 156, 164–65

Loguen, Cherry: children sold, 43; motherhood, 48–49

Loguen, Jermain: abuse of, 11, 49; critique of slavery, 79; hunting and fishing, 61; separation from family, 43; tribute to mother, 48–49

Love, Hunton, 18

Marriage: abroad, 47, 50; ceremony, 55; jumping the broom, 55; permission to marry, 53; set up housekeeping, 85; slave owner interference in, 24, 53–54, 56; view of, 56

Marshall, Alice, 78

Martin, John Sella, 44, 145

McGee, Edward, 147

McGee, Sarah, 137–38, 147

Miscarriages, 57

Music: African influences, 181–83; banjo, 52, 120, 181–82, 184, 185, 186, 188, 201, 203; coerced performances, 185–87; Congo Square, 202–3; critique of, 181; drums, 182–83, 203; fiddle, 183–84, 186–87, 189, 192; Gilliat, Simeon, 187; improvisation, 181, 184–85, 187; patting, 190–91; ring shout, 108, 187–88; songs, 112, 113–14, 121, 181, 184–85, 188

Nat Turner's Rebellion, 103–4, 111, 155, 156, 164–65, 170

New Orleans, 181, 202–3; slave market, 11, 25, 44, 49, 169

Norfleet, Lizzie, 90

Northup, Solomon: cotton, 33; cotton picking, 13, 14, 34–35, 134; dancing, 52, 187, 190–91; family separation, 44–45, 169; fancy trade, 25; fiddling, 186–87; fish trap, 76; food, 71, 72–73, 74, 75; material goods, 86; Patsey, 170–71; punishment, 171, 186; slave cabins, 82, 85; slave sales, 25; sugar cultivation, 17

Olmsted, Frederick Law, 7, 24, 83, 89, 90, 135, 136

Organic intellectual, 154, 166–67, 171

Parker, Theodore, 171–72

Paternalism, 126–27, 162; critique of, 129, 131; uses, 129–31, 140

Pregnancy: fieldwork and, 57–59; health problems, 57; reducing workload during, 58; rewards for, 58; trash gang and, 58

Quilting, 194–94

Randolph, Peter: critique of master's religion, 98; family separation, 98; literacy, 107; punishment, 98; religious conversion, 106; religious worship, 97, 120–22

Rebellion: Prosser, Gabriel, 117; Turner, Nat, 103–4, 111, 117–19, 120; Vesey, Denmark, 103, 110, 117, 120

Religion: African Methodist Episcopal Church, 109–10; biblical typology, 113–15; black churches, 109; camp meetings, 108; Christmas, 112; conjure, 100–101, 102; conversion, 106–7; criticisms of slave owner's religion, 98, 115–17, 129; discomfort with slave religion, 99, 102, 111; funeral

Index 219

practices, 101–2; Islam, 104–5; literacy and, 106–7, 163–64; praise house, 110–11; religious revivals, 99, 107; ring shout, 108, 187–88; slave resistance and, 101, 103–4, 110, 111; spirituals, 112, 113–14, 121; used to defend slavery, 126–27; West African religion, 99–102; worship, 97–99, 111–12, 120–22

Reynolds, Mary, 13, 14, 25, 55, 80

Rice: gender division of labor, 7; growing of, 16, 18–19, 20; harvesting, 19–20; pace of work, 5; slave management, 4–5, 50–51, 58, 85, 134; slave trade and, 41, 46, 104; task system, 4–5, 135

Richmond, VA, 21–22, 26, 27, 62–64, 86, 87, 99, 143–44, 179, 180, 187

Rollins, Mandy, 7

Rollins, Parthena, 44

Sexual coercion, 24–25, 54, 167–68

Slave breeding, 24

Slave children: clothing, 31, 88–89; domestic work, 28, 61, 137; fieldwork, 9, 10, 13, 17, 19; food, 61, 74, 80; hiring of, 23; punishment of, 11, 49, 79, 137–38, 159; recreation, 61, 196–97; sale of, 25, 40, 42–45, 62, 64, 98, 111, 129, 137; work performed by, 7–8, 60

Slave family: importance of, 39, 48, 50, 51; naming patterns and, 48; owners' interference in, 23, 48, 61; separation by sale, 2, 23, 25, 39, 41–43, 44–45, 46, 62–64, 98, 111, 129, 130, 137; structure of, 46, 47; survival of, 49–50; work and, 59–60

Slave hiring: dual mastery, 23; family separation, 23, 143; independence, 22–23; living out and, 21–22, 86–87; mistreatment, 23; negotiation, 143; reasons for, 20–21, 23; Richmond, 21, 86–87; working conditions, 22

Slave management, 125, 131, 134, 142; advice literature, 131–32; black drivers, 17, 18; classification of hands, 3–4, 14; domestic work, 136–39; gang labor, 4, 17, 161; negotiation, 5, 44, 135, 139–40, 141–42, 143, 144; overseers, 4, 70, 133, 140–41; pace of work, 4, 11, 12, 14; plantation mistress and, 28–29, 127–28, 136–39, 141–42; resistance to, 44, 133, 134–35, 142, 143–44; rewards, 14–15, 59, 68; task system, 4–5, 135–36; threat of violence, 18, 113, 131; violence, 10–11, 12, 15, 28–29, 44, 49, 111, 125, 137, 144, 169–71

Slave quarters: changes to, 84; conditions, 81, 83, 84; construction of, 85; double pen, 82; furniture, 85–86, 92; health and, 84; root cellar, 84; size, 84

Slave women: breastfeeding, 60; breeding, 24; clothing, 88, 89–90, 91, 92; gender division of labor, 6–7, 19; lying-in period, 59; motherhood, 43, 49, 130; plowing, 7; reproduction and workload, 57–59; sexual coercion of, 24–25, 54, 56, 167–68; wet nurses, 26–27

Smith, James, 86

Steward, Austin: food, 71, 73; punishment of, 28–29; work, 61

Stringfellow, Thornton, 127

Stroyer, Jacob: religious beliefs, 112–13; slave owner power, 192

Sugar: cutting cane, 17; growing of, 15–16, 17; labor demands, 16;

processing of, 16, 18; working conditions, 16

Tobacco: decline in production, 20; growing, 4, 8, 9; picking, 10; processing, 21, 86, 87; uses, 31, 75, 192; worming, 9

Walker, David, 115
Watson, Henry, 84
Webb, Mary, 7
Wet nurses, 26–27
Williams, Nancy, 9, 52, 89
Williams, Rose, 54

About the Authors

PAUL E. TEED is Professor of History at Saginaw Valley State University specializing in the American Civil War era. He is the author of four other books, including *Joseph and Harriet Hawley's Civil War: Partnership, Ambition and Sacrifice* (2018). In 2012, he was selected as Distinguished Professor of the Year by the Presidents Council, State Universities of Michigan.

MELISSA LADD TEED is Professor of History at Saginaw Valley State University specializing in nineteenth-century U.S. women's history. She is the author of several scholarly articles as well as coauthor (with Paul Teed) of *Reconstruction* (2015).

www.ingramcontent.com/pod-product-compliance
Lightning Source LLC
Chambersburg PA
CBHW070336240426
43665CB00045B/2122